The Athletic Trap

THE ATHLETIC TRAP

How College Sports Corrupted the Academy

Howard L. Nixon II

JOHNS HOPKINS UNIVERSITY PRESS   BALTIMORE

© 2014 Johns Hopkins University Press
All rights reserved. Published 2014
Printed in the United States of America on acid-free paper

2   4   6   8   9   7   5   3   1

Johns Hopkins University Press
2715 North Charles Street
Baltimore, Maryland 21218-4363
www.press.jhu.edu

Library of Congress Cataloging-in-Publication Data

Nixon, Howard L., 1944–
The athletic trap : how college sports corrupted the academy / Howard L. Nixon II.
pages cm
Includes bibliographical references and index.
ISBN 978-1-4214-1195-8 (hardcover : alk. paper) — ISBN 978-1-4214-1196-5 (electronic)
— ISBN 1-4214-1195-4 (hardcover : alk. paper) — ISBN 1-4214-1196-2 (electronic)
1. College sports—Corrupt practices—United States. 2. Universities and colleges—
Corrupt practices—United States. I. Title.
GV351.N59 2014
796.043—dc23   2013017624

A catalog record for this book is available from the British Library.

*Special discounts are available for bulk purchases of this book. For more information,
please contact Special Sales at 410-516-6936 or specialsales@press.jhu.edu.*

Johns Hopkins University Press uses environmentally friendly book
materials, including recycled text paper that is composed of at least 30 percent
post-consumer waste, whenever possible.

*For Sara, who is the best research and instruction librarian I know
and who has always encouraged me*

CONTENTS

I would like to thank my editor, Greg Britton, for his excellent insights and suggestions and for his encouragement and support. His suggestion of the subtitle was especially helpful in sharpening my focus in preparing the manuscript. I would also like to thank Greg Nicholl for his assistance during the production process. I have appreciated the commitment to quality of all of the board members and professionals associated with Johns Hopkins University Press. In addition, I want to thank Towson University for granting me a sabbatical leave to complete a large portion of the preparation of this manuscript. Associate Dean of the College of Liberal Arts Irena Makarushka and my department chairs, Sam Collins and Beth Clifford, deserve special thanks for their encouragement to pursue a sabbatical to work on this project. There are many other colleagues, including Bill Tsitsos and Carol Caronna, who listened and responded to my comments about college sports and helped me develop my analysis. However, I must single out my closest colleague, my wife Sara Nixon. She is the best research and instructional librarian I know, and her constant encouragement and help motivated me to write this book and apply for a sabbatical to work on it. She is probably tired of all my recitations of my text as I sought to sharpen it and make it more compelling. I must add a word of thanks to my many sport sociology students. Their distinctive perspective of college sports always reminds me of the reason why we need to work harder to make college athletics more reflective of the interests of genuine student-athletes.

ABC	American Broadcasting Company
ACC	Atlantic Coast Conference
AGB	Association of Governing Boards of Universities and Colleges
AIAW	Association for Intercollegiate Athletics for Women
AQ	automatic qualification
BCS	Bowl Championship Series
BTUs	big-time universities
CAA	Colonial Athletic Association
CFA	College Football Association
CLC	Collegiate Licensing Company
C-USA	Conference USA
FAR	faculty athletics representative
FARA	FAR Association
FBS	Football Bowl Subdivision
FCS	Football Championship Subdivision
IAAUS	Intercollegiate Athletic Association of the United States
IGT	intercollegiate golden triangle
IOC	International Olympic Committee
LHN	Longhorn Network
MAC	Mid-American Conference
MEAC	Mid-Eastern Athletic Conference
MLB	Major League Baseball
MVSU	Mississippi Valley State University
NAIA	National Association of Intercollegiate Athletics
NBA	National Basketball Association

NCAA	National Collegiate Athletic Association
NFL	National Football League
Pac-12	Pacific-12
SEC	Southeastern Conference
SIC	Special Investigative Counsel
SUNY	State University of New York
SWAC	Southwestern Athletic Conference
UCSD	University of California, San Diego
UMES	University of Maryland Eastern Shore
UNC-A	University of North Carolina at Asheville
UNCC	University of North Carolina at Charlotte
WAC	Western Athletic Conference

The Athletic Trap

Commercialization, College Sports, and the Athletic Trap

Under the headline "Division I Schools Spend More on Athletes than Education," a *USA Today* story that would probably mystify many people outside the United States began: "Public universities competing in NCAA Division I sports spend as much as six times more per athlete than they spend to educate students."[1] Why, they might wonder, would U.S. institutions of higher education devote so much attention and money to sports? Even Americans most caught up in the hoopla of big-time college sports would have difficulty explaining this strange paradox.[2] After all, colleges and universities are supposed to be committed to educating us for the serious challenges of the twenty-first century. Yet, even as these institutions tout their commitment to their educational mission, they shift relatively large sums of money away from this mission to fund athletics.

The same day that the *USA Today* story appeared, the *Chronicle of Higher Education* reported that the credit-rating agency Moody's Investor Services had issued a bleak assessment of economic prospects in the higher-education sector for the coming twelve to eighteen months.[3] Thus, while institutions faced increasing economic and financial pressures, they continued to make major investments in athletics and run up growing deficits. Indeed, during the recent severe economic downturn, many universities paid coaches extravagant salaries that far exceeded those of faculty members and even their presidents. While academic buildings deteriorated, universities constructed huge and sometimes luxurious buildings for athletic competition. Furthermore, while they have seemed to be consumed with enhancing their brand and moving up the *U.S. News & World Report* rankings, universities have also risked tarnishing their image by recruiting coaches and ostensible student-athletes who have had little concern about the academic integrity of the institution where they work and play.

The story is a familiar one. Yet despite all the attention that the problems and risks of college sports have received in the past, universities competing in or aspiring to big-time status in sports have not learned the lessons of these negative experiences or come to grips with the campus forces that sustain them. College and university presidents and trustees continue to engage in actions and make decisions that reproduce the problems of the past. Disturbing stories —about the skewed spending patterns, the scandals, the distortions of values and mission—keep repeating themselves.

This book focuses on university presidents and trustees as pivotal players in athletics, leaders who have the authority to control and change the direction of big-time college sports on their campuses. Despite this authority, presidents and trustees—whether willingly or reluctantly—give athletics preferential or special treatment. Especially in programs that are the most commercialized, these officials are in an athletic trap of their own making, one that they are either unwilling or unable to escape. This book attempts to answer how this trap has enabled athletics to take over the academy and what can be done to free most colleges and universities from these commercial influences that distort academic values.

Higher Education, Commercialization, and College Sports

Understanding the paradoxes, problems, and the athletic trap in college sports requires an understanding of how commercialization has been intertwined with the evolution of athletics in higher education in the United States. Many segments of higher education today are commercialized, from bookstores to medical centers and scientific research institutions. Commercialization has meant that colleges and universities have pursued relationships with corporate partners in the private economic sector to finance equipment, facilities, projects, and personnel and to outsource services. In recent years, commercialization of the academic side of colleges and universities has raised questions and concerns about the influence of these outside interests on academic integrity. But commercialization is not a recent development in higher education.

Former Harvard president Derek Bok observed that commercialization arose on college campuses as a result of the development of college athletics.[4] From its early years in the middle of the nineteenth century, college athletics has become increasingly commercialized. The relationship between commercialized athletics and the academic mission of colleges and universities has long been uneasy and even rocky, often leading critics to challenge institutional investment in commercialized sports programs. As a result, college presidents and governing boards are constantly involved in promoting or controlling commercialization in athletics and in trying to balance the athletic-academic relationship.

The involvement of institutions of higher education in highly commercialized sports is unique to the United States.[5] This commercialization began innocently enough.[6] An entrepreneurial railroad owner and land developer saw the commercial benefits of a competition between Harvard and Yale students in a crew race on a lake in New Hampshire. The race was seen as a way to get wealthy families and friends of the Harvard and Yale rowers to use his railroad and consider purchasing his New Hampshire vacation properties.[7] In addition to intercollegiate athletic competition being used for this business entrepreneur's commercial purposes, the athletes were "professionalized" because they had the opportunity to earn "lavish prizes" and have access to "unlimited alcohol" as a result of their participation.[8]

These modest beginnings have evolved into today's commercialized college athletics. This first sports event was not even a competition between colleges because it simply involved students from two different institutions and existed outside the scope of institutional control. Other early competitions between college students did not involve promoters and prizes and were run by and for the student participants, sometimes with faculty members invited to participate as well. These affairs were quite informal and looked much like today's student-run club sports.[9] These vigorous and sometimes highly aggressive activities at elite institutions may have appealed to privileged young men because they gave them a chance to learn about and display their manhood.[10]

A relatively informal model of intercollegiate competition similar to the early U.S. model generally characterizes college sports outside the United States today. Although contemporary club sports on many U.S. college campuses retain much of the more informal elements of early college sports, U.S. colleges and universities started reshaping the informal model in the 1870s. After they began to take control of intercollegiate teams in the 1870s, "official" university athletic programs became more bureaucratic and commercialized. Thus, the emergence of institutionally sponsored intercollegiate athletics brought with it a shift in their control from student participants to the institutions they attended. College and university administrators became interested in intercollegiate athletics when they noticed that these student games were attracting public attention, which raised the possibilities of increased revenue and media coverage. In the 1870s, leagues and conferences were organized to regulate and promote intercollegiate competition in several sports, including track, rowing, baseball, and the new sport of American football. By the 1880s, college sports involved professional coaches, the sale of tickets for sports events, the use of trainers, and efforts to get alumni to provide financial support for athletics. At the end of the 1880s, most institutions had athletic committees consisting of some combination of alumni, professional coaches, students, and a few faculty members to oversee or control their athletic programs.[11]

College athletics was run by college administrators and coaches by the end of the nineteenth century, with significant input from alumni on some campuses. Then, as now, faculty members and students rarely had much influence in athletic decision making. Administrators and alumni sought control because they did not think students could run athletics responsibly or effectively and in line with institutional interests. In addition, administrators did not want to share control with faculty members because faculty complaints about issues such as professionalism, financial mismanagement, poor sportsmanship, and violence threatened to derail the growth of athletic programs.

In the early part of the twentieth century, football was already a lucrative enterprise at some schools. For example, in 1915 the Yale football team earned more than $1 million (in current dollars).[12] This fact points to an ostensible oddity in the growth of commercialized college athletics. Many of the prominent college sports teams then were at established elite institutions, such as Harvard, Yale, and the University of Chicago. Like college presidents elsewhere, the presidents of elite institutions a century ago sought more students and saw athletics as a way to broaden the appeal of their institutions. A few did have serious reservations about the growth of sports on their campuses. They worried about the damage to the academic integrity and overall reputation of their institutions, and football was typically singled out for the sharpest criticism. Its brutal play was not well regulated and resulted in frequent injuries and even deaths, and its best players were subsidized by various groups, including fraternities and alumni. Some players were not even students. These "tramp athletes" were paid for their services as they went from campus to campus, much like contract workers.[13]

Harvard president Charles W. Eliot was among the most outspoken early presidential critics of college sports. His tenure as president of Harvard from 1869 to 1909 paralleled the period that witnessed the creation and growing popularity of college football, and he did not like what he saw, calling football a "brutal, cheating, and demoralizing game." He tried repeatedly to abolish the sport on his campus but was overruled every time by his trustees.[14] Unlike President Eliot, most college presidents during this early era of college sports either kept their concerns to themselves or openly extolled the virtues of their sports programs, especially when students expressed their support and their teams were successful.

In the late nineteenth century, institutions with limited visibility or prominence, such as Notre Dame, significantly increased their national visibility by competing against college football powers such as Harvard. The continuing surge in popularity of college football into the twentieth century was a driving force in the entrenchment of organized athletics on the campus. Although it was becoming increasingly popular, football was an ongoing problem for college presidents because it seemed to embody all the criticisms that had been directed at college sports. President Theodore Roosevelt was among the fans of the sport, but with mounting deaths and rampant professionalism, he considered abolishing football on college campuses.

Yet this crisis of college football and college sports soon subsided. Colleges passed resolutions to reform rather than ban the sport, and innovations such as the forward pass opened up the game and made it less violent. Most crucially, though, the Intercollegiate Athletic Association of the United States (IAAUS) was formed in 1905 to regulate football and college sports in general.[15] This new organization established rules to increase institutional control, academic integrity, ethical behavior, and the well-being of student-athletes. The IAAUS morphed into the National Collegiate Athletic Association (NCAA) in 1910. The NCAA remains today the most powerful regulatory body in American college sports, even though it has continued to face sharp criticisms for its role in promoting the commercialization of college sports. While it has shepherded the continuing commercial growth of college sports, it has not been successful in eliminating many of the basic financial, academic, and ethical issues that animated opposition to college sports in its early years.

The injection of more order into college sports, the increasing enthusiasm that students, alumni, and fans expressed for "their" college teams, and the increasing media coverage of college sports made it easier for college presidents and their governing boards to support athletics. This support helped presidents fend off criticisms and, at the same time, made it difficult for them to express their own reservations. They may not have believed their own publicly expressed justifications of college athletics, but by the 1920s they recognized that college sports had developed into a popular and powerful institution as commercial entertainment. This was a golden age, when college football and its stars began to compete with the stars of the national pastime, Major League Baseball.[16] The Great Depression and wars caused temporary dips in the popularity of college sports, but with the increasing investment by the media, corporate sponsors, and the institutions themselves in sports, it became an entrenched institution and a prominent segment of American popular culture. Today we refer to its most popular forms as "big-time" college sports, and this realm is distinguished not only by its popularity but also by its level of commercialization and seriousness of competition. This realm promises the biggest rewards and also poses the biggest problems for college presidents and governing boards. Public debates about college sports and the major scandals in college sports have almost always involved the athletic programs sponsored by big-time universities and by universities aspiring to big-time status.

Two Models of College Sports

When the NCAA came into being in the early part of the twentieth century, it formalized the amateur status of student-athletes, legally treating them as students and forbidding them from being paid employees. In 1956 the organization constructed a compensation mechanism, the athletic grant-in-aid or athletic scholarship. It was a form of financial aid based not on academic qualifications or need but strictly on athletic ability.[17] This treatment of college athletes reflects fundamental contradictions that are embodied in two different models of college sports.

These two models emerged as interest in college athletics grew on and off campus and athletics became more commercialized. The *collegiate model* conceptualizes college athletics as an enterprise organized around the interests of student-athletes. This model focuses on the welfare of student-athletes both in the classroom and on the athletic field, though it concentrates on the student part of student-athlete. It is often cited by college leaders and NCAA officials as part of their public justification for sponsoring athletics. By making college sports an extension of the academic mission, this model emphasizes the academic and career accomplishments of athletes as students who have taken their studies seriously and have used their academic and athletic experiences to propel them to success in their careers.

A contrasting conception of college athletics is the *commercial model*, which focuses mainly on the uses of college sports for commercial purposes. It reflects the realities of big-time college sports programs, which depend on the recruitment of blue-chip athletes and star coaches who can produce victories and championships for a school. Winning is necessary to attract fans, funding, media exposure, and corporate sponsorship and to generate significant amounts of revenue. This model focuses on the athletic skills and accomplishments of student-athletes rather than their success in the classroom. The commercial model has created a big-time college sports world populated by highly paid coaches, star athletes playing in front of huge crowds and national television audiences, intense pursuit of high school prospects, sports media personalities, corporate sponsors and partnerships, branded merchandise, expensive tickets for premium seats and prime-time games, federal tax write-offs for donors, conferences constantly seeking better deals with television and sponsors, schools jockeying to be in the most lucrative conferences, and debates about whether college athletes at the most commercialized level should be paid to play as professional athletes are. This is also a world in which some schools and people have been willing to go to great lengths and even cheat to be competitively and commercially successful. On its fringes are people who alter high school transcripts and test scores, who take tests or write papers for athletes, who offer illegal inducements to star high school athletes to get them to play for a particular school, who use college games in their legal and illegal gambling businesses, and who try to get athletes to fix the outcomes of games. This world also includes actions by university officials to cover up transgressions by athletes, coaches, and other athletic and university personnel in order to protect their reputations, the reputation of the institution, and the competitive status of the athletic program. Such behavior represents the fallout from the excesses of the commercial model.

The contrasts between the commercial and collegiate model are striking. In focusing on how college sports took over the academy, I pay special attention to how the commercial model of college sports has often made the collegiate model and academic concerns less important. The commercial model initially gained a foothold on college campuses because college presidents were looking for ways to attract more students. They needed a way to popularize the ivory tower and make it more appealing to the American public. Sponsoring athletics was seen as a way to do this.[18] Sports events attracted media attention. They also attracted the interest of business leaders who were increasingly becoming members of governing boards of colleges and universities and were important sources of external financial support. In addition, sports offered a way of widening the pool of prospective students by appealing to those who wanted to relieve the stresses of their studies with opportunities for entertainment.

College presidents tried to balance their commitment to the academic integrity of their institutions and the collegiate model with their desire to create new revenue streams and make their institutions better known. They turned to sports for these financial and status enhancement purposes and, in doing so, shifted institutional priorities toward the commercial model. They may have continued to publicly embrace the collegiate model, but by increasing their commitment to commercialized athletics, they tacitly accepted the influence of the commercial model. They were beginning to fall into the athletic trap.

Allowing the commercial model to drive their sports programs has enabled some universities to achieve national prominence through sports, but the commercial model has also created headaches for college presidents and other college officials.[19] In the early years of college sports, college presidents had to deal with issues of tramp athletes, financial and academic corruption, and football violence. These early years have left more than a century of periodic violations of NCAA rules in their wake.

The desire or need to recruit and retain outstanding athletes and keep them academically eligible has created strong temptations to cheat. The commercial fortunes and competitive status of big-time athletic programs are at stake, as are the careers of athletic directors, coaches, and aspiring athletes. Even academically prestigious institutions that compete at the big-time level or aspire to big-time status are not immune from these temptations. Just as Harvard had to deal with tramp athletes in the nineteenth century, institutions such as the University of North Carolina, Ohio State University, and the University of Southern California have faced penalties for NCAA rule violations in more recent years. As President Eliot of Harvard discovered, the powerful lure or enticing promise of commercialized college sports can create serious dilemmas for college presidents. Once they embrace the commercial model, it may become increasingly difficult to avoid the challenges to the collegiate model that the commercial model can create. The trap has been set.

While the names of the schools and people in the headlines change in the stream of stories about the tribulations of big-time college sports programs, persisting cultural and structural factors make these tribulations recurring issues. In examining these cultural and structural factors, we will consider how they are related to the commercial model and how they contribute to the challenges in athletics faced by college presidents and governing boards.

The Athletic Trap

The *athletic trap* is my conceptual device for framing the dilemmas posed for college presidents and their institutions by the excesses of the commercial model. I do not want to imply that all college presidents with big-time athletic programs are caught in this athletic trap in the same ways, to the same extent, or with the same implications. Clearly, though, any college or college president with lofty aspirations about commercialized college sports could become trapped because the lure of having a successful and profitable big-time sports program can be very powerful. Of course, many presidents find themselves in the athletic trap the day they are hired because their new institution has an established big-time athletic program. Like any trap, once a school is caught, it can be difficult to extricate itself without experiencing some pain.

The grand vision of big-time college sports is that the entire university will be able to bask in the reflected glory from highly visible sports success. The lure of the athletic trap includes the promise of specific institutional rewards from big-time sports success, such as more athletic revenue, more student applications, more loyalty from alumni, more money from donors, more student spirit on campus, and an easier time getting the attention of legislators and the governor during budget negotiations at the state capital. Yet these kinds of promises, like dreams, can be illusions. The *institutional enhancement rationale* is the idea that athletics will yield important benefits, and this rationale has been used to justify institutional investment in college athletics. Asserting claimed benefits of having a big-time athletic program could reflect or alleviate the ambivalence that presidents might have about the presence of commercialized sports at an institution of higher education. Regardless of such feelings of ambivalence, though, presidents may feel compelled to assert some sort of institutional enhancement rationale because big-time sports programs already exist at their institution and have a loyal following or because their university is about to start a big-time sports program. Starting such a program or moving to a higher level of NCAA competition can cost a lot of money, which requires some justification. After all, not every student, faculty or board member, alumnus, prospective donor, or legislator is a sports fan or a fan of big new investments in a college sports program.

All kinds of claims of benefits may be expressed about athletics, but once a program is established, the fans, alumni, trustees, boosters, politicians, media, and sponsors most interested in these programs will ultimately judge them in terms of wins, losses, and rankings. The pressure to win can lead to major compromises of the academic integrity of the institution and even result in a ceding of significant control of athletics to athletic departments and coaches or even to boosters and other interests outside the institution. Former Harvard president Derek Bok believed that most college presidents felt some discomfort about having to make academic compromises to maintain a successful athletic program. These compromises might include admitting less academically qualified applicants on the basis of their athletic prowess or diverting money from need-based or academic scholarships to athletic scholarships. He wrote that however they actually perceive athletics, college presidents may "feel they are trapped in a system they are powerless to change."[20] When this happens, they are in the athletic trap.

The athletic trap has an emotional component. After all, winning in sports and the attention it attracts can be very exciting. Yet the athletic trap is fundamentally a structural matter—namely, a structure of financial, social, and political obligations that ties institutions and presidents to existing and future athletic commitments. Financial obligations, for example, include having to pay the salaries of athletic personnel and the cost of athletic scholarships, to honor long-term contracts for coaches and athletic directors and the stipulations of athletic donors, to pay debt service for expensive construction projects, and to sustain the ongoing maintenance costs for facilities and equipment. These are formal contractual and legal obligations.

In addition, there are more informal but still compelling social and political obligations. They include promises to wealthy donors, boosters, alumni, and politicians to support or enhance athletics. As athletic programs move to higher levels of competition, financial, personnel, and capital requirements increase. With these developments, presidents may have to become more passionate in expressing their institutional enhancement rationales, and the grip of the trap may intensify. Believing in the institutional enhancement rationale may lead college presidents down the path of increasing investment in and more enduring commitments to college athletics. Of course, they do not walk this path alone. Their real or apparent enthusiasm for athletics is likely to be shared by trustees or board members and influential and wealthy donors and boosters, as well as by many students.

At any given time, athletic programs in the big-time college sports world may be struggling competitively and financially. Once they have fallen into the athletic trap, though, it is hard to reduce the amount of institutional commitment to big-time programs, to move to a lower level, or to eliminate programs. It happens from time to time, especially in a difficult economy, but more often than not, big-time programs tend to stay at this level.[21] Once an athletic program has become established at the Division I level, has a budget of many millions of dollars, and has a loyal following of wealthy and powerful alumni, donors, and politicians, presidents may feel obliged to express athletic commitment. They realize that they might lose some internal backing if their support for athletics diminishes. They also recognize they could undermine their status or power with external constituencies if they voice reservations about athletics or appear to break promises about supporting their big-time athletic programs. These promises are implied by public expressions of the institutional enhancement rationale.

Losing the support of powerful external constituencies is likely to be more consequential for a college president than losing the support of students and faculty on some campuses would be. Scaring away big donors or antagonizing wealthy and powerful alumni or politicians generally causes more headaches and more perceived job insecurity for presidents than dealing with "no-confidence" votes from the faculty or with student protests. In fact, at big-time universities, faculty members usually play a minimal role, have limited interest, and have little power in athletics.[22] Student voices may be louder about changes in athletics, but their voices become louder and more influential when they become alumni, begin donating to the institution, and serve on institutional committees and boards.

When presidents do not see an easy way out their institution's and their own commitments to athletics, they are in the athletic trap. Thus, continually making highly publicized statements of support for athletics can lead to the trap or reinforce it. Having expressed such support so frequently in the past, a president risks credibility, respect, and support by reversing course and trying to scale down or eliminate big-time sports programs that have become too costly or have engaged in serious corruption. On the other hand, when an athletic program gets caught in a major scandal, presidents are held accountable. Scandals can range from recruiting violations and academic cheating to cover-ups of rape, sexual abuse, drug abuse, and other crimes. If presidents have been outspoken advocates or cheerleaders for corrupt programs, they are especially vulnerable to being swept away by the house-cleaning that rids the campus of their guilty colleagues in athletics and administration. Having or claiming no prior direct knowledge of the corruption typically has little bearing on the fate of presidents in these cases. The president is supposed to be in charge, and being caught in the trap is not an excuse that absolves presidents of their perceived responsibility as the top university official.

Justifying (More) Investment in College Sports

Despite the complexities and dangers of the athletic trap, presidents continue to express support for athletics and embrace opportunities to expand their athletic program. In recent years, there has been a trend of adding football programs, despite the cost of football, the possibility of big financial deficits, and the risk of tight university budgets in a difficult economic period. Between the economic collapse in 2008 and 2011, seventeen colleges and universities added football teams, and seven institutions dropped football.[23] Eight of the new teams were added in 2011, and fourteen more were scheduled to begin play between 2012 and 2014. Most of the added teams were at small colleges or universities, in the NAIA,[24] or in the NCAA Division III. Three of the dropped teams competed at the Football Championship Subdivision (FCS) level,[25] and the financial cost of football played a role in these decisions.

Various explanations were given by presidents, athletic directors, and others in college sports for the decision to add football.[26] Some saw football increasing enrollment or attracting more males to help rectify significant gender imbalances in the undergraduate student body. At bigger institutions, claims were made that adding football could increase institutional visibility and prestige. The University of North Carolina at Charlotte (UNCC) is an example. A relatively young institution (created in 1963), UNCC had grown to twenty-five thousand students and was projected to grow to thirty-five thousand over the next two decades. Its basketball team had been relatively successful, so it decided to field a football team in 2013, which would compete at the NCAA Division I FCS level.

The president and trustees believed that football should be part of their strategy to elevate their institution to major university status. UNCC was in a state with established and highly regarded research universities such as UNC at Chapel Hill, Duke, NC State, and Wake Forest. All of these institutions had football programs at the higher Football Bowl Subdivision (FBS) level. The UNCC leadership saw football as a means to expand and strengthen ties to their alumni and build new relationships with employers in the region. The chancellor of UNCC,[27] Phillip Dubois, was aware of the possible risks of launching a football program, but he was generally very optimistic about what it could do for his university: "Your academic opportunities open up when you're perceived as an institution of significance and quality, and if you do football right you'll be able to help achieve that."[28] He went on to say that he thought that more stature as a university would make corporate and business leaders and employers in the Charlotte area more likely to hire UNCC students and have them as interns. He also thought that the corporate sector would be more interested in working with faculty researchers and in forming other kinds of partnerships with the university. He and other university officials believed that football would help their institution achieve these outcomes by making the Charlotte and regional community look at UNCC with more interest and respect. The athletic director added that having football would give UNCC more options as it considered how to position itself in the conference realignment mix that has become a major force of change in big-time college athletics in recent years.

The case of UNCC illustrates the kinds of arguments that college presidents often make to justify both new and existing investments in college athletics. We can see the optimism implied by these expressions of the institutional enhancement rationale. These arguments are meant to suppress initial concerns and reinforce the commitment to athletics. Presidents at some institutions may have an empirical basis for believing in the institutional enhancement rationale. We know, for example, that big-time athletic success has sometimes resulted in more publicity, a higher profile, more student applications, more donations (largely to athletics), and wider or stronger ties to the community. Furthermore, it is easy to see why presidents might get caught up emotionally in athletics, since sports contests can be very exciting and inspire strong feelings of institutional pride and pride in athletic teams, at least for the moment. For example, it is exciting to see 50,000 to 100,000 people pack a stadium or to see your indoor arena full. It is also exciting to see your teams win and attract media attention. This excitement and the anticipation of various benefits fuel the commitment to athletics. Presidents look forward to big donations, fruitful partnerships, and political support when they see prominent alumni, wealthy members of the business community, and powerful politicians cheering for their athletic teams.

There is no other activity sponsored by a university that attracts this much attention or creates this much excitement. Still, presidents who make unqualified assertions of the institutional enhancement rationale may have no actual justification for them. Most teams lose money, only some can win, and fans of those teams marked by a lack of success can sometimes get frustrated. Student applications, donations, and state allocations may not increase, and the spikes in public attention and campus morale after big wins usually do not last long on most campuses. Nevertheless, presidents may be committed to athletics for various reasons. They need to find ways to propel their institution forward as they contemplate their next strategic plan. They may need new strategies for growth or new ways to make the institution more attractive to prospective students or donors. Offering a popular form of entertainment, having winning big-time teams, and moving up the rankings in the big-time college sports world may seem to be a solution to some of their challenges of institutional leadership. Their athletic commitment may increase because they are caught up in the strong emotions of the moment that athletic entertainment can inspire or because they have suspended the rational and critical thinking they apply to other decisions.

Presidents might initially think that they can treat athletics in the same way they treat other kinds of institutional decisions and commitments, but they are likely to discover that they are qualitatively different. It can be a challenge for presidents to approve cuts to academic budgets or programs or of faculty, but downsizing or cutting entrenched big-time athletic programs may be more difficult. Athletics is an external activity of the university. Alumni, boosters, the business community, the public, and others can identify and get involved with athletic teams, and winning and losing make sports relatively easy to understand. People who do not work on campus or with campus officials are unlikely to have much knowledge of or interest in academic and other institutional decisions. Thus, internal and athletic decisions are likely to have a different context and dynamic for presidents.

Part of the athletic trap for presidents is the realization that they must make athletic decisions in a way that is different from other kinds of decisions and that they face constraints on their athletic decisions that are different from and possibly greater than the constraints on their decisions in other areas. In addition, major athletic decisions are likely to require more public justification beyond the campus than many other kinds of institutional decisions do. Being in the athletic trap may mean that presidents think they have to express a commitment to their big-time athletic programs even when they have serious reservations about them.

When a commitment to athletics is expressed more on the basis of unfounded optimism or emotion than reality, it becomes more ideological than rational or empirical. It does not matter whether the claims about institutional benefits from athletics are true. As an ideology, the institutional enhancement rationale is supposed to be accepted without question because everyone is supposed to know that athletics is a good thing for the university. Passion or biases justify belief in this case. Belief in the institutional enhancement rationale is parallel to a belief in what sociologist Harry Edwards called "the Dominant American Sports Creed."[29] The creed was expressed as a general justification for sports in America. Its main tenets were beliefs about the benefits of sports participation (e.g., it builds character, prepares participants for life, and teaches discipline). In his research, Edwards found these beliefs to be vaguely defined or largely unsupported by systematic evidence. Some may have been true, at least some of the time, but the important thing is that they were accepted because they resonated with what people wanted to believe, not because evidence supported them. This is the nature of the institutional enhancement rationale when there is no empirical basis for it.

While claims about the benefits of big-time athletics can convince people of the importance of supporting a significant investment in athletics, these public claims have not prevented problems from arising in athletics or insulated presidents from them. Assertions are not necessarily reality, and presidents lose traction with their claims when people begin to see that they do not ring true. Initial supporters of the establishment or improvement of athletic programs may become unhappy when they see expenses escalate, budgetary pressures result, losses pile up, expectations dim, star athletes or coaches caught in scandals, or the school embarrassed by negative media attention. Disappointment and disillusionment are likely to intensify when institutions succumb to ethical, moral, or legal problems in athletics. Being caught in the trap does not make dealing with these problems any easier. An obstacle to taking strong measures to rein in athletics is that even unhappy, disappointed, and disillusioned athletic supporters often continue to support failing or troubled athletic programs. These people may become unhappy with the people they see causing these problems, but their loyalty to the athletic programs themselves is much less likely to diminish. This kind of support for athletics further complicates the president's efforts or intentions to exert control. All of this is part of the athletic trap.

Presidents are not delusional in their view of athletics. In their role of cheerleader for their institution, however, they may not be as rational or calculating in their decisions about big-time sports programs as they might be about support for a new or existing institute, an academic program or department, or an academic building. They may want to treat sports like other areas of the university. Once in the trap, though, they may feel compelled to express their unwavering commitment to athletics and give preferential treatment to big-time sports programs because prominent and wealthy institutional friends favor them. Thus, the athletic trap may compel presidents to claim their enthusiastic support for big-time sports programs over which they are, in fact, unable to exert much control.

The Grip of the Athletic Trap

James Duderstadt is a former president of the University of Michigan, which is one of America's top research universities. Michigan also has long been an athletic power in college sports. Duderstadt recognized the intrinsic value of athletic competition for student-athletes.[30] At the same time, he pointed to serious shortcomings in big-time athletic programs. He sharply criticized big-time football and men's basketball as commercial entertainment businesses, noting their corruption of academic values, their lack of relevance to the academic mission of the university, and the deviance of athletes and coaches.

Despite such harsh criticisms from a former insider and rhetoric from the NCAA about reform,[31] there is little evidence that the NCAA or its big-time members are moving away from the commercial model that has been associated with significant problems in big-time college athletics. The commitment of the NCAA to the commercial model seems self-evident, if not self-serving. As for the universities, they are likely to be caught in the athletic trap once their leaders publicly assert their commitment to commercialized athletics and develop relationships that reinforce this commitment. Being caught in the trap means that these universities and their leaders are unlikely to back away from the commercial model. For example, I have questioned university and athletic administrators about the sometimes-controversial mandatory student athletic fee. Their response has almost invariably been that they understand the ethical concerns and sympathize with students already burdened with high tuition costs, but at the same time they are not willing to give up or reduce a valuable revenue stream for athletics.

The deepening of formal and informal obligations makes it very difficult to escape the athletic trap.[32] For example, the institutional enhancement rationale can lead institutions into a financial arms race. More money is always needed to hire better coaches and athletic directors, recruit the best athletes, and have the best facilities. Then, to justify escalating investments in sports, schools need to win and achieve national prominence. This in turn will likely give coaches and athletic directors more power. Their requests for money, other resources, and concessions in admissions and other areas will be given more weight as the need to win and gain a higher ranking becomes more pressing. As a result, control over athletics may subtly, unintentionally, and steadily shift away from presidents.

As the commercial model takes hold, big-name coaches, athletic directors, and powerful athletic boosters such as alumni, trustees, and wealthy athletic donors are likely to increase their power. Television and corporate sponsors will also play a bigger role in athletic programs guided by the commercial model. This commercial orientation generally means a primary emphasis on football and men's basketball at the expense of women's sports and less commercialized and less-revenue-generating men's sports.[33] Thus, the athletic trap implies both an entrenchment of the commercial model and a bias toward the financial, personnel, and facility needs of the most commercialized programs, usually football and men's basketball. Even the substantial legal clout of Title IX has not displaced these men's sports from their top-tier status. What has happened instead is that non-revenue men's sports have been underfunded or cut to allow for the addition or increased funding of some women's sports.[34]

Presidents who are already in the athletic trap or who are making commitments to create the trap may have an abstract or intellectual understanding of the possible risks of big-time sports programs. However, they also may be naïve in thinking that they and their institutions will escape the fallout from striving for athletic success. Once they have decided to work at a major university or to seek big-time or elevated status for athletics, they will find it is difficult to reverse course. People who study bureaucracies tell us that formal structures usually are difficult to dismantle once they are put in place and especially when they are established for a while. Contractual commitments to people and facilities, established loyalties, and the chance to generate revenue and publicity all keep big-time athletic programs in place. Furthermore, promises, raised expectations, and new resource commitments keep institutions on the path of building up their athletic program. The aspirational process in athletics is similar to the process of pursuing a research-university model that has appealed to so many primarily undergraduate regional comprehensive universities.[35] Indeed, some of these aspiring research universities may be "mid-majors" also seeking more prominence in athletics. The ultimate goal in both pursuits would seem to be more prestige, which can take precedence over the educational mission or academic integrity of the institution. Thus, the commercial model creates a combination of aspirational and structural factors that make big-time college sports commitments a trap.

Commercialism, Critics, and Reformers

Throughout the history of college athletics, critics have seen the need to reform or even eliminate college athletics as a result of commercialism and its perceived and real corrupting influence. The Knight Commission on Intercollegiate Athletics has received attention over the past two decades for its reform efforts. The Knight Commission was founded in 1989 with money from the John S. and James L. Knight Foundation in response to a previous decade of major scandals in college athletics.[36] It focused mainly on how the excesses of the commercial model and academic corruption were undermining the academic integrity of institutions with big-time athletic programs. It has brought together prominent people in college sports to discuss its problems and ways to resolve them. The Knight Commission has sponsored conferences and published research reports and policy papers on college sports. In its models of reform, it has emphasized the key role of presidents in taking control of athletics, reining in the excesses, and reforming it. Its desire to see presidents assert control apparently has been shared by the NCAA, which has historically been the dominant force in college athletics. In 2003 and 2010, it chose former college presidents as its leader. Not surprisingly, both NCAA presidents, Myles Brand of Indiana University and his successor Mark Emmert of the University of Washington, led institutions in major athletic conferences.

Critics have often pointed to excessive commercialism as the underlying cause of major problems in college sports. This is not really surprising, since the NCAA and its most prominent and powerful member institutions have long been committed to a commercial model of college sports. Commercialization turned college sports into popular entertainment and enabled the most successful programs to reap the benefits promised by the institutional enhancement rationale. The model of college sports as entertainment has helped the most commercialized programs and their universities to become household names and popular brands. Thus, the primary beneficiaries of this commercial model have understandably also been strong proponents of commercialized sports programs. Their successes at the big-time level of college sports encouraged other institutions to follow their lead. The money and prestige earned by the top programs has given hope to less prominent programs that they will also be able to reach the heights and reap the rewards of the big-time in college sports. As a result, neither the successful nor those aspiring to success in the commercialized college sports world have been willing to undertake major reforms.

Seeing the benefits of commercialization, NCAA members have been reluctant to bite the hand of commercialism that has fed the growth of college athletics. Yet competing in big-time college sports is expensive. The quest for competitive success has led institutions into arms races of continually escalating spending that only the most competitively successful at the highest levels of their sport have been able to win. Only a relatively few schools earn enough from athletics to balance their athletic budgets. The problem is that schools want to stay in the race, but they are having difficulty keeping up financially and competitively. NCAA officials and college presidents decry the irrationality and destructiveness of the arms race, but very few seem to have figured out how to compete at a high level and keep costs under control. And no one has figured out how to stop the arms race. This is a major challenge of reform for the NCAA, college presidents, and their governing boards. Reforming the commercial model and getting rising costs under control are likely to make it easier to deal with the issues of academic integrity and cheating that have made the headlines over the history of college sports. This challenge, though, is complicated by the powerful athletic aspirations and existing obligations represented by the athletic trap.

The athletic trap raises the question of how much flexibility universities and presidents have in trying to give the collegiate model priority over the commercial model when making decisions about their athletic programs. Is there a point at which presidents of universities with big-time programs find the obligations of the athletic trap so big and so entrenched that it is no longer possible to sustain an illusion that the collegiate model is more important than the commercial model? Can the grip of the athletic trap seem so tight that escape routes are not readily apparent, even when problems are emerging or getting much worse? It is difficult to answer these questions precisely, but they suggest the tightrope that college presidents and the NCAA must walk to sustain college athletics as a big-time enterprise and also to protect the perception of academic integrity among NCAA member institutions.

At the most commercialized Division I level of the NCAA, presidents and governing boards are already caught in the athletic trap. This explains why presidents do not act preemptively or decisively when their athletic programs suffer financial distress, begin to show signs of corruption or a scandal, or manifest some other kind of fallout from the stresses of commercialized athletics. The question is how presidents can create commitments and obligations that give them some flexibility in decision making and allow them to act relatively quickly and decisively and without serious repercussions for their institution. How can they make the athletic trap less of a trap?

Critiques of big-time college sports have pointed to the patterns of corruption and exploitation at institutions in the athletic trap. Two of the most searing recent critiques are journalist Mark Yost's book *Varsity Green* and historian and Pulitzer Prize–winning author Taylor Branch's analysis of college sports in an *Atlantic* magazine article called "The Shame of College Sports."[37] Yost wrote about how commercialism in college athletics has created a culture of corruption and has led to the exploitation of young and poor inner-city athletic stars, who are the raw material and entertainment product of college athletics. Branch's critique was aimed at the underlying commercial structure of big-time college sports and the corruption and exploitation it spawns. It is has generated some strong counterarguments that question its validity and fairness.[38] However, Yost and Branch joined a long list of critics of big-time college sports.

Charles Clotfelter recognized the pros and cons of big-time college sports programs, but he also saw their entertainment function as a valuable adjunct to the academic mission.[39] His systematic, empirically based analysis is a striking contrast to the most trenchant criticisms of college sports. It reminds us to be careful in generalizing about the effects of big-time college sports. On the one hand, big-time college athletics has been a display of commercial entertainment with a history of embarrassing stories about excess and corruption. On the other hand, many respected universities over the history of college sports have enjoyed financial, status and other institutional rewards from competing in this realm. Although they may not always say so,[40] institutions have also seen the value of commercialized sports as entertainment for their students, alumni, and the community. Part of the reason that reform efforts have largely failed is that institutions have been caught in the athletic trap and have been able to rationalize their involvement in big-time sports with various forms of the institutional enhancement rationale.

Looking Ahead with a Focus on Presidents and the Athletic Trap

The issue of presidential control has long been on the minds of reformers, and it figured prominently in the models constructed by the Knight Commission to try to gain control over academic and economic corruption in college athletics.[41] The NCAA has gathered presidents of universities with big-time programs to talk about how to embody more of the spirit of the collegiate model in college athletics. Exerting significant presidential or NCAA influence in this direction has not been easy, though. Rules have been passed to toughen initial and continuing academic eligibility standards and to punish teams with low graduation rates. However, the basic commercial structure of big-time college athletics, which tempts people and institutions to break rules and to cover up irregularities, remains intact.

It is an old story, but reform clearly is needed in college sports. This book proposes a new model of reform that places presidents at the center of reform efforts and the governance of a reformed landscape of college sports. However, it also shows how the entrenched power structure in college sports and the athletic trap stand in the way of achieving genuine reform.

Part of understanding the dilemma of the athletic trap is the tension it represents between the collegiate model and the commercial model of college athletics. Big-time sports programs often have many very loyal fans, and some are wealthy and influential on campus and in the community. Diehard fans love their favorite college sports teams, and for many their loyalty to the university revolves entirely around their passion for its sports teams. At the same time, there are many students, faculty members, trustees, alumni, legislators, government officials, and members of the public who care most about the academic reputation and operations of the university and expect universities to honor their academic obligations first.

Because a disproportionate amount of the attention that many universities receive from the media and the public centers on athletics, it is easy to forget that athletics is not the main interest or concern of these universities. Universities today face many serious challenges, such as accounting to legislators, balancing budgets, responding to the needs and demands of increasingly diverse student bodies, and making themselves more accessible and affordable. This is the complex environment in which universities operate and in which the athletic trap is situated. It is also the environment that university leaders must understand when they make decisions about their athletic programs. A major issue is how much control presidents and their governing boards will have over these changes and whether their efforts are responsive to the academic mission of their institutions.

In some ways, this book is a cautionary tale for presidents, governing boards, and their institutions. Presidents are actually quite familiar with it in many cases. In fact, presidents may acknowledge the possible pitfalls of big-time athletics as they also plunge into commitments and relationships that will constitute an athletic trap for them in the future. I am sure that presidents usually feel confident that their athletic programs will avoid the pitfalls and do the good things that the institutional enhancement rationale promises. On the other hand, there are presidents who are not so confident and may be worried about where big-time athletics has taken their institution or will take it in future. They may feel an obligation to appear enraptured by athletics. At the same time, they may believe that the athletic trap has left them with few options in their efforts to keep athletics under control.

Making athletic decisions involves an array of relationships in the athletic arena. I frame the context of these decisions as a social network of relationships linking universities, their athletic programs, and the governing bodies of college sports to rich and powerful media corporations and other private businesses, such as corporate sponsors and merchandisers. I call this network the intercollegiate golden triangle (IGT).[42] Chapter 2 discusses the main actors in the IGT sectors of college sports, media, and private business and what draws them into this network. Dealing with the IGT is a major aspect of presidential efforts to make athletics on campus honest, financially viable, and a worthy element of the institution's primary educational mission. The array of relationships represented by the IGT is a major component of the structure of the athletic trap.

Chapter 3 examines how the IGT shapes the business of college sports, considering the dynamics of the college sports business in the IGT as a manifestation of the commercial model. Chapter 3 shows how the interplay of power, status, and money in the IGT affects college sports and also what it means to be in the athletic trap. In addition, the chapter examines capitalistic influences in the college sports business, its exploitation of student-athletes, and the influence of athletic boosters.

Chapters 4 and 5 discuss the fallout or problems created by the commercial model and the business of college sports. Chapter 4 focuses on the arms race, economic inequalities, and financial pressures. Chapter 5 examines deviance, corruption, and major recent cases of scandal in big-time college sports programs. It also considers how the athletic trap contributes to deviance and scandals by corrupting values, decisions, and actions.

The perspective of presidents and institutional control is a recurring theme in the first five chapters. In the sixth chapter, it is the central theme. Chapter 6 examines the various roles and relationships that define the networks of presidential responsibility and influence and affect how presidents deal with athletics. This chapter looks closely at the challenges presidents and governing boards face as they try to lead their institutions and keep athletics under control. A big part of this challenge is trying to balance the collegiate and commercial models of athletics so that the institution does not lose track of its academic mission. The entanglements and constraints of the athletic trap for president will become more apparent in this chapter.

Chapter 7 presents a model for reforming big-time college sports and eliminating its worst problems. It recommends ways to lessen the grip of the athletic trap and reduce the serious fallout that the influence of commercialism, the IGT, and this trap can spawn. It also presents a vision of college sports in general that embodies the collegiate model to a much greater extent than college sports does today. The model does not offer a commercialism-free world of college athletics, but it restricts big-time commercialism to a smaller domain within college sports in general and proposes some radically different ways of operating in this domain. NCAA officials and many college presidents have joined reformers in calling for major changes in big-time college sports in recent years, especially in the aftermath of a series of distressing scandals. The reform model I present should provide a realistic and pragmatic way to think about the reform process.

There are cases of universities where big-time athletics appears to have not only taken over the academy but also corrupted it in major ways. Even where college sport has not literally taken over or taken down the academy, it surely has had a significant impact on many institutions of higher education. In some cases, it has distorted the institutional mission and priorities, tarnished reputations, and created serious financial and ethical issues. The athletic trap that can result from big-time commercialized sports programs can bind the president and institution to an array of constraints and pressures that may not be in the best interest of the institution or the president.

My Perspective

I have been directly involved in college sports in some capacity for most of my adult life. I have played a college sport for a couple of years, served on athletics councils at the various universities where I have been a faculty member, served as the faculty athletics representative (FAR) at my current institution, conducted research about various aspects of college sports, taught many genuine student-athletes as well as less serious athletes in the guise of students in my classes, and cheered for many college sports teams as a fan. In formal and informal capacities, I have also had numerous chances to talk to university presidents, athletic directors, coaches, and student-athletes about their involvement in athletics and their athletic hopes and expectations, and I have gotten to know some of these people fairly well.

I have also studied and taught the sociology of sport as a college professor for forty years, which has been a period of exceptional growth and change in college sports. As a sport sociologist, I have felt compelled to examine what I have seen in college sports as objectively as possible and with critical analytical eyes. My research and writing have examined various aspects of college sports. I have studied Title IX and gender influences, the role conflicts of student-athletes as students and athletes, the meaning of the pain and injuries that college athletes experience, and the current commercialized structure of college sport, its implications, and efforts to reform it. Indeed, I once began a book about small groups with an extended example of a sports team to demonstrate the importance of teamwork in achieving success. In addition to all this, I taught a seminar for the past few years about the organizational dynamics of higher education. Thus, I have combined personal involvement in college athletics with research, writing, and teaching about sport and higher education. The range of these experiences has provided valuable insights about the value, possible pitfalls, and complexities of college sport. I think that these experience have kept my observations and analysis connected to the real world of college sports. I have tried to use my experience and expertise to write a book for anyone with an interest in big-time college sports, from the harshest critic who wants to see it go away to the biggest fan who wants it to remain as popular as ever.

CHAPTER TWO

The Intercollegiate Golden Triangle

The idea of the intercollegiate golden triangle (IGT) that I introduced in chapter 1 is an essential conceptual tool throughout this book. It is a way of seeing and referring to the dominant structure of money, power, and prestige in commercialized college sports.[1] The IGT is a social network of relationships linking universities, their athletic programs, and the governing bodies of college sports to rich and powerful media corporations and such other private businesses as corporate sponsors and merchandisers. Professional sports leagues and other major players in the marketplace of commercialized sports are also part of this network. Although IGT is not part of the popular lexicon for discussing college sports, the idea it represents is not new.

Barry Smart first used the term *golden triangle* to refer to an "indivisible trinity" of professional sport, television, and corporate sponsors in the global cultural economy of sport from which all three partners derived substantial economic benefits.[2] I borrowed from Smart and used the term extensively as an integrating theme in my analysis of commercialized sports and the forces of change in the global cultural economy.[3] Others have used similar ideas to refer broadly to dominant structural forces in commercialized sports.[4] In this book, I have narrowed my application of the golden triangle idea to college sports.

This concept serves both a descriptive purpose and an analytical one in clarifying and explaining what is driving the operation and development of big-time college sports in the United States. The IGT is the foundation of commercialism in college sports. This network of commercial ties has enabled college athletics to grow in size, stature, power, and wealth as a segment of the cultural economy in the United States. Institutions of higher education have been able to make money and increase their public visibility through sports, and media and private business enterprises have generated profits and prestige as a result of their relationships in the IGT. Commercialized college sports have become a significant segment of the entertainment business, as people have been willing to pay to attend live contests, watch or listen to broadcasts, and purchase assorted products associated with college sports teams or contests.

The IGT is the structure that has substantially expanded the market for college sports. As universities, the NCAA, and athletic conferences have become increasingly dependent on media and private business investments, they have accepted the commercial influences accompanying these relationships. Observers of college sports have criticized this commercialism almost since the first time institutions of higher education started charging admission for sports events, and the criticism escalated when colleges and universities began making more money from sports through their relationships with the media and private businesses. Although successful big-time sports programs have become increasingly expensive and have damaged the reputation of more than a few institutions, the promise of assorted institutional benefits from sports prominence has motivated many schools to try to support big-time operations.

The main sectors of the IGT involve sports, the media, and private businesses. The major actors in the sport sector include universities sponsoring commercialized athletic programs; their athletic departments, programs, and foundations; athletic conferences; the National Collegiate Athletic Association (NCAA); and professional sports leagues. Entities such as the Bowl Championship Series (BCS) have been spawned by powerful players in the IGT—in this case, powerful football schools and conferences.

Our interest here is mainly in the athletic programs that compete at the most commercialized level of the NCAA, Division I. These are the big-time athletic programs, and I refer to the universities that sponsor these programs as *big-time universities* (BTUs). The *media sector* involves the various media outlets that report, broadcast, and advertise college sports. This sector includes network and cable television, radio, newspapers, magazines, and emerging Internet media. I call the sector including corporate sponsors the *private business sector*, or simply the *business sector*, notwithstanding the fact that the media sector also includes private for-profit businesses. While the social network of the college sports industry is very large and diverse, I focus on relationships within the IGT that directly or indirectly connect the sport, media, and business sectors through relations of money, power, and prestige.

Money is the glue that binds the various sectors of the IGT to each other. The college sports business exists because all of the parties involved think they can make money from college sports, and the IGT exists because the partners in this network think they can directly or indirectly make money from their relationships with each other. The basic financial structure of the IGT can be described in terms of revenue streams linking the different sectors.

The college sector earns money from its media and marketing rights contracts. The NCAA makes hundreds of millions of dollars from its television rights contracts, and the conferences and individual athletic programs also make substantial amounts of money from their relationships with the commercial sports media. The NCAA, individual athletic programs and universities, and athletic conferences also make money from the private business sector of the IGT through sponsorship contracts, licensing agreements for the sale of branded athletic gear and other branded merchandise, and vendor relationships. Television and other media, such as the Internet, newspapers, and magazines, make money from fees for televised, online, and print ads placed by private business sponsors. Private businesses purchase ad time and space from sports media because they believe that they will increase sales and profits by reaching the college sports audience. This audience is attractive to advertisers because it is relatively well educated and affluent.[5] Parenthetically, professional sports leagues *save money* because BTUs shoulder the costs of recruiting and preparing athletes to play in these leagues. In effect, big-time college sports programs serve as the minor leagues for professional sports.

Although most BTUs already have a big-time sports program in place when a president is appointed, some of these new presidents make the decision to elevate the existing sports program to a higher level. Those trying to move up in the college sports hierarchy often nurture hopes that their institution will someday achieve the kind of sports success that will make it more known, more respected, and better supported by alumni and donors. Whether or not they voluntarily choose to pursue or be in the big-time of college sports, presidents at BTUs and aspiring BTUs face the challenge of balancing their primary commitments to the academic mission of their institution with the assorted demands of its relationships in sport and the IGT. The levels of commercialism that the IGT makes possible and that are associated with big-time status are also a source of many potential challenges for presidents. Being in the IGT helps explain why presidents may feel pressure to continue pursuing success in big-time college sports despite pitfalls and problems. It is difficult to walk away from the financial and contractual commitments and public expectations that big-time status implies. This difficulty of walking away from these obligations and expectations is the athletic trap. Thus, being in the IGT is part of the explanation of how universities fall into the athletic trap.

Big-Time Players, Money, and Financial Linkages in the IGT

The NCAA has long been the dominant player in the sport sector of the IGT. In a speech to the NCAA's annual convention in 2006, the late NCAA president Myles

Brand asserted the need for the NCAA to be "more aggressive" in seeking additional revenue, in selling its championships to new media outlets and the Internet, and in securing new corporate sponsors.[6] In stating the NCAA's business plan, he implicitly described the structure of the IGT and acknowledged the dependence of big-time college sports on revenue from its commercial partners in the IGT. This speech is noteworthy and revealing: Brand, a former college president, who had tried for many years to rein in commercialism in college sports, was obviously caught in the same athletic trap as that faced by many presidents in his organization whose institutions had big-time athletic programs.

We would expect media and private business enterprises in the IGT to be primarily or exclusively oriented to making money through their relationships in the IGT. It may be a little more difficult to accept that money is an important or primary motive of the NCAA and universities in college sports. After all, the NCAA and universities often assert high-minded motives for being involved in commercialized college sports. The pursuit of commercialism through the IGT, however, effectively makes college sport a business, and businesses exist to make money. Consider how much money flows through the NCAA each year. According to a *USA Today* analysis, the NCAA generated at least $860 million in revenue in FY2012, mainly from multimedia and marketing rights contracts.[7] By 2012 it had accumulated more than $500 million in net assets, with an endowment fund of more than $260 million in unrestricted assets. *USA Today* estimated that FY2012 expenses were more than $800 million, with an all-time record $503 million distributed to Division I institutions and conferences. Thus, one could argue that the power of the NCAA to regulate college sports derives mainly from the money it makes for its big-time members. This may be why its late president asserted the importance of finding new revenue streams and making more money, because more money could help the NCAA maintain its power in the sport sector of the IGT.

The financial motives of universities are somewhat different from the motives of the NCAA, the conferences, and other actors in the sport sector of the IGT, and they are significantly different from the financial motives of the media and business sectors. On the one hand, universities do not have the same distributive function that the NCAA and conferences have in what they do with the sports revenue they generate. On the other hand, they are different from their profit-oriented media and business partners in the IGT because universities are not supposed to be trying to profit from their activities.[8] They are accorded tax-exempt status because they are treated under the law as not-for-profit entities. Universities do expect their commercialized sports programs to generate enough income to pay for themselves and also to subsidize the nonrevenue programs in the athletic department. Even though most big-time athletic programs do not meet this expectation, they nevertheless engage in commercial activities that produce millions of dollars. These commercial activities could be construed as being similar to business ventures, and the large sums of money that flow through the sport sector of the IGT could look like the profits that private businesses generate. Of course, the profits of private businesses are taxed, and some legislators have raised questions about why universities are able to escape taxes on revenue from commercial activities that seem so similar to those of for-profit businesses.

Thus, universities are in the delicate financial, legal, and political situation of needing to make money from sports without looking like they are businesses. They also have to justify using funds from sources unrelated to sports activities to pay for athletic programs when athletic revenue falls short of expectations. This complicated financial structure of athletics at BTUs represents an especially complicated challenge for the presidents who have ultimate campus responsibility for ensuring that their universities' financial balance sheets are in the black.

Underpinning the financial structure of the IGT is popular interest in college sports and, in particular, big-time sports teams. Colleges initially got into the college sports business because they recognized that the public was attracted to college sports events. Seeing this interest also motivated the media to cover and invest in college sports and motivated businesses to sponsor college sports and sell college sports merchandise. Less interest in college sports translates into smaller media audiences and fewer potential customers reading, watching, or hearing sponsors' ads. Significantly smaller audiences and fewer customers would shake the foundation of commercialized college sports and the IGT. This may be a proverbial elephant in the room. Even with some recent evidence of declining attendance in college football and basketball,[9] there has been little talk in the IGT about college sports losing its prominent place in popular culture or the entertainment economy in the United States.

As long as the IGT investors believe that Americans still love big-time college sports as a form of entertainment, they are likely to ignore short-term dips in attendance. After all, they can believe that the economy will improve and put more money in people's pocketbooks. They can also assume that unpopular bowls will add popular new gimmicks to attract more fans or that consistently unpopular bowls will be dropped from the crowded bowl schedule and strengthen overall interest in the remaining bowl games. Furthermore, the people who run and invest in college sports may see a shift from seats in the stadium to eyeballs on the Internet or other media delivering college sports events to fans. While universities rely on ticket sales and want to see their stadiums and arenas full of cheering spectators, the media and business investors in college sports are likely to see enough profits to maintain their interest as long as large numbers of people are paying attention to college sports events in either live or mediated forms, are exposed to the ads, and buy the branded merchandise. In addition, having signed long-term contracts with the NCAA and other organizations in the sport sector of the IGT, the college sports media, sponsors, and merchandisers are caught at least for a while in an athletic trap of their own. It involves a set of obligations that is structurally similar to the kind of trap that binds the sport sector to its current investment in college sports.

A decline in attendance cannot be so easily dismissed though. For some programs, it could foreshadow troubles that make it difficult for them to remain competitive or financially viable. When some programs fail and are not replaced by new programs at other institutions, there are ripple effects on scheduling and conference viability. If the governing bodies of college sport ignore these changes, such ripple effects could turn into a tidal wave that could significantly disrupt the current financial structure of big-time college sports and the IGT.

The IGT as a Network of Money, Power, and Prestige

The IGT is not just a financial or economic network. It is also a network of status relations in which members within each sector vie for prestige. The quest among universities for higher rankings in the annual *U.S. News & World Report* surveys is paralleled at the top level of athletics by the competition for a spot in the national rankings for football and men's basketball teams. Competition can be fierce in this status system because universities know that athletic success can be a useful currency to reap status and rewards only if that success is widely recognized. Recognition makes athletic success a currency that can be used to burnish a university's brand, attract students and donors, and generate alumni and popular support. These are the kinds of institutional enhancements that presidents promise when they talk about their commitment to big-time athletics. Universities with teams consistently in the national rankings in football or men's basketball are able to translate that recognition into power within the NCAA and other important college sports circles, and they command the most interest from the media and business sectors of the IGT.

The media make it possible for college sports teams to gain national recognition or prestige. Prestige implies brand recognition in marketing terms and is a useful commodity for building and maintaining the competitive success of an athletic program. Coaches utilize this reputational capital when recruiting talented athletes. Similarly, presidents, fundraisers, and admission directors often seem to believe that having a successful big-time athletic program will help open doors for them as they try to impress legislators, members of the business community, prospective donors and students, and trustees.

Flows of prestige, money, and power represent the basic structure of the IGT and also reveal why the IGT has so much influence over college sports. Actors in the IGT compete for these rewards within and across its three major sectors. This competition results in prestige, financial, and power hierarchies in each sector. The stratification of the IGT means that the money, goods, and services that flow through the IGT do not flow evenly to the various actors in this network. As a result, some actors have more resources to translate into competitive success on the field or in the athletic marketplace, and this success can be used to exercise power and gain prestige.

The universities and athletic programs with the highest status in the IGT are generally the most competitively successful members of the elite conferences of football and men's basketball.[10] Football Bowl Subdivision (FBS) football teams are at the highest and most commercialized level of the NCAA Division I and may be eligible to compete in bowl games at the end of the season. Beginning in the late 1990s, the most highly ranked college football teams had a chance to play in the Bowl Championship Series (BCS), which was created by the major athletic conferences to determine a national champion. NCAA Division I football teams in the Football Championship Subdivision (FCS) compete in a playoff system to determine their national champion. The FCS generally includes less prominent mid-major schools in less prestigious and less commercially successful conferences than those in the FBS.

The Elite 6 conferences in the FBS have had automatic qualification (AQ) status in the BCS.[11] These conferences are where most of the top-ranked teams are found. In 2012 they were the Atlantic Coast Conference (ACC), Big East, Big Ten, Big 12, Pacific-12 (Pac-12), and the Southeastern Conference (SEC). Notre Dame is a special case in football because it has historically remained an independent and has not had a conference affiliation in this sport. The Elite 6 conferences have generally had the most ranked teams in men's basketball as well as football, which is an indicator of their elite status.

The Elite 6 conferences generate the most revenue for their members and enjoy the most national prestige. While the influence of the IGT on these big-time programs may be obvious, less obvious is the influence of the IGT and the big-time programs on less commercialized and less competitively successful athletic programs and their institutions. The stratification of intercollegiate athletics into different realms separated by traditional reputation, success, wealth, and power and by more or less favored status in the IGT is an important fact about college sports in the

United States. Just as individuals strive to move up the social class hierarchy, institutions of higher education and their athletic programs also strive for such mobility in the world of college athletics. They believe that the institution as a whole will bask in the reflected glory of being regarded as a big-time player in college sports. While we generally applaud ambition as a virtue embedded in the American Dream, the desire to move up the college sports hierarchy and be among the best can have adverse effects when ambition exceeds resources and capabilities.

The College Sport Sector: Universities and Athletic Programs

Each of the major sectors of the IGT network is more complex than I have so far suggested. Because much has already been written by scholars and journalists about each of these sectors, I try here only to show how selected actors, patterns, and issues in each sector illustrate the basic character and important implications of the IGT.

In the college sports sector, the dominant institutional actors are public universities. Their teams are disproportionately found in the rankings of big-time college football and basketball. This is especially true for the large flagship and historic land-grant universities. Regional or comprehensive universities also compete at the Division I level of college athletics, but they are generally affiliated with less elite mid-major basketball conferences and compete in the less prestigious FCS rather than FBS. Mid-majors occasionally reach unexpected heights in basketball, such as when mid-major Colonial Athletic Association conference members George Mason University in 2006 and Virginia Commonwealth University in 2011 made it to the Final Four of the men's basketball tournament. FCS teams also occasionally defeat FBS teams in football, such as when Appalachian State beat the University of Michigan in 2007 and James Madison University defeated Virginia Tech in 2010. These upsets are especially noteworthy because they are relatively unusual and because the mid-majors and FCS teams have much more modest athletic budgets than their more prestigious big-time opponents. The higher-status teams in football and men's basketball generally use their superior wealth, prestige, and power to hire better-known coaches and athletic directors, to recruit more talented athletes, and to win more.

The mid-major and FCS institutions are on the outside looking in at the elite, but they usually invest a lot less than their elite counterparts in their pursuit of athletic success. Thus, presidents with mid-major and FCS programs may feel the grip of the athletic trap and the arms race, but the consequences of not succeeding usually are less significant for them and their institutions. Their athletic budgets and deficits are typically more modest and more manageable, and the expectations for athletic success are lower. Still, athletic aspirations that presidents cultivate or that powerful trustees or donors push on them may lead to far more athletic spending and far greater expectations, which can tighten the grip of the athletic trap at these institutions. This is especially likely to be true when institutions add a football team, seek to move from a lower NCAA level to Division I or to the FBS, or try to increase their prominence in football.

Size, structure, mission, history, resources, reputation, and its vision of itself are among the factors that can influence a university's ambitions in athletics and how well it does. University leaders and sports boosters often believe that consistently winning at progressively higher levels of big-time college sports will propel the institution into the ranks of the nationally known and respected. Of course, most of these dreams are largely unfulfilled, because the climb to success in college sports is expensive and often rocky. However, the UNC at Charlotte story related in chapter 1 and similar stories of aspiration in college sports have shown that the institutional enhancement rationale can be compelling. While universities may conduct systematic feasibility studies and use student input to guide their athletic decisions,[12] clearheaded and fact-based rational thinking and responsiveness to students is not always a part of the decision-making process in relation to sports.

Even elite small colleges playing at the least commercialized Division III level of the NCAA and the eight very old institutions that formed the Ivy League in the mid-1950s display some seriousness about sports.[13] They like to win and controversially give preferential treatment in admissions to applicants with solid athletic credentials. These student-athletes tend to become involved in campus social networks mainly made up of other athletes and, not surprisingly, tend to do worse academically than their high school grades and standardized test scores predicted.[14]

Although elite small colleges may become trapped in athletics to a certain extent, this trap is not nearly as consequential for them as it is for universities competing at higher levels and with more invested in athletics. They are generally insulated from the worst financial, academic, and legal consequences of athletics because they compete at the least commercialized level of college athletics, do not engage in the kind or intensity of athletic recruitment that results in serious cheating, and have large endowments to cover athletic deficits. At these institutions, it is assumed that athletics is part of the educational mission and that it will be largely or almost entirely subsidized by general university funds. In embracing the collegiate model of college sports, elite small colleges provide a significant contrast to institutions with more commercially oriented approaches to athletics. Their less commercial orientation places them outside the big-time college sports world, which is why they will not be a significant focus in this book. On the other hand, their approach to athletics will be an important emphasis in the model of reform proposed in chapter 7.

I focus on two types of universities in the more commercialized realms of college sports, which are separated by a large gap in the big-time college sports hierarchy. One type includes the elite BTUs. These universities, at the NCAA Division I level with athletic budgets that may exceed $100 million, are affiliated with the most prestigious conferences, receive large shares of NCAA and conference revenue distributions, have extensive national media coverage, are frequently in the football and men's basketball top twenty-five rankings, have big-name coaches, supply a large share of the All-Americans and professional sports draftees, play in front of huge and often packed stadiums and arenas, and have wielded the most power in their conferences and in the NCAA and BCS. A second type includes universities that compete less successfully in the NCAA Division I or compete in a less prestigious conference and want to achieve elite status. Mid-majors and FCS schools are also in this second group. There are far more of these nonelite universities than there are elite BTUs.

The athletic department budget for FBS schools averages about 5 percent of the overall institutional budget. This percentage may not seem like a very big number. Averages can be misleading, though. This average does not tell us how much revenue is produced by individual athletic programs or how much money they spend. To get an idea of how much money is made and spent by individual schools at the highest or most commercialized level of college sport, consider the athletic budgets of three members of this elite: the University of Texas, Ohio State University, and the University of Alabama. According to Equity in Athletics Data reported to the U.S. Department of Education for 2010–2011,[15] Texas generated revenues of $150.3 million and spent $133.7 million, which produced a surplus of $16.6 million. Ohio State produced $131.8 million in revenues, had expenditures of $122.3 million, which resulted in a surplus of $9.5 million. Alabama generated revenues of $124.5 million and spent $105.1 million, producing a surplus of $19.4 million.[16] These schools are members of three of the Elite 6 conferences. In 2012 Texas was in the Big 12; Ohio State was in the Big Ten; and Alabama was in the SEC.[17]

Texas, Ohio State, and Alabama were part of a small financial elite in the Elite 6 conferences because they generated athletic surpluses. According to NCAA statistics,[18] in FY2010, only 22 of the 120 schools in the FBS at that time produced a surplus. Furthermore, the average amount of revenue generated by these FBS programs was $35.3 million and the average amount of expenditures was $46.7 million. In addition, less than 7 percent of all Division I athletic programs produced a surplus between 2004 and 2010. To cover athletic deficits, FBS institutions provided a median amount of $9.8 million in subsidies in 2010, which was about 1 percent of the total university budgets at this level.

According to one estimate, a majority of schools in the six major conferences had double-digit percentage increases in their athletic budgets between FY2010 and 2012.[19] These increases are often driven by a fear that big-time athletic programs will become less competitive if their school does not increase its athletic investment each year. This fear drives the arms race of constantly increasing expenditures in big-time athletics. Among the less elite, there is an almost quixotic quality to the belief that spending more will significantly elevate an institution, its athletic programs, and its sports brand in the IGT. After all, becoming a brand that has a national cachet and is highly attractive to the media and business sectors can take time. It can be expensive and frustrating to invest enough to keep up with the schools with established programs that can generate the most revenue, afford the best coaches, and recruit the best athletes.

Two cases in a *USA Today* story about nonelite athletic programs reveal the challenges of trying to keep up in Division I with a small athletic budget.[20] Mississippi Valley State University (MVSU) spent $4.2 million on athletics in 2011 and relied on a university subsidy of $2.4 million. The University of Maryland Eastern Shore (UMES) spent $4.9 million on athletics in 2011 and had a university subsidy of $4.2 million.[21] Both are historically black universities, which have historically been underfunded institutions. At the beginning of the 2010–2011 season, the MVSU men's basketball team had to practice in a middle-school gym twenty minutes from campus because its own gym's roof had a leak which caused the floor to warp. The team was unable to afford repairs for four months, until after it had earned $800,000 in guarantees for playing (and losing to) four top teams. Although it struggled through its 2010–2011 season compiling a record of 13–19, MVSU did well the following year, with a seventeen-game winning streak in the Southwestern Athletic Conference (SWAC) and a 21–13 record. Despite its limited resources, the team achieved some success between 2007 and 2012, with two NCAA and one NIT postseason tournament appearances. The team was still looking for its first postseason win, but just playing in the postseason is generally seen as a badge of honor for mid-majors. MVSU apparently was unable to duplicate this level of success in football, winning only one of its nine games in 2011.

UMES was not nearly as successful as MVSU in men's basketball, and it had not had a football team for more than thirty years. UMES competed in the Mid-Eastern Athletic Conference (MEAC), and its basketball record for 2010–2011 was 8–21. It was even worse in 2011–2012, dropping to 7–23.

These two cases illustrate what it is like to live in the financial basement of big-time college athletics. It is possible to be a winner in one of the big-time sports but harder to field successful teams in both men's basketball and football. It is also difficult to sustain success from year to year, which can affect revenue. Budgets are balanced with guarantees from big-name teams who invite the lesser teams to play on their courts or in their stadiums because they expect to pick up a win when, as the host, they play their less prominent visitors. These nonelite schools also depend heavily on institutional subsidies, which represent 58 percent of the athletic budget for MVSU and 85 percent for UMES. Winning obviously makes a difference for their precarious budgets. At the lower echelons of big-time college sports, successes must be squeezed from a shoestring budget and from rosters of undersized and less heralded athletes. Training and playing facilities are unlikely to attract star coaches or blue-chip athletes. Their greatest successes tend to come in conference competition, where they are competing against teams with comparable resources. Or they may succeed in sports that attract little public attention. For example, UMES gained little national recognition for its two consecutive NCAA championships in women's bowling in 2011 and 2012.

MVSU and UMES compete in conferences with little clout in the NCAA and almost no national visibility; and they have relatively meager athletic budgets, even for FCS schools. Yet schools in the most competitive mid-major conferences and nonelite FBS schools also reside in a very different world of money, power, and prestige in comparison to the schools at the top of the big-time college sports hierarchy. The financial dimension of this contrast is illustrated by the gap in athletic spending and subsidies between top mid-majors and nonelite schools in the FBS and the expenditures and subsidies of the FBS financial elite.

The Colonial Athletic Association (CAA) is one of the most competitive mid-major FCS conferences. Two of its teams, George Mason and Virginia Commonwealth, competed in the Final Four of the NCAA men's basketball tournament in 2006 and 2011, and four of its football teams—Delaware, James Madison, Richmond, and Villanova—won FCS national championships between 2003 and 2009.[22] NCAA data for public institutions indicated that in 2011 Delaware spent $36 million on athletics and had an institutional subsidy of $28.5 million; George Mason spent $18 and had a subsidy of $14.7 million; James Madison spent $31.1 million and had a subsidy of $25.7 million, and Virginia Commonwealth spent $21.5 million and had a subsidy of $16 million.[23] George Mason and Virginia Commonwealth did not have football teams in 2011. A typical expense budget of a nonelite FBS school is illustrated by Marshall University. It is a member of Conference USA and spent $26.1 million on athletics in 2011 and had a subsidy of $12.5 million. Thus, even at FBS institutions, subsidies—mainly from student athletic fees—cover a substantial portion of expenses, while at FCS schools, subsidies typically cover a majority of the expenses.

Ohio State and Texas are among the relatively few schools providing no subsidies for athletics. While Alabama's athletic subsidy from the university was $5.2 million, none of this money was from student fees.[24] Thus, being among the biggest of the big-time athletic programs in the sport sector of the IGT can be financially rewarding for institutions; such programs neither drain institutional resources nor put a financial burden on students. For most other schools in the NCAA, budgets are much more limited, and substantial deficits are common when subsidies are not taken into account.

The disparities in competitive resources between the elite "haves" and everyone else, the "have-nots," in big-time college sports prompted the president of the University of Texas to raise the idea of restructuring NCAA competition on the basis of these economic differences.[25] Although the NCAA president said he was not advocating this split, it reflected the persisting reality of substantial stratification in the FBS as well as in Division I in general. Of course, those in the less advantaged strata of big-time college sports often see their athletic status and opportunities quite differently from how the Texas president sees his. They celebrate their relatively rare victories against more highly ranked teams and appreciate the chance to gain visibility (and financial guarantees) from competing against the elite.

It would be less expensive to compete at the Division II or Division III level, but as the athletic director of tiny University of North Carolina at Asheville (UNC-A) said, "Staying in Division I is a huge benefit; it brings a lot of attention to our small school. How do you put a price tag on getting your school recognized on a national level?"[26] UNC-A had just played in its second consecutive NCAA men's basketball tournament. Of course, competing at the highest level of college sports has a real price tag. It can be very expensive for smaller and less endowed institutions, and it requires institutional subsidies for all but a relative few. Many presidents may privately worry about how they can balance their institution's finances so that they can continue to sustain their commitment to big-time athletics. When they look at the red ink in the athletic budget, they may wonder whether there are enough practical as well as symbolic benefits to justify their institution's commitment to the big-time world of athletics. However, the athletic trap can make it difficult to escape these commitments, at least in the short term.

Other Players in the College Sport Sector

Other major players in the college sport sector of the IGT are the NCAA and the conferences. The BCS has also been an influential player in this sector over the past two decades. The NCAA has been the primary governing body in college athletics for more than a century. It describes its mission mainly as rule making and governance.[27] Established in 1906 as the Intercollegiate Athletic Association of the United States (IAAUS), it was renamed the National Collegiate Athletic Association in 1910. At first, it concentrated on bringing order to the college sports world. Excessive violence and deaths in football led to calls for its abolition, and the exploitation of athletes was a serious concern. NCAA efforts to create order through its governance have not been completely successful, since a range of financial and integrity issues continue to arise in college sports. The NCAA has been much more successful in fostering growth and commercialization. The establishment of a full-time professional staff and a permanent headquarters greatly facilitated this growth and commercialization.[28]

NCAA members made the director position full-time in 1951 and built a national headquarters in 1952 to centralize control over college sports. Under full-time professional leadership, the NCAA sought to rein in recruitment and financial aid practices with new regulations and more vigorous enforcement and to play a central role in controlling the increasing number of postseason bowl games and championships. It also had a mandate to deal with the influence of the new medium of television on college sports. It created three divisions with different administrative rules and levels of competition in 1973, and in 1978 Division I members voted to divide into two subdivisions, which became the FBS and FCS. The NCAA wrested control of women's sports from the Association for Intercollegiate Athletics for Women (AIAW) in the early 1980s when it began offering championships in women's sports. The increasing differentiation of the structure of the NCAA reflected the stratification of college sports into more and less commercialized realms. The relationship of the NCAA to television has significantly affected the increasing commercialization and stratification in college sports.

NCAA members began restricting televised football broadcasts in 1953 through a Football Television Committee. This control over television exposure and access to revenue significantly increased the power of the NCAA over its members and also gave it substantial leverage in its negotiations with television networks. From 1965 to 1981, the American Broadcasting Network (ABC) was granted the exclusive right to televise regular-season college football games.[29] Universities with major football programs, however, became increasingly unhappy with the way that the NCAA was handling television rights and revenue.

In 1979 the College Football Association (CFA) was formed to represent the interests of the major football programs, and its members included all the major programs and their conferences except for the Big Ten and Pac-10.[30] After the CFA began negotiating its own contract for televising games of its members, various legal skirmishes between the CFA and the NCAA ensued, culminating in a court case that reached the U.S. Supreme Court in 1984. In this court case, two CFA members, the University of Oklahoma and the University of Georgia, sued the NCAA over control of television broadcast rights.[31] As a result of this decision, the NCAA lost its monopoly position in college football television rights negotiations, and the CFA became a major player in the IGT. It negotiated television contracts for its members and distributed television revenue, and it provided a forum for the discussion of common issues affecting the most commercialized football programs. Like the NCAA, though, it faced complaints from ambitious members. When Notre Dame decided to go out on its own and the SEC chose to pursue a separate TV contract, the CFA fell apart, voting to disband in 1997.[32]

The BCS filled the void left by the demise of the CFA. Disagreements over who got to compete in the BCS and the national championship game in turn led to a playoff system, beginning in 2014.[33] All of these powerful structures in big-time football effectively excluded the NCAA. Most of its power today derives from controlling the purse strings of the biggest single moneymaker in college sports, the NCAA Division I men's basketball tournament, called "March Madness."

The NCAA had nearly eleven hundred member universities and colleges in 2012, with approximately one-third in Division I. Only 120 schools were full-time members of the FBS in 2012, with 7 additional schools either in the midst of transitioning into the FBS or waiting to join the queue.[34] The question is how well the NCAA leadership will be able to maintain order among member institutions with widely divergent athletic budgets, reputations, and competitive and commercial opportunities. There has been talk in recent years about the need to reorganize the NCAA,[35] but powerful figures in the sport sector of the IGT have not publicly pushed for a restructuring. For example, in 2011 the commissioners of the dominant conferences in the Elite 6 stated that structural change would not be an issue "until you have a group of core presidents, athletic directors, commissioners and coaches who were willing to embrace real change . . . and are shot down."[36] Parenthetically, presidents of different types of Division I institutions sit on the president's commission and other leadership bodies and committees of the organization.[37] They are supposed to establish the organization's agenda and help assure the academic integrity of college sports. Because the NCAA has never been a democracy, though, future organizational changes in the NCAA will most likely reflect the wishes of its most commercially and competitively successful members.[38]

The NCAA has largely been a spectator as college sports has undergone some major changes in recent years. These changes have involved an ongoing series of Elite 6 conference realignments in which conference commissioners have been the pivotal players.[39] Conference commissioners have gained or lost power according to their skill at playing the conference realignment game. Those who have not played this game well enough have lost their job. This was the fate of Big East commissioner John Marinatto in 2012, and his was the fifth leadership change in Elite 6 conferences over a five-year period.[40] The job of conference commissioners can be daunting in an unstable environment of frequent shifts of conference affiliations. They must be media-savvy negotiators in their dealings with potential media partners. They must be entrepreneurial in putting together the most lucrative packages with TV networks and cable companies. They must have teams that compete in exciting games with each other and are successful against teams in competing conferences so that they can attract large media audiences. They also need to find a balance between strong football and strong basketball schools and a relative competitive balance in both sports within their own league. With more money in major football bowl games and media contracts, though, football strength has seemed to outweigh basketball in the recent era of conference realignment.

The turmoil in the Big East illustrated the importance of football. Several schools with strong basketball programs and established or aspiring football programs left or contemplated leaving the conference to have a chance to reap more revenue from conferences generating more football revenue. Left behind were schools with rich basketball traditions but less prominent football programs or no football program at all. These schools worried about the long-term stability of the conference as it is maneuvered to replace departing members.[41] In late 2012, seven basketball-only Catholic school members, which were among the strongest basketball schools still in the Big East, departed to form a new basketball alliance.[42] Its revenue potential was limited by not having football members, but these universities wanted to be in a conference that focused on their mutual commitment to (men's) basketball. The loss of these schools added to the woes of the Big East, as it sought to protect its brand and secure its future financial viability.

The struggles of the Big East demonstrate a complicating aspect of realignment decisions. It is that shifting conference affiliations may have different implications for teams in football and men's basketball. The competition among conferences for prominence and wealth in the IGT has led to efforts to recruit more attractive members from other conferences, leaving less elite conferences with the challenge of attracting enough schools to have a viable competitive league. Realignment efforts by conferences have been encouraged by the game of musical chairs that individual institutions have been playing for years, as they jump from conference to conference in an effort to move up the college sports hierarchy. Sports economists have called this phenomenon of conference hopping *churning*, referring to the movement of top and bottom teams out of conferences and into new ones.[43]

The presidents of institutions in the elite conferences expect their commissioners to attract and retain the major football powers that are a magnet for television money. Commissioners keep their jobs by taking care of men's basketball and being entrepreneurial in football. When presidents do not see enough media attention and money flow into their conference, the commissioners lose their trust and their jobs. Presidents sometimes face criticism from the sports public and sports commentators for trying to exercise their authority over conferences and other realms in college sports.[44] Sports insiders may resent these moves because they do not respect the sports knowledge of presidents. In the bigger picture of college sports, though, presidents are ultimately the ones who are accountable on their campuses for keeping their athletic programs competitively and financially on track and out of trouble. Thus, there is the irony that presidents are criticized not only for acting decisively but also, when problems arise in athletics, for not acting decisively enough.

The hierarchical order of conferences can be seen in the average amount conference members spend on athletics in the different conferences.[45] Average athletic expenditures per school among the top fifteen Division I conferences in 2011 varied from the fifteenth-place Missouri Valley Conference at $14.59 million per school to first-ranked Southeastern Conference at $75.74 million per school. The Big East was at the bottom of the Elite 6 at $40.76 million per school, which may give some insight into the challenge Big East commissioners have faced in trying to compete with the more elite conferences in football. These numbers are also a way of seeing the cost of being in the athletic elite. It seems, though, that ambition is a bigger factor than cost when more competitive schools leave weaker conferences for stronger ones, since there is the anticipation of bigger returns on their athletic investment.

There may be an upside to realignment for some institutions that could lessen some of the adverse publicity. A study by University of Georgia doctoral students suggested that realignment could have positive academic and institutional effects for institutions that move to more prestigious conferences.[46] Schools moving to a new conference typically were able to be more selective in admissions because they attracted more applicants, and they increased their admission yield rate. Ironically, universities engaging in churning may be criticized for moving to a more prestigious conference to get more media attention and money, but being in a more prestigious conference may confer on churning institutions more prestige, which has academic benefits of increased selectivity, student quality, and retention. The institutions in this study that enjoyed the biggest benefits were ones that moved to the Atlantic

Coast Conference. These kinds of possible benefits are important because they are part of the institutional enhancement rationale used by presidents and others to promote big-time college sports.

The realignment process could have profound effects on the landscape of college sports, possibly resulting in a contraction of conferences into a few super conferences made up of the biggest of the big-time programs. Super conferences are a potentially serious concern for the NCAA because they could further erode its power and increase the stratification of college sports.[47]

The rise and fall of the CFA and the BCS and conference realignment reflect the dynamic organizational environment of big-time college sports. Whatever the shape of the college sport sector, it is likely to have conferences among the most powerful players. The conferences, after all, were the foundation of the CFA and the BCS. They created the playoff system that replaced the original BCS format, and they will retain their power over college football under this new system. In anticipation of the changes created by the new playoff system, the elite conferences began negotiating long-term relationships with the major bowls to be sure their top teams had a place in one of these bowl games. Such placement would guarantee these conferences more television revenue. If one of their teams qualified for the national playoff, a second conference team would have a chance to play in another big-money bowl game. While conferences were assuring their place in the reorganized environment of college football, the NCAA once again found itself with no formal role in the postseason for top football teams.[48]

The Media and Private Business Sectors

Although print media such as newspapers had much to do with the initial popular and commercial growth of college sports, television has been more associated with this growth since the middle of the twentieth century. Television exposure and money are the reasons why the college sector of the IGT has become so dependent on television and why television has been able to increase its influence over college sports. The case of ESPN offers important insights into the nature of the media relationship to the sport sector of the IGT.

Two well-regarded *USA Today* sports reporters provocatively titled their 2011 article about ESPN and college sports "Is ESPN the Main Force behind Realignment in College Sports?"[49] They noted the conspiracy theories asserting that ESPN had been working behind the scenes to orchestrate membership shifts in the conferences to increase the popularity and commercial value of the games it broadcasts. While ESPN executives denied having this kind of power, there is little question that

ESPN had achieved a substantial and pervasive influence over college sports. It was a business partner to various conferences and BTUs, and its contracts were worth a total of $700 million to college sports in 2012.

ESPN has had extensive power as a major broadcast, print, and online news outlet, and it has been in the curious position of being responsible for the sports programs and sports business deals that it reports as sports news. Andy Geiger, a former athletic director at Ohio State University, was quoted as saying, "We're doing business with an entertainment company whose only way of surviving involves the number of eyeballs watching the screen. That is the driving force in what I see as all the decisions being made (about college sports)."[50] While some critics were worried about the close relationship between conference commissioners and ESPN executives, one former college president asserted, "If I'm a president, I want the commissioner to be having that conversation."[51] He suggested that commissioners should know whether particular realignment moves or decisions about conference championship playoff formats will help or hurt their status with the media.

University presidents agreed to a contract with ESPN in 2008 that involved exclusive television, radio, digital, international, and marketing rights for the Fiesta, Orange, and Sugar Bowls from 2011 to 2014[52] and the BCS title game from 2011 to 2013. In 2012 ESPN reportedly paid $160 million for the broadcast rights for the five BCS games, which was about 55 percent more each year than the prior $82.5 million per year contract with Fox. As previously noted, estimates of the value of the TV payout from a four-team FBS playoff ranged from $600 million to $1.5 billion per year.[53]

Some of ESPN's business dealings have created unhappiness in the elite circles of the college sector. For example, it established a twenty-year, $300 million partnership arrangement with the University of Texas for the Longhorn Network (LHN), which initially was to involve the LHN in broadcasting high school and other games. Conference rivals saw this as giving Texas an unfair advantage in the hotly contested recruitment of athletes, and reportedly contributed to Texas A&M's decision to leave the Big 12 conference in which Texas was a member. Although controversial, the desire of the University of Texas to have its own network was shared by conferences and other schools. The Big Ten Network had been in existence for several years when Texas set up the LHN. The Pac-12 was planning its own network as well,[54] and most of the other Elite 6 conferences had lucrative television rights deals.[55]

Although ESPN's power in the IGT has prompted some to call it a monopoly,[56] it is not the only powerful force in the media sector. ESPN has ties to all of the Elite 6 conferences but has exclusive broadcast rights only in the ACC. ESPN has shared the BCS terrain with Fox in recent years, and it has not been able to get the exclusive rights for the Division I men's basketball tournament. Most recently, it lost the rights bidding war to CBS and Turner Sports. The contracts for this tournament were worth $10.8 billion over fourteen years to the NCAA, making this tournament the NCAA's and college sport's most lucrative business venture. This contract involved television, Internet, and wireless rights.[57] ESPN had to settle in 2012 for a deal with the NCAA to broadcast the Division I women's basketball tournament and other NCAA championships, which was worth $18.8 million.[58]

Comments by different parties to the media contract for the men's basketball tournament reveal interesting differences in perspective among major players in the IGT.[59] It may have been public posturing, but the NCAA expressed how the agreement would provide student-athletes across all three divisions with "a range of championship opportunities, access to funds for personal and educational needs, and (in Divisions I and II) athletically related financial aid." On the other hand, the president of CBS News and Sports referred to how the deal assured his network's standing "as a year-round leader in sports television well into the next decade." He also pointed to the "new strategic partnership that not only makes this prestigious property an ongoing core asset in our stable of major television events but a profitable one as well." He looked forward to working with Turner Broadcasting to combine its "industry-leading media assets to maximize the value of the great NCAA championship." The Turner Broadcasting president of sales, distribution, and sports observed that his network was "well-positioned to monetize (its) investment in NCAA programming across three nationally distributed networks," which made possible maximum exposure for the tournament. This business talk by the CBS Sports and Turner Broadcasting executives is an interesting contrast to the NCAA's references to student-athletes. Each party expressed its own interests, but all three had a common interest in making this deal profitable.

Revenue for men's college basketball is channeled through the NCAA, while college football money tends to be channeled through the conferences and the BCS and to a few prominent programs well connected to the media sector. The schools' take from television broadcast rights has swelled since Clemson University and the University of Georgia agreed to split the $3,000 payout that ESPN offered for the right to televise their football game in the fall of 1980.[60] In 2011 Clemson and the other member schools in the Atlantic Coast Conference began reaping the rewards of their twelve-year $1.86 billion contract with ESPN and ABC.[61]

Other elite conferences had even more lucrative contracts in place. For example, the Pac-10, which became the Pac-12 in July 2011, agreed to a twelve-year contract with ESPN and Fox in May 2011 to triple its media rights for football and basketball.

The contract was the most lucrative for any conference in college sports at that time, paying $225 million per year and a total of $2.7 billion beginning in the 2012–2013 season. The conference did not sell the rights to all its football and men's basketball games, because it wanted to be able to show them on the new network the conference was planning.

Big audiences and huge contracts make it easy to see why the media sector is so important to the sport sector in the IGT. The importance of the private business sector may be less evident. However, the media sector is able to invest in sports because private businesses see the sports section of the newspaper, televised sports events, and online sports sites as places where they can effectively reach their intended markets. The college sports media market is especially attractive because of its size and its demographics. Not surprisingly, college sports tend to be most appealing to those with college degrees and to those who have relatively higher incomes.[62] These are two characteristics that are especially attractive to corporate sponsors. Bigger and more affluent audiences enable the sports media to charge higher advertising rates and generate more revenue from advertisers. More media revenue has meant bigger contracts for broadcast rights for college sports telecasts.

The private business sector of the IGT consists of corporate sponsors and other businesses that see college sports as a way to make a profit. The connections that sports consumers draw between corporate brands and college sports and specific schools and teams help these corporations expand the market for their products. Private businesses also hope to increase consumer awareness and sales of their product lines in campus communities by donating money, products, and services to athletic programs on campus. In addition to corporate sponsors, private businesses in the IGT include merchandisers, who enter into licensing agreements with universities to sell official university branded sports gear to the public; retailers, who sell licensed college sports gear to the public;[63] sporting goods manufacturers, who contract with universities to be the exclusive suppliers of sports equipment or apparel to their athletic teams; video game manufacturers, who are licensed to produce NCAA-branded products; and the construction companies that build and renovate sports facilities.

The popularity of March Madness has made it a magnet for advertisers and a popular EA Sports video game.[64] In 2010 the tournament was the second biggest postseason sports opportunity for advertising revenue, generating more ad revenue than the Major League Baseball (MLB) playoffs and World Series, the National Basketball Association (NBA) playoffs and Championship Series, and all thirty-five college football bowl games. CBS earned $613.8 million in ad sales revenue in 2010 for March Madness, which was a 4 percent increase over the previous year. The record was $643.2 million earned in 2008. Only the National Football League (NFL) playoffs and Super Bowl earned more from sponsors, generating $793.8 million for the league broadcast partners in 2010. The NBA earned $417.7 million, and MLB earned $345.3 million in advertising dollars in 2010. Between 2001 and 2010, CBS collected $4.85 billion in March Madness advertising money from 281 advertisers. Compared to the $3 million advertisers paid for thirty-second ads during the 2012 Super Bowl, advertisers paid $1.22 million for thirty-second ads during the final game of the 2010 NCAA men's basketball tournament, down somewhat from the $1.26 million rate in 2007. Football has also been a popular investment for advertisers. In December 2009 and January 2010, college football bowl games generated $318.9 million in ad revenue.

Who are the biggest advertisers in the private business sector of the IGT? For March Madness, they were auto manufacturers, whose investment was about 17 percent of the total ad dollars generated by the tournament in 2010. General Motors (GM) was the biggest sponsor, paying $47.2 million. It was followed by AT&T ($35 million), Coca-Cola ($25.3 million), Capital One ($24.2 million), and Hewlett-Packard ($21.8 million). All of these companies were on the Fortune 500 list of top corporations in 2011, with GM at no. 8, Hewlett-Packard at no. 11, AT&T at no. 12, Coca-Cola at no. 70, and Capital One at no. 134. The status of these companies should not be surprising, since ad buys are expensive for this major sports event. However, their relationship with college sports reflects how closely major college sports are tied to the most successful corporations in America through the relationship of the sport sector of the IGT to the media sector. These relationships reflect the intertwining of interests across the major sectors of the IGT and make big-time college sports financially viable as well as a popular success.

As a practical matter, the dependence of the sport sector on investments from the media and private business sectors means that college presidents must be responsive to the expectations and demands of their media and corporate partners in the IGT. These ties are necessary to sustain the competitive and financial momentum of their big-time athletic programs. As a result, we see cases where teams play at the times that accommodate television scheduling rather than the academic schedules of student-athletes. We also see universities cancel classes so that students can attend big games; college sports arenas and stadiums and other campus buildings display the logos of corporate sponsors; college stores use shelf space to stock licensed athletic gear instead of books and academic supplies; and athletic departments outsource their websites to commercial firms. Faculty members are often wary about having academic interests and values compromised by ties to private businesses. Nevertheless, most college presidents realize that their precarious athletic budgets would be stressed even more if they did not have ties to the private business community. In addition, seeing people on and off campus wear and use athletic gear with their university brand is heartening to presidents, who are typically interested in spreading the university brand more widely.

BTUs typically utilize external marketing firms to disseminate their brand. IMG College is the top collegiate marketing firm and provides a range of services to more than two hundred clients in college sports. Its clients include the NCAA, its eighty-nine championships, NCAA Football, major conferences, and elite and subelite colleges and universities.[65] IMG College generates nearly $450 million in annual sales through a range of services. For example, it represents its clients in a diverse array of economic activities and transactions. They include managing multimedia rights, licensing, events, hospitality, marketing, stadium and arena development, stadium seating plans, ticketing, sales, and consulting. It also produces radio programs, manages telecasts, publishes the most college sports publications, and is the biggest manager of university athletic websites. Duke, Kentucky, Michigan, Notre Dame, Ohio State, Texas, and UCLA are among the elite BTUs on its client list. IMG College is a division of IMG Worldwide, which is a powerful global management and marketing business with interests in sports, entertainment, fashion, and news media.

IMG's client list and its wide range of commercial activities on behalf of its clients clearly show the extent of its influence over the sports sector of the IGT. One college sports expert suggested that its rapid recent expansion of its sports business placed IMG behind only ESPN and CBS as a force in the college sports business.[66] With the resources of a major global corporation, IMG was able to make its way to the top echelons of the IGT in a fairly short period of time. Apparel companies such as Nike and Adidas are also important to college sports, with payouts to top programs for exclusive use of their products worth millions each year.[67] In addition, many other types of businesses play significant roles at national, regional, and local levels. They are sources of revenue and vehicles that connect the NCAA, conferences, and universities to products, services, revenue, and consumers. However, the amount of financial investment and the scope of services place ESPN, CBS, and IMG College at the top of the IGT hierarchy.

The IGT, Presidents, and the Athletic Trap

The IGT emerged in college sports when colleges and universities concluded that they could be more successful in promoting and making money from athletics by forming commercial partnerships with the media and private businesses. Colleges and universities may have assumed that they would be able to keep their commercial ties in perspective and still maintain their commitment to a collegiate model of college sports. In this model, educational purposes are more important than commercial motives. As college athletics has evolved and become increasingly commercialized, though, the dependence of universities on their partners in the media and private business sectors has increased. Furthermore, the organizations in the sport sector that represent the athletic interests of the BTUs have become more and more commercially oriented. NCAA presidents have lamented growing commercialism while fostering it at the same time. They have recognized how important commercial activities are to the current and future popularity and financial viability of big-time college sports. Presidents of BTUs have generally seemed to arrive at the same conclusion.

Dependence on the media and private business sectors of the IGT can be problematic for NCAA and college presidents trying to convince the public or faculty and students that college sports are primarily about student-athletes and educational opportunities. Presidents may personally feel some ambivalence about their institutions' commercial ties and activities in the IGT because they are concerned about how many institutional resources and how much of their time are devoted to athletics vis-à-vis academic and other areas of the campus. At many BTUs, presidents also know that some faculty members seriously question their institution's athletic commitments. They see money invested in athletics when academic facilities are subpar, faculty salaries are not competitive, academic departments and programs are inadequately funded, money is insufficient for student financial aid, star athletes struggle in the classroom, and embarrassing misdeeds occur in athletics. Faculty members also may be suspicious about the motives of their institution's media and private business partners.

Faculty members seem justified to have these concerns and suspicions. At BTUs, big-time athletics often receives a disproportionate amount of attention, and academics and the commercialized world of the IGT seem to be fundamentally at odds with one another. The IGT is ultimately about commerce, and this commerce is only indirectly or peripherally connected to the collegiate model of college sports. However, being a university with a big-time athletic program or big-time aspirations requires ties to the IGT. The challenge for the NCAA and the presidents is to get as much as they can from their commercial partners in the IGT, while they balance the appearance of their commitment to the collegiate model with the realities of the commercial model. Presidents of BTUs may be able to maintain only the appearance of a commitment to a more amateur conception of college sports because the commercial demands of sustaining big-time status in college sports inevitably conflict with the conception of sport for its own sake or for the sake of student-athletes.

Although athletics can be a source of revenue and has intrinsic appeal to many people as entertainment, these are not the kinds of arguments that presidents typically make to justify big-time athletics on their campus. They seem to be more comfortable talking about how big-time athletic success can indirectly benefit their campus by extending and enhancing the university's brand in the higher-education marketplace. They see it as a way to get more and better applicants, build community and political support, and raise campus morale. They like to talk about their scholar-athletes, even if they are disproportionately found in less commercialized sports.

After having bought into their own institutional enhancement rationale, institutional leaders discover that pursuing success can be very costly. They also find that once they make major investments in athletics, they cannot easily reverse course. This inability to change direction is the case even when spiraling costs have stressed the budgets of many institutions and scandals have tarnished the reputation of a significant number of others. Presidents cannot easily reverse course because they have made the kinds of expensive and binding long-term and public commitments that have placed them in the athletic trap.

The allure of athletics is that many people notice when sports teams win on a national stage. The trap is that winning consistently on this stage is elusive and very expensive because many other schools have the same aspirations. This is a zero-sum game, especially when winning national or even conference championships is the yardstick of success. It is easy to see why hopes and dreams are typically or eventually tempered by more disappointing realities. This is why presidents may come to view athletics more as a headache than as a help. Their teams lose. Their athletic programs generate large deficits. Their athletes and coaches get into trouble. The sports media portray them in a harshly negative light. Corporate sponsors commercialize the campus in ways that upset some faculty members. Alumni and boosters try to inject themselves into key campus decisions about athletics and funding priorities. It can be complicated and frustrating for presidents to guide their institution through some or all of this.

Corporate executives in the media and private business sectors of the IGT are unlikely to understand or care much about how their glamorization of the college sport sector can contribute to the athletic trap for college presidents. They pay big sums of money to the college sports sector and the most prominent BTUs because it is a profitable investment. However, the money and prominence they offer the NCAA and universities for being successful are precisely why the collegiate model cannot compete with the commercial model in the IGT.

CHAPTER THREE

The Business of College Sports

The existence of the intercollegiate golden triangle (IGT) implies that there is much more to big-time college sports than what spectators or viewers see when they watch a football or men's basketball game. These games are embedded in a network of relationships involving college presidents, athletic directors, coaches, marketing specialists, athletes and their families, trustees, alumni, fundraisers, serious fans and boosters, politicians, the NCAA, conferences, media, corporate sponsors, and other private businesses. In addition, hanging around the fringes of big-time college sports are shadier characters, including overzealous boosters offering illegal inducements, would-be agents, and gamblers and fixers who want inside information or an edge in determining the outcomes of the games on which they bet. Professional sports leagues, such as the National Football League and the National Basketball Association, are also part of this world because they are members of other golden triangles linked to the IGT.[1] They depend on a steady flow of talent from the colleges and frequently whisk away the most successful big-time college athletes, especially in basketball, before they complete their college eligibility.

While much of the U.S. public may not fully see or understand the complexity of big-time college sports or the IGT, many people seem to understand that big-time college athletics is not a purely amateur endeavor imbued with ideals emphasizing the education or welfare of student-athletes. They read about the intense recruiting of star athletes and star coaches and the million-dollar contracts secured by top coaches at even the mid-major level. They know how expensive it can be to pay for season tickets to see their favorite team play. If they are identified as loyal fans, they are likely to receive solicitations asking for their donations to support "their" team. They see the logos of major corporations displayed around the venues where teams play. If they follow closely enough, they also learn that star athletes at prominent universities are not always serious about their studies and that they often leave school before their eligibility expires or they have a degree in hand. Worse, they may read that prominent universities sometimes get caught in embarrassing cases of corruption involving their sports program.

A Knight Commission survey conducted in late 2005 showed most of the public believed that college sports were highly commercialized, paid coaches too much, were at odds with academic values and traditions, and were excessively controlled by corporate sponsors and the media.[2] A majority also said that universities should reduce their spending on big-time football and basketball and had concerns about the pressures on athletes to use performance-enhancing drugs to play hurt. Furthermore, 44 percent said they thought that college sports were "out of control." This last statistic is actually a significant improvement over responses to this question in a 1990 poll (75 percent felt this way) and in a 1993 poll (52 percent held this belief).

Even with widespread recognition of substantial commercialization, there appears to be increasing public confidence that college sports is getting its house in order. This might explain why 83 percent of the respondents to the Knight Commission's 2005 survey expressed an overall positive opinion about college sports, despite their concerns. The public seemed to understand that college sports was a business, to question some of its business practices, and to have worries about the athletes. Nevertheless, none of this diminished a favorable view of college sports for most respondents.

Perhaps their ready or uncritical acceptance of many of the justifications asserted by presidents and other proponents of college athletics explains why the public does not care much about how universities conducted their sports business. More than three-quarters of the respondents in the Knight Commission survey believed that BTUs generated profits from their sports programs; 84 percent believed that winning in sport resulted in more alumni donations; 55 percent thought that athletic success improved the quality of applicants; and 42 percent believed that spending more on salaries and operating expenses enabled teams to win more.[3] The fact that existing evidence did not consistently support these beliefs is not really important.[4] People live in a world of their perceptions and biases.

It may be relatively easy to convince loyal fans of big-time college sports about the virtues of college athletics, whether or not they are true. Serious fans see college sports and their favorite teams through the filter of their sports passion and dedication. Believing that college athletics is worthwhile reflects their values. Sports and teams with well-established traditions may be relatively insulated from serious public criticism by the public embrace of these traditions and by the entertainment value of watching big-time college sports. Fans can blame individual coaches, athletic directors, presidents, and even some athletes for problems that are publicized from time to time, but their love of the sport itself may not be diminished by these perceived aberrations.

Presidents, though, cannot so easily dismiss financial shortfalls, poor graduation rates, or cases of corruption. They have to answer to trustees and regents and to alumni who do not want the reputation of their alma mater besmirched by excesses or misdeeds in athletics. At the same time, presidents cannot ignore wealthy and influential donors and boosters who expect the university to field successful big-time athletic teams. Presidents with less established or less prestigious athletic programs especially feel the crunch when problems arise in their athletic program and when their teams do not win enough. These latter presidents may find their alumni, boosters, and fans less patient and less forgiving.

Running an institution with a big-time sports program involves a juggling act with different stakeholders having different perspectives of sports. Presidents with established and successful elite big-time sports programs are more likely than their counterparts with less established and less successful programs to be able to keep all the balls in the air. Having a history of playing a sport at a high level and winning fairly consistently generates economic resources needed for success and builds strong loyalties that can help schools weather the bumps of occasional poor seasons or even highly publicized scandals. More elite BTUs have more of this kind of capital, which helps them ride out the tough times. This capital also gives them more clout in the college sports business and the IGT. Being successful and popular makes athletic programs attractive to prospective investors in the sport, including the media and private business sectors of the IGT.

Accommodating the Commercial Model in Big-Time Athletics

NCAA and university leaders have often defended the collegiate model and tried to protect the image of college sports from more commercialized characterizations. They have faced a barrage of criticism in recent years about commercialism in college sports from journalists with a variety of perspectives.[5] Proponents of big-time college sports have had a difficult task trying to argue that commercialism can co-exist with the collegiate model. The commercial and collegiate models imply very different conceptions of the nature and purposes of college sports. They represent a clash of values. Universities are supposed to be essentially about teaching, research, and the educational needs of students and society. They may do other things, but they are supposed to be lesser priorities. Intercollegiate athletics is about training for, playing, and winning sports competitions. While students play these games, their enjoyment or education is not the purpose of athletics at the big-time level.

Opponents of big-time college athletics criticize the crass commercialism embodied in the predominant commercial model. It is contrasted with the idealization of the academy as an ivory tower. The collegiate model at least connects sport to education. The commercial model makes no pretense of this connection. However, the idea that universities are only about purely academic pursuits does not describe the modern university in America. The modern American university is a multiversity, which is a complex organization with tentacles reaching in many different directions. Clark Kerr introduced the multiversity concept in 1963.[6] It was meant to convey how higher education had evolved from more classical forms to an institution that was in tune with the dynamic economic and social changes that accompanied the spurt of postwar industrialization in the mid-twentieth century. The creation of government-funded land-grant universities in the latter part of the nineteenth century planted the roots for the emergence of the multiversity in the United States. These institutions opened the doors of higher education to a more diverse student population, and they expanded the mission of universities to include funded research and public service.

Large research and comprehensive universities today are not single communities unified by traditional academic pursuits of scholarship and teaching. They are typically loosely connected collections of communities with a variety of missions, constituencies, and stakeholders. They exist within a single organizational framework and supposedly are committed to a common albeit vaguely defined university mission. Yet they typically compete with other campus departments and programs for status and resources. This kind of fragmented, entrepreneurial, and outward-looking organization was fertile ground for the development of commercially oriented athletic programs in the late nineteenth century. Big-time athletics remains the most thoroughly commercialized area on BTU campuses. This extent of commercialism contributes to the discomfort more traditionally minded members of the academic community and some presidents feel when thinking about athletics on their campus.

The public apparently has not been too bothered by commercialism in athletics, but it has had some serious questions in recent years about the priorities of colleges and universities as educational institutions. The public recognizes the need to have a college education to be successful today, but it has become dubious about how much colleges and universities care about the education of their students. A national survey of American adults conducted by Public Agenda for the National Center for

Public Policy and Higher Education in December 2009 revealed that only 32 percent of respondents believed that colleges today mainly cared about education and
about assuring that their students had a good educational experience. A majority
believed that colleges could spend less and still maintain a high quality of education,
that students have to borrow too much money to pay for college, and that there are
many people qualified to go to college who do not have the chance to do so.

Comparing more recent results with prior surveys since 2000, the researchers
found two trends going in opposite directions. On the one hand, there was an
increasing perception of the importance of college, while, on the other, there was a
declining confidence that a majority of qualified and motivated students will have
the opportunity to attend. The access and affordability issues combined with the
perceived importance of a college degree may explain why relatively more respondents in 2009–49 versus 39 percent—believed that their state's public college and
university system needed to be "fundamentally overhauled" than believed that their
state's higher-education system should be "basically left alone." Finally, 60 percent
said that colleges were like businesses and cared mostly about the bottom line.

Thus, the polls reveal that the unhappiness a relatively large segment of the
public has with public higher education today has not translated into dissatisfac-
tion with increasing spending on athletics. This is despite the fact that the athletic
department gets a relatively large portion of its revenue from mandatory student
fees on many campuses, and some institutions have upgraded their athletic program with money from student fees. Presidents of many public BTUs explain that
they must raise tuition and fees because declining state support and a bad economy
have squeezed institutional budgets and jeopardized the quality of education. They
seldom explain why they continue to charge or even increase student athletic fees,
which have nothing to do with their students' quality of education.

The public so far has seemed to give these presidents and universities a free pass
regarding athletic fees and spending. Its love of college sports seems to have insulated college athletics from general criticism of higher education. People are aware
of commercial excesses in athletics, but they have largely accepted the commercial
model. Perhaps they implicitly understand that the college sports they love depend
on money and commercialism. Thus, NCAA and campus leaders' worries about
public perceptions of too much commercialism or spending in athletics appear to
be largely unfounded at this time.

Public universities have had to make some tough financial decisions in the difficult economic climate of the past several years, but most BTUs have remained in the
athletics arms race and have been reluctant to cut back student athletic fees. I have
spoken to college presidents and athletic directors who have acknowledged the fi-

nancial strain on students and parents trying to keep up with college costs. However, the athletic directors believe that they cannot compete at a big-time level without student fees, since they typically believe they barely have enough money to cover their current costs and compete successfully. Presidents are often sympathetic to athletic directors, although they may be more willing to hold the line on student fees as the financial squeeze tightens on their campus. In general, though, the athletic trap means that presidents have to accommodate the needs of athletic programs. This implies accepting the commercial model as the way to meet those needs.

When they are hired by BTUs, presidents are unlikely to miss the significance of athletic traditions, major financial investments in athletics, or the well-known and influential actors associated with the athletic program. The stadium and basketball arena typically occupy a lot of real estate on or near campus, and athletic banners and trophies are usually prominently displayed in these venues or the athletic field house. The athletic hall of fame may include members who became professional athletes and many others who distinguished themselves in business or the professions. The athletic department portfolio will also include ties to various commercial partners in the IGT.

The boards of trustees of BTUs often are supportive of athletics, and some members may be former athletes. Former athletes are especially prominent among the members of the athletic boards that help the athletic department raise money. The members of these boards frequently have business backgrounds or business ties,[7] and most are comfortable with the commercial model of athletics. They are likely to be impressed with presidents who are ambitious and entrepreneurial and understand the business logic of efficiency, productivity, and moneymaking.

When presidents publicly embrace the commercial model of athletics as a means to build the university brand and make it better known and more respected, they have accepted the idea of college sports as an entertainment spectacle. They may have accepted this idea enthusiastically or with private reservations, but in either case the belief they had no choice is a reflection of the hold of the athletic trap. Presidents of BTUs typically find that prominent alumni, trustees, and prospective donors like the idea of having their institution in the sports headlines. These people enjoy watching their football and men's basketball teams compete and win on a big stage. When their teams win, presidents may find themselves becoming cheerleaders with as much excitement as loyal fans. They might talk about the importance of the collegiate model, but the vision of amateur sport this model embodies pales in comparison with the much more exciting reality of the sports spectacle that the commercial model makes possible. Presidents of BTUs typically bow to the realities of big-time commercialized sports.

Some faculty members may criticize presidents for being too willing to accept commercialism in athletics or elsewhere in the university. These faculty members often are unhappy about spending a lot of money on athletics and have various concerns about big-time athletics on their campus. They also may be opposed to the business model that is frequently embraced more generally in higher education in this era of the academic marketplace. They rarely are selected to serve on presidential search committees and rarely exert much influence over athletic decisions on their campus.[8] Presidents are less likely to risk alienating trustees than faculty members because they know that defying the board could cost them their job.[9] Defying or ignoring faculty members rarely has such dire consequences.[10]

Thus, debates on BTU campuses about athletic spending or commercialism in athletics may be largely symbolic or philosophical. These kinds of issues may be argued in faculty senates and editorial columns, but they typically do not have much impact on commitments to big-time athletics or the commercial model. People love to watch big-time college sports, which means that they love the entertainment spectacle that the commercial model makes possible. Whereas alternatives offered by the collegiate model do not have the capacity to be as entertaining for a large audience, adoption of the commercial model has enabled the college sports business to grow and prosper.

Athletics as Commercial Entertainment

For TV, college sports is a long-running reality show with a reliable audience. The most commercialized college sports of football and men's basketball have a passionate following around the country, which reach peaks during bowl season and March Madness. They have made successful big-time coaches and athletes idols in the popular culture. These big-time sports have also made their universities popular brands in the cultural economy. Commercialized college sports are part of the institutional and cultural fabric of the United States; as Clotfelter has argued with his data, critics are not likely to diminish their luster for the public or make them disappear anytime soon.[11]

Television executives like sports because they are cheaper to produce than are scripted shows with professional actors. They like college sports because they attract a relatively educated and affluent audience. Universities accommodate the interests and demands of television because they want and think they need television money and exposure. Not to be confused with educational television, college sports telecasts are commercial products of the IGT that reflect commercial entertainment values and the interests of those most invested in these products.[12] As commercial commodities, college sports telecasts are manufactured, marketed, purchased, and sold as entertainment to the public. As a result, televised college sports events often seem to be less about the live competition or athletes on the field or court and more about a spectacle constructed to make the event appeal to as many people as possible.

Television orchestrates what we see and hear. Television sports executives negotiate the matchups of teams and when their games will be played. Television sports producers and directors choose the camera images and angles we see, feed information to announcers, decide when games will be interrupted by TV timeouts, and make sure that the telecast fits in the number of ads that have been contracted. The NCAA, conferences, and competing schools often get opportunities to promote themselves in their own ads, but the primary thrust of ads and the telecast is to sell viewers on the importance of consumer culture and the consumption of advertised products. Announcers are usually careful not to say things that might alienate or anger viewers. Announcers are not journalists.

Spectators attending live events are also exposed to commercialism, but they are freer to choose what they look at or listen to and how they interpret the action as they watch the game. The college sports business is rooted in commercialism, and the sports media try to make sure the public does not miss its importance. Commercial motives shape the ways we experience college sports, since the media sector of the IGT is focused on putting commercial values and products at the center of its broadcasts.[13]

Clotfelter observes that commercialized entertainment has long been part of the "real mission" of BTUs, with benefits as well as costs to universities.[14] He points out that, on the one hand, commercialized athletics can be enjoyable as entertainment, may be a source of state pride, and might emphasize important values such as racial equality, diversity, cooperation, and merit versus inherited status as a basis for success. On the other hand, these kinds of values are not universally learned by participants or spectators, and other values such as winning at any cost and cheating to win could be learned instead. Thus, accepting the commercial entertainment function of big-time college sports as part of a university's mission can be a mixed blessing. It surely is a significant departure from the academic and service missions that even modern multiversities are supposed to have. Perhaps for this reason, few universities include sports in their mission statement.[15]

The reluctance of universities to acknowledge publicly the role of commercial sports entertainment in their mission is not difficult to understand. It is one thing to use commercialized sports entertainment for assorted university purposes but quite another to say it is part of what you are as an institution of higher education.

The uneasy integration of the entertainment culture of big-time college sports into the academic culture of the university was the topic of a provocatively titled session at the Aspen Ideas Festival in June 2012: "College Sports at a Crossroads: Entertainment or Education?" While not a new debate, the people who organized this gathering of "some of the most interesting thinkers and leaders from around the U.S. and abroad" obviously thought such a discussion was still salient.[16]

The Business of College Sports in the IGT

Even though the public seems willing to overlook its concerns about commercialized college sports, the NCAA and universities still seem a bit defensive at times in asserting the value of college sports. They typically use their advertising minutes during sports telecasts to focus on educational programs and facilities, students, and the ways student-athletes take advantage of their education. While universities are serious about their educational mission, such media messages do not change the basic fact that these universities invest substantial resources in an entertainment enterprise with a dubious connection to the educational mission. Commercialized college athletics is fundamentally about the business of marketing and sales: marketing and selling the NCAA and the universities, college sports, and commercial products, from licensed gear to the assorted products of advertisers.

I remember a time years ago when professors recoiled at references to their universities as businesses involved in marketing, sales, and branding, to students as consumers, and to teaching as the delivery of a commodity. Many of my liberal arts colleagues still do. However, all of this is part of the contemporary reality of "universities in the marketplace," which is the title of former Harvard president Derek Bok's book about the commercialization of higher education.[17] Bok observes that commercialization was once largely confined to activities outside the academic core of the institution, such as athletics. Today, though, it is interwoven into the institutional fabric, with financial market incentives influencing many important areas of the university, including medical education, scientific research, business schools, undergraduate admissions, emerging distance education initiatives, and the hiring of increasing numbers of (much less expensive) adjunct and part-time faculty members.[18] By introducing institutions of higher education to commercialization, athletics may have had an insidious influence on the traditional academic culture of these institutions. Athletics provides a ready model for other commercially oriented and entrepreneurial "self-support" units on campus.[19]

Commercialization in athletics and other areas of the university has been driven by such factors as privatization, murky academic missions, competition, and the desire to make money from the things that are produced in and by universities. It has created what David Kirp called the "New U," and what is new and worrisome, he asserted, is the "raw power that money directly exerts over so many aspects of higher education."[20] Some faculty members have been quite creative in marketing themselves as public intellectuals or in turning their intellectual products into marketable goods. Presidents often huddle with other administrators to try to identify new commercial ventures and possible revenue streams. They also discuss the programs that may have to be cut because they no longer attract enough students and cannot pull their weight financially. At the same time, though, they are willing to subsidize athletic programs that do not cover their costs by using general university funds and student fees that could support struggling academic programs.

It is difficult to argue that athletics is about education when athletic departments and programs are guided more by the principles of business administration than by academic values. While athletic departments may not literally be businesses like their for-profit counterparts in the IGT are, athletics structurally and culturally has more in common with businesses than with the academic departments and other campus programs.[21] It is more bureaucratic, has a more regimented culture than the traditional academic realm, and has a more hierarchical system of authority. The NCAA is not a democracy, nor are athletic departments or teams. Student-athletes will have to learn how to think critically and make decisions for themselves in their liberal arts courses because this kind of thinking is not encouraged in big-time athletics.

The NCAA, university athletic departments, and athletic conferences may value business logic and commercialism, but they do not want to look too much like businesses for financial and legal reasons or for public relations purposes. Even if the public is not too bothered by the commercialism in college sports, legislators and courts could cause problems for universities and big-time college sports if they see college sports primarily as a business. College sports organizations have been able to enjoy significant tax exemptions because college athletics has generally been viewed by legislators and the courts as an adjunct of educational institutions, which are granted tax-exempt status. These organizations periodically dance with danger, though. Legislators have made proposals to require universities to pay taxes on income generated from commercial sports because athletics has not been clearly tied to the educational mission of universities. These proposals have not gained much traction yet, perhaps because universities probably would be able to find accounting methods to hide athletic revenue and circumvent these kinds of laws.[22] However, the history of commercialism and ties to the IGT make it difficult for the college sports sector to argue it is not in the college sports business.

The media and private businesses will continue to invest in big-time college sports as long as they remain popular. Yet, as business investors, they do not care if some parts of the sports sector fail, as long as there are conferences, schools, and teams that maintain a large fan base and retain a strong brand. Thus, conferences, schools, and teams compete fiercely not only on the field but also for the loyalty of fans and for favorable status in the eyes of sports media and private business investors. Presidents try to assure this loyalty and stature by spending a lot of money on a first-rate professional staff with star coaches and athletic directors, on first-rate facilities, and on scholarships for talented athletes. They also join with other presidents in making commitments to spend the necessary money on savvy entrepreneurs to lead their conferences. Those who want more from college sports find that they need to spend more, just to keep up. This is the essence of the arms race. Star coaches and athletic directors and savvy conference commissioners are rewarded well when they succeed.

Colleges and universities and the NCAA may be sincere in their commitment to the collegiate model, the idea of the student-athlete, and the academic integrity of college athletics. At the same time, the NCAA and its member institutions that compete at both the most commercialized level and at the mid-major level are also quite serious about the business of college sports. They are committed to success on the field and in the athletic marketplace. Thus, the rhetoric about the collegiate model is likely to be superseded by the realities of the commercial world of college athletics when college presidents, athletic directors, conference commissioners, and the NCAA make key decisions about the business of college sports.

Elite Dominance in the College Sports Business: An Illustration

The NCAA and college sports are dominated by the economic interests of the elite in the college sports establishment. This dominance is illustrated by the case of a proposal for a full cost-of-attendance scholarship for student-athletes.[23] On the surface, it would seem like a reasonable proposal for all schools because it would cover the cost gap between amount the NCAA designates as a full scholarship and the actual cost of tuition and fees, room and board, and books needed to attend a school. This is especially relevant for out-of-state student-athletes who have to travel to and from college.[24] The proposal emerged from a retreat of presidents of schools in the Elite 6 conferences and was backed by the NCAA president. While seemingly a reasonable answer to those calling for more compensation for athletes in commercialized programs, its practical effect was to pinch the budgets of the have-not schools even more. The scholarships were supposed to be an option, but only the richest athletic programs could afford to pay them. Although the NCAA Board of Directors had earlier approved this proposal, it was tabled by the board at the NCAA's annual meeting in January 2012. The board was responding to opposition from more than 160 member schools.

This case illustrates how the haves make decisions without much concern or sympathy for the plight of the have-nots. In fact, the reaction of some presidents to the tabling motion shows the mutual irritation felt by the have-nots and the haves toward each other. Presidents with nonelite programs complained that this was an additional cost that was not offset by cost reductions elsewhere. It would have made it tougher to compete and the arms race even more of a burden. In effect, it was another barrier to making it into the elite.

Presidents in the college sports establishment were not interested in opening the door to their exclusive club. The lack of sympathy for the have-nots was summed up by the University of Georgia president. He remarked that, "A lot of people want to be in Division I but do not want to do Division I."[25] One of his peers said that Division I had grown too big and had too many members. He implied it was being unduly influenced by the votes of schools that do not belong there because they lack the resources to compete at this level. This seemed like class warfare to some, and it explains the desire of the richest and most powerful to separate their big-time programs from the have-nots and the rest of the NCAA. Parenthetically, the elite conferences seem to have the same attitude. They only want members who can afford the cost of doing business at the elite level of college sport or can enhance the conference brand.

Although the elite and nonelite in college sports clearly have quite disparate economic interests, there is one area they have in common—namely, the exploitation of student-athletes. This exploitation is a central factor in sustaining college sports as a viable economic enterprise. In fact, there is a broader exploitation of students in big-time college sports, if we consider the imposition of mandatory student athletic fees. Thus, the NCAA and all schools that compete in big-time college sports have a fundamental bias against the economic interests of students in general and rely on student exploitation to maintain their economic and financial viability.

The Exploitation of Student-Athletes

In the debate about college sports at the Aspen Ideas Festival, the NCAA's vice president and chief policy adviser, Wally Renfo, had the job of responding to two of the sharpest recent critics of his organization and big-time commercialized college sports.[26] Taylor Branch, a prominent civil rights historian, had authored a scathing and sweeping attack of the college sports business in a 2011 article in the *Atlantic* titled the "The Shame of College Sports."[27] New York Times op-ed columnist Joe Nocera frequently took on the NCAA for its monopolistic control over college sports and its exploitation of college athletes.[28] Branch and Nocera both zeroed in on the exploitation issue. Craig Robinson, coach of the Oregon State men's basketball team, also sat on the panel and added fuel to their criticisms. He said that trying to balance the "educational part" and the "entertainment part" made him unusual in the fraternity of big-time college coaches. He thought most of his colleagues were in college coaching for the money. He believed that even if 100 percent of his players graduated, he would still lose his job if his team did not win enough. He did not think being the brother of First Lady Michelle Obama would make much difference.[29] This perception is consistent with the greater influence of the commercial model than the collegiate model.

Renfro defended the NCAA by redirecting criticism to some member institutions and asserting the freedom student-athletes have to make their own choices. For example, he said that member schools, rather than the NCAA, have been responsible for a lot of the problems in college sports, such as recruiting academically underprepared student-athletes and seeing them fail. In fact, the NCAA did establish measures to raise academic standards for student-athletes and athletic programs. He also said that athletes voluntarily decide to play at NCAA schools knowing that their compensation will be limited to an athletic scholarship. This argument was meant to address critics who thought student-athletes were inadequately and unfairly compensated.

Renfro's arguments did not convince his critics or address deeply rooted concerns about how the college sports establishment exploits student-athletes. The challenge in trying to defuse these criticisms is twofold. First, the power of the NCAA as well as the conferences is ultimately rooted in their commercial rather than their academic success. Second, transforming the status of college athletes from amateur to professional could also fundamentally transform the structures of money, status, and power in the college sports business.

NCAA leaders may be sensitive to criticism about how they have run college sports, but they have been able to deflect most of this criticism and keep big-time college sports popular and commercially successful. However, the treatment of athletes may be an issue that makes the leaders of big-time college sports squirm a bit more than other issues raised by critics. The college sports establishment has historically undervalued the contributions of student-athletes as athletic labor and inflated the value of coaches, administrators, conference commissioners, and other paid staff members. The most money flows into the most commercialized level of college sports, but student-athletes at this level are not rewarded any more for their talents or success than are athletes at lower levels of the big-time college sports hierarchy.

The rich and powerful BTUs could claim they were trying to remedy this inequity for big-time college athletes by proposing the full-cost-of-attendance scholarship option. Those who could afford the option would pay for it, and those who could not would opt out. The opposition of the have-nots on financial grounds made them seem like they were less concerned about student-athletes than their bottom line. Thus, the elite schools were the champions of student-athlete welfare, and the have-nots were caught up in money issues. To the have-nots, though, this proposal was a way to drive them farther down the big-time college sports hierarchy.

This proposal might have seemed like a concession by the college sports establishment to proponents of the pay-for-play argument, which would turn athletes into wage-earning employees of the athletic department.[30] The University of Nebraska president made it clear, though, that this was not what he had in mind. He asserted that college athletes were students who played sports and should have their educational costs fully covered. He added that if they wanted to be paid for being athletes, they could become pros.[31] Of course, turning pro is an option only for those good enough and mature enough to play basketball overseas or in a minor league. Football players have no similar options.

The Nebraska president's argument expressed a common sentiment felt in the college sports establishment.[32] Yet it was more of an assertion of values than an economic explanation about a practice in a realm of college sports where economic motives are paramount. Extolling the collegiate model and offering platitudes about athletes as students and amateurs are clearly at odds with the realities of a college sports business organized around a commercial model.

There may be compelling practical or economic arguments about why the best athletes cannot operate as free agents in the college marketplace, but the commercial growth of big-time college sports has made it more difficult to argue that athletes do not deserve a bigger share of the growing financial pie. Whatever their intentions, the NCAA president and the presidents in the elite conferences essentially conceded this point when they proposed the full-cost-of-attendance option. The NCAA made an even bigger concession to commercialism in 1956 when they created the athletic grant-in-aid. This athletic scholarship was financial aid based on athletic merit but not academic merit or need.[33] The NCAA and college sports establishment were not willing to admit that this was pay for play then, and it has never made this admission since that time.

Commercialized sports programs have been able to use the promises of a "free education" and the chance to continue their athletic careers on a big stage to recruit talented high school athletes to play big-time college sports. These promises have not been enough to mollify critics of the exploitation of college athletes. This exploitation is more complicated than the idea that college athletes do not get adequately compensated for their efforts, sacrifices, and successes in commercialized college sports programs. The economic concept of "rent" suggests a more sophisticated conception of this exploitation.[34]

Star athletes in big-time college sports provide a rent for their institution by producing athletic success, favorable publicity, revenue, and other rewards for their schools that generally far exceed the value of what they receive in compensation from athletic scholarships. The difference between the benefits they produce and the amount they get compensated is the rent. It can be interpreted as a form of economic exploitation when the grant-in-aid received by star athletes is far less than the amount of money and prestige their athletic performance generates for athletic directors, coaches, presidents, and their school. Another way of putting this is that rent is a form of exploitation because the amount institutions get from their star athletes is highly disproportional to the amount they invest in them. More talented athletes in more commercialized programs produce more rent. Rent explains why coaches and institutions are willing to take risks and even cheat in recruiting star athletes and in accommodating their academic and other nonathletic deficiencies.[35]

College athletes are idealized in the collegiate model as amateurs and students, but the commercial model that dominates big-time college sports is based on the exploitation of these student-athletes. While fans and boosters might view it as an interesting bit of trivia that some star athletes are also serious and successful students, what they love most about them in the most commercialized realms of college athletics is how entertaining they are. Their enthusiasm seems largely unaffected by the relatively poor or perfunctory academic performance of many of the biggest stars or by criticisms that they are not paid enough for their athletic performance. Thus, the NCAA and college presidents do not get a lot of pressure from the sports public to treat athletes more responsibly and fairly.

The NCAA often touts the rising graduation rates of student-athletes.[36] It also understandably boasts when one of its legendary football programs achieves the top ranking in the football polls and in graduating its players. In 2012 Notre Dame became the first to earn this dual distinction.[37] Publicizing these kinds of educational accomplishments is a way for the NCAA to convey a positive image of big-time college athletics for the media and sponsors and to demonstrate to critics that they are serious about the collegiate model.[38] In this vein, the NCAA also has stiffened the penalties for schools that do not meet tougher academic or graduation standards, and it has provided financial assistance to less affluent schools to help them improve the academic performance of their student-athletes. These educational accomplishments, policies, and programs do not, however, demonstrate the primacy of the collegiate model in the college sports establishment. Nor do they negate the realities of exploitation in big-time college sports.

Exploitation is an especially serious issue for big-time college athletes who come from disadvantaged families and neighborhoods and arrive on campus with barely adequate academic preparation, serious learning deficiencies, and little serious academic motivation. Even the best academic support programs may not be able to get many student-athletes from disadvantaged backgrounds up to speed academically. Their adjustment is complicated by the role conflicts that they face as students and athletes and their intention to leave college early to become professional athletes. In 2012 the Center for the Study of Race and Equity in Education reported that graduation rates for minority male athletes at many Elite 6 conference schools were disturbingly low and substantially less than the rates for their white counterparts.[39]

The NCAA likes to say that almost all college athletes go pro in something other than sport.[40] The failure to obtain a solid education and a degree leaves many athletes in big-time college sports programs with little to show for their investment.[41] They find that pursuing an "eligibility education"[42] does not equip them to compete successfully in the very tough job market they face after their athletic eligibility has expired.

Although NCAA vice president Renfro essentially argued that student-athletes make their own choices about the use of their athletic scholarship, the environment of big-time college sports is structured to make it difficult to be a serious student and a serious athlete, especially for those least prepared for a college education. I do not think that coaches or presidents think of themselves as intentionally exploiting athletes, but the commercial model drives them to recruit high school prospects for their athletic rather than academic potential. Then they try to get the most they can from their investment. The fact that they are willing to recruit from junior colleges with dubious academic reputations to circumvent NCAA initial eligibility standards seems to confirm the underlying commercial motives of schools in big-time college sports. This kind of recruitment belies their expressed commitment to having genuine student-athletes on their big-time teams. Notwithstanding the fact that many student-athletes in big-time programs earn their degrees, quite a few others do not. In addition, athletic demands prevent many big-time athletes from taking advantage of academic opportunities to the same extent as other students not involved in athletics.

The Influence of Athletic Boosters

Presidents of BTUs understand that the presumed benefits of big-time athletics come from winning. They also know that big-time teams need talented athletes to win, and on many BTU campuses presidents seem willing to accept some compromises of academic integrity in recruiting star athletes as part of the formula for winning. They also seem to accept some degree of exploitation as a necessary part of this winning formula. Star athletes can help teams win, but the best athletes are often attracted by star coaches and first-rate facilities, which can be very expensive. Athletic departments try to cover their rising expenses with money from ticket sales, game guarantees, their conferences, independent media contracts, relationships with commercial partners in the IGT, donors, and other sources. In recent years, private donations from alumni and boosters have become an increasingly important source of revenue for big-time sports programs.

At many BTUs, boosters,[43] booster clubs, and athletic foundations have become key elements in helping the athletic program raise money to improve facilities, provide a big enough compensation package to attract star coaches, give coaches the latest technology such as training equipment and video devices, and balance the athletic budget. These bodies are often officially part of the athletic department but sometimes are independent 501(c)(3) nonprofit organizations. All serve as fund-raising arms of the athletic department. They involve large numbers of volunteers, who have been the most loyal and generous supporters of athletics. These athletic boosters often rub shoulders with the president, may work closely with athletic administrators, and participate in activities that cultivate new donors.[44]

Boosters can provide money to fill gaps in the athletic budget, and they give the large gifts to capital campaigns that are used to build or upgrade athletic facilities. Between 2002 and 2008, athletic programs raised almost $4 billion for capital expenditures.[45] In addition, their business contacts help attract corporate sponsors, and their political contacts may help universities with relations with legislators and governors. At universities at the FCS or mid-major level, presidents and athletic directors may see major infusions of private donations as the only way to move up the college sports hierarchy.[46] Their varied contributions can make boosters very powerful figures at both established and aspiring BTUs. Presidents know they must cultivate these people and keep them happy. Universities have sought more help from private donors in recent years as the arms race has continued escalating and as institutional subsidies and other funding sources have decreased.

Fundraising campaigns in athletics do not rival institutional capital campaigns at major research universities, but on many campuses they have become very ambitious. The *Chronicle of Higher Education* found that fifty-five of seventy-three Elite 6 conference schools that responded to its survey had collectively raised a total of $1.1 billion in cash donations for athletics in 2007–2008.[47] Among the most successful in generating these cash donations were Texas (nearly $46 million), Florida (over $45 million), Louisville (over $40 million), Tennessee (over $38 million), and Georgia and Virginia (over $36 million). More than two dozen athletic departments were pursuing or planning an endowment campaign, with the University of California at Berkeley ($500 million), Duke ($350 million), Boston College ($250 million), Texas ($200 million), and Louisiana State ($155 million) leading the way.

These schools might have wanted to emulate Stanford, which had an athletic endowment worth over $500 million. At that time, it was generating about $25 million per year for the athletic department.[48] This money helps Stanford spread more money across its entire athletic program and explains why Stanford won its eighteenth straight Learfield Sports Directors' Cup in 2012 as the most successful athletic program overall in the NCAA. However, only the richest institutions or ones with the biggest athletic ambitions have channeled large portions of their athletic donations into endowments in recent years. As immediate operational and capital needs have increased, more donations have gone into the athletic operating budget. Data from 2008 indicate that only 10 percent of contributions went into endowments.[49]

These data are incomplete and give a snapshot of a single year, but the names of the schools that were cited should not be surprising. It takes a lot of resources to compete in an elite conference, but being in an elite conference has its rewards. Elite conferences have ties to major players in the media and business sectors that generate money and exposure for member schools. These things are part of the winning formula for big-time teams. Having winning teams in the media spotlight makes it easier for universities to convince prospective donors that athletic programs deserve their money.

There is a price for these gifts. There is often an implicit or explicit quid pro quo. Many donors and particularly those making big gifts expect something in return.[50] It is a common practice for major athletic programs to trade the right to buy football and men's basketball tickets for a minimum annual donation. Bigger donations usually mean better seats. The *Chronicle of Higher Education* survey cited earlier found that 40 percent of donations to the most prominent athletic programs paid for seats or suites.[51] The biggest donors typically want more than prime seats, though. The rewards have ranged from dinners with star players to access to practices usually closed to the public and chances to travel with team and be on the sideline during games.

These arrangements can be very intrusive, but donor demands substantially escalate when they want to have their name on a building, want to be appointed to the board of the athletic foundation, or want to be at the table when key decisions are made about the athletic program. Big donors expect their money to buy them attention and influence, and they are usually powerful people accustomed to having other people listen to them.[52] When donors see themselves as being ignored or rebuffed by the beneficiaries of their largesse, they can become upset and withdraw their support. This turn of events has happened frequently at big-time programs, including well-publicized cases at the University of Connecticut and the University of Oregon.

At Connecticut, the case involved the CEO of a capital management firm who was a big football booster and had given $7 million to UConn's football program. When he was not given a voice in the decision to hire a new football coach, though, he became unhappy and threatened to withdraw a $3 million gift and have his family name removed from the football complex.[53] The decision, he reportedly said, "hurt and embarrassed his family."[54] He changed his mind after a contingent including the incoming president met with him. It is not clear what they offered him to change his mind, but their conversation apparently was reassuring and soothed his hurt ego.

The Oregon case involved a major figure in the IGT, Nike cofounder and longtime CEO Phil Knight. He was a University of Oregon alumnus and gave tens of millions of dollars to his alma mater's sports programs. His contributions were an important reason why Oregon was able to move up into the top rank of college football.[55] When Oregon players wear uniforms or footwear he donated, they were paying him back with advertising the Nike logo in front of national television audiences. Beyond this payback, though, he also had regular access to the president and coaches and the athletic program. Needless to say, critics worried about this influence.

Phil Knight did not always get his way at Oregon, and in 2000 he withdrew his donation for the renovation of the football stadium, cut his ties to the university, and invested his money elsewhere for seventeen months after the university became involved in an anti-sweatshop consortium that made Nike one of its prime targets. He was unhappy with the athletic director who had failed to take his side in this conflict. He reconciled with the university and reinstated his pledge when the university withdrew from the consortium and got rid of its athletic director. A revealing part of this story is that the athletic director's contract was bought out with the help of another big booster, who was then hired as the new athletic director. Conflict of interest appears in a variety of ways in this case and seems to be part of the quid pro quo on some campuses.

Presidents realize that athletic gifts do not contribute to the academic mission. In fact, there is recent research showing that athletic giving, especially for football, can adversely affect academic giving.[56] This research suggests that presidents might want to reexamine their premise that successful big-time football programs and the athletic giving associated with them are necessarily good for the university, financially or otherwise. In addition to hurting efforts to raise money for academic purposes, athletic donations can drive a wedge in the culture of the campus.[57] Glistening new athletic facilities and highly paid coaches often stand in stark contrast to aging classroom buildings and research labs and stagnant and much lower faculty salaries. The athletic trap nevertheless obligates presidents to take care of athletics in ways they are unable to tend to the academic plant or faculty. Boosters want winning athletic programs and seem much less interested in what is happening elsewhere on campus.

Boosters sometimes become overly enthusiastic or meddlesome and put universities at risk of being subject to NCAA penalties (see chapter 5). The possibility of overzealous and wayward boosters is why most athletic departments remind boosters, fans, and other friends of their athletic program about relevant NCAA rules involving contacts with current student-athletes, prospects, and others related to the recruited student-athletes.

Presidents often believe they must accept the risks of going after big donors. They view winning as the key to getting the institutional benefits that big-time sports programs are supposed to bring. They know that winning requires money, and donors can be a critical source of money for successful athletic programs. Recent research suggests, though, that the perceived effects of winning and alumni giving may be exaggerated at many schools.[58]

Using sophisticated statistical procedures, Anderson found that winning in football had institutional benefits, but the benefits differed according to the status of the teams. The positive effects of winning in football were more numerous and stronger for the schools with teams in the elite conferences. In comparison with teams in other conferences, teams in the Elite 6 conference saw stronger positive effects of winning in football across a range of variables: alumni giving for the athletic operating budget and for the university's general fund, the total amount and rate of alumni giving, academic reputation, applicants, selectivity in admissions, and first-time out-of-state enrollment. Teams not in the Elite 6 conferences saw stronger positive effects of football wins on first-time in-state enrollments and the average SAT score of incoming freshmen.

Anderson suggested that his results may indicate that alumni of more prominent football schools are more affected by football wins than are their counterparts who graduate from schools with less prominent football programs. Winning for the lower-profile schools may have a bigger effect on prospective in-state applicants because it can give these schools more visibility in their local region. Schools with higher-profile teams already have this visibility, and winning in football may make a school more appealing to out-of-state students in a wide geographic area already familiar with a school's name.

Anderson offered a caveat for those who might want to jump to the conclusion that it is worth investing in big-time football programs, especially at the highest levels of the sport. He said that even though his study found more and stronger effects than those found in prior research, these "spillover effects" were not sufficient to warrant athletic spending. His results showed that schools already in the elite realm of college football benefited most. Alumni of other schools did not seem impressed much by football wins at lower levels. At schools in the Elite 6 where alumni gave more as a result of winning in football, Anderson argued that the bump in donations did not cover the costs of competing at this most expensive level of the sport. Thus, spending more to win more to get alumni to give more so that a school can spend more in the arms race is a circular logic that ultimately does not propel most schools to a place where they win regularly and balance the budget. Even for the relatively few schools in the financial elite of big-time college sports, being in the elite means having to depend more on private donors to stay competitive in the arms race. As we have seen, investing more effort to get athletic donations could hurt academic fund raising at many schools.

Presidents, the College Sports Business, and the Athletic Trap

The NCAA sent a packet of materials to the fifty presidents attending the summit it was sponsoring at its headquarters in Indianapolis in 2011 to help them get ready to discuss some thorny issues in big-time college sports. These materials set the tone of the upcoming meeting by warning that without "strong and swift action," the current threats could continue to grow and undermine the future viability of the collegiate model of athletics in which they were all involved.[59] The NCAA president was referring to a conception of intercollegiate athletics that emphasized the centrality of the student-athlete idea. However, we know that college sports at its highest levels, where most of the power is exercised and most of the money is generated through relations with the IGT, conforms more to a commercial model. Thus, we can be sure that while student-athletes might have been on the minds of the NCAA and the presidents attending this summit, the primary concern was actually sustaining the commercial—not the collegiate—model of college athletics. The commercial model is the basis for the college sports business.

College presidents frequently have to perform a difficult balancing act in commercialized college sports to maintain at least an appearance of a commitment to educational purposes in athletics in an environment that is organized to use college sports for commercial purposes. This appearance is meant to satisfy the academic community, but it probably is not so important to the most ardent fans, boosters, and donors involved in their athletic program. Nevertheless, presidents need to meet broader institutional expectations of alumni, governing boards, and legislators. These various stakeholders might have different expectations, but those involved in the governance of the institutions expect the colleges and universities they support, run, or fund to be successful and respected as academic institutions.

Balancing academics and athletics is a lot easier for presidents of elite institutions with well-established reputations, big endowments, and strong internal and public support than it is for most other presidents, who lead less prestigious and less wealthy institutions. The presidents of most universities at the Division I level of NCAA sports do not have the luxury of having the financial and public support they need to be among both the most respected academic institutions and the top football and men's basketball powers year after year. It is costly to be highly ranked every year in the *U.S. News & World Report* survey or to be in the top twenty-five in football and basketball and unusual to be in the elite in all of these rankings year after year.[60]

College presidents are advocates or cheerleaders for their most commercialized sports teams because they envision various benefits, enjoy the hoopla, or do not see any choice on a campus with an established program or with influential boosters who seek a big-time program. Presidents in the college sports business are entrenched in a wide array of relations across the various sectors of the intercollegiate golden triangle that are accompanied by obligations, demands, and expectations that constitute the athletic trap. As long as presidents are committed to being in the college sports business, there is no escape from this trap. The challenge for presidents is to try to keep the trap from overwhelming their other responsibilities.

Part of being in the trap is keeping up in the arms race. The arms race can significantly inflate the stress levels of college presidents and athletic directors by creating financial problems and affecting decisions about athletic and university resources. The motivation for the arms race, its major manifestations, and its implications in big-time college sports are the primary focus of the next chapter.

CHAPTER FOUR

The Arms Race, Inequalities, and the Pressures of the College Sports Business

The lack of public interest in the problems facing big-time college sports may explain continued popular support for these sports, but it does not make these problems go away. They include real and serious financial, ethical, and legal problems. Unlike the public, the people who run or are responsible for college sports cannot so easily ignore them. Many problems are a consequence of the commercial model's influence in college sports and the powerful motivation to make enough money to afford success in big-time sports. The athletic trap is a by-product of the commercial model, in which winning is a central element. Because campus leaders believe that winning translates into money, status, and power for the institution as well as for the athletic program, winning is the holy grail of big-time college sports.[1]

Athletic success requires that athletic departments spend money on salaries and benefits, facilities, athletic scholarships, team travel, recruiting, game-day expenses, marketing and fundraising costs, medical expenses, and guaranteed payments to opponents.[2] The arms race is driven by the assumption that outspending your competitors leads to more wins.[3] Two areas where expenditures have skyrocketed in recent years are coaches' salaries and the construction and renovation of facilities, with an increasing number of big-time football and basketball programs hiring coaches for millions of dollars and assuming capital debt in the tens or hundreds of millions of dollars.

Athletic departments derive income from various sources, including ticket sales, donations, local marketing income, local media rights fees, their athletic conferences, the NCAA, and institutional subsidies (such as funds from the general university budget and student fees). In addition, athletic departments generate revenue from licensing fees for logos on university-branded clothing and the sale of university sports "gear," concession sales during games, endowment and investment income, and contracts with manufacturers such as shoe companies and other apparel makers.[4]

The arms race puts universities in the college sports business in a precarious position unless they are among the relatively few institutions with the stature and endowment to be able to offset rising expenses with sufficient income. The arms race results when institutions try to keep up financially in the college sports business.[5] This fallout may not be fully anticipated when universities decide to add a football team to their sports line-up, upgrade the status of their athletic program, or compete in a more prestigious conference.

Presidents, boosters, and the athletic department typically expect to be successful, although they realize it may take some time when they are moving up to a higher level. Their optimism and patience, however, are often tested by the demands and challenges of the college sports business and by the arms race. Participating in big-time college sports generally leads to the arms race, which becomes part of the athletic trap. This financial trap involves a seemingly endless feedback loop of rising expenses. A university becomes entangled in a set of commercial and financial relationships in the IGT that become reinforced over time by the need to win. This need to win creates the need for more or better resources, from personnel to facilities, and these resources cost more and more money over time. The grip of the athletic trap gets a lot tighter when an institution decides to hire a star coach to an expensive long-term contract or to build or renovate an athletic facility. Presidents implicitly understand they are in the athletic trap when they cannot see a way out of the obligations and problems the arms race has created for them.

A factor reinforcing the perceived need to join the arms race is the fact that the top teams in college football are the biggest spenders as well as the biggest revenue producers. Equity in Athletics data collected by the U.S. Department of Education revealed that the top NCAA Division I football teams in the six seasons up to 2009 were among the top ten spenders and top ten revenue producers.[6] These are the teams, such as Texas, Alabama, and Ohio State, whose budgets we looked at in the second chapter.

In 2009 thirteen universities earned more than $50 million from football, and FBS football teams earned $2.5 billion overall that year.[7] In 2010 more than $470 million in new revenue and more than $1 billion in surplus were generated by major college sports programs.[8] It might seem surprising then that, with all this money, relatively few athletic departments earn more money than they spend. We expect Division II and III athletic programs to have to subsidize athletics with institutional funds, and we also might expect programs outside the FBS to have to rely on subsidies to balance their athletic budgets. The reality is that most athletic programs at the most commercialized FBS level of college sports also have to rely on institutional subsidies.

Institutional subsidies from general funds and student fees have increased at many institutions in recent years, despite tight state budgets and the substantial belt-tightening that many state universities have had to endure. According to a *USA Today* database, the athletic programs at the 218 public institutions that were in the NCAA Division I over the previous five years received a total of approximately $2 billion in subsidies in 2010.[9] This was an inflation-adjusted 3 percent more than 2009 and 28 percent more than 2006. These subsidies constituted approximately one-third of the total amount of revenue in college athletic budgets. Overall, the numbers show that the idea of the profitability of big-time athletics is a myth. This point reinforces the idea of the risk associated with the arms race for most institutions.

Almost $6.2 billion was spent on athletics in 2010 at the 218 schools in the database, which was 3 percent more than 2009. Total revenue grew by 5.5 percent between 2009 and 2010. When we combine these numbers with the statistics about costs, deficits, and subsidies, two conclusions jump out. First, the big-time programs generating surpluses are doing very well. Second, the others at the big-time level are struggling and need help from their institutions and students to stay afloat financially. In fact, only 22 of the 218 Division I institutions in the NCAA database were self-supporting in the 2009–2010 school year. That is, slightly more than 10 percent generated more money than they spent, when institutional and government support are excluded.[10] The total number was 8 more than the previous year but 3 less than the year before that. The median net surplus for these 22 self-supporting programs was approximately $7.4 million in 2010, while the median net deficit for the 98 other institutions at the highest or FBS level was $11.3 million. This gap of $18.7 million between the 22 programs that were self-sufficient and the 98 others in the FBS that were not was $3.1 million more than the previous year. Parenthetically, eight of the twenty-two institutions in the financial elite did not receive any allocated funds or subsidies from their university,[11] which meant that fourteen did.

Leading the way in the financial elite in 2010 was the University of Oregon, with a surplus of $41.9 million, based on self-generated income of $119.7 million. Recall that Oregon's football program leaped into the top ranks of college football after major infusions of money from alumnus and Nike billionaire Phil Knight. Despite this generosity, Oregon's athletic program also received $2.7 million in revenue from university funds, including student fees. Such subsidies may be understandable at universities struggling with athletic deficits, but they are more difficult to understand when athletic programs are highly profitable and when many states and state universities were facing difficult decisions in trying to balance budgets in a persisting weak economy. In Oregon, for example, the fortunes of the University of Oregon football team were soaring, but the state's public university system continued to struggle financially, ranking forty-sixth in the country in per-student funding in 2010.[12] There had been a 44 percent decline in public support between the mid-1990s and 2010.

The "Star Wars" Arms Race

College presidents have been criticized for their increasing salaries, especially during tough economic times. However, presidents at many BTUs earn less than their football and basketball coaches or the NCAA president.[13] My colleague Bill Tsitsos and I have called the competition in hiring coaches the "star wars arms race."[14] By 2010 in football, this arms race had escalated to the point where university-based salaries of head coaches had reached $5 million for the Alabama coach, and this amount did not include external compensation from boosters and other sources.[15] The twenty-fifth best-paid college football coach in our study made $1.9 million. NCAA data indicate that in fiscal 2010, the median total compensation earned by football head coaches was $1.4 million and the median cost of all their assistant coaches was almost $2 million.[16] Furthermore, the average salary of football head coaches in the Elite 6 conferences rose from $1.4 million in 2006 to $2.125 million in 2011.[17] The star wars arms race is further illustrated by the facts that between 2006 and 2012 the number of FBS football coaches earning salaries of at least $5 million rose from zero to two, the number earning at least $4 million increased from zero to four, the number earning at least $3 million went from one to thirteen, the number earning at least $2 million rose from nine to forty-two, and the number earning at least $1 million went from forty-two to sixty-six. During this time period, the pay of FBS head coaches increased 70 percent to an average of $1.64 million.[18]

In basketball, the best-paid coach (at Louisville) among the sixty-eight in the 2011 NCAA Men's Basketball Tournament earned $6.1 million that year, with $3.6 million of that amount from a one-time bonus. Second on the list was the Duke coach, who earned more than $4.2 million. Number 25 earned $1.35 million. According to NCAA data, the median total compensation earned by major college basketball coaches was $962,000 in 2010, and the total compensation earned by all their assistant coaches was $472,000 that year.[19] The richest athletic programs may be able to afford these salaries because they generate a huge amount of money from their assorted commercial ties in the IGT that depend on their athletic success.

The assumptions driving the star wars arms race have some basis in fact. There is research showing that coaches who successfully recruit the most talented athletes tend to have the most competitive success and that being successful in athletic competition tends to make a program more attractive to the most talented athletic prospects.[20] This self-reinforcing pattern suggests that major athletic programs or those aspiring to this status must hire coaches who can attract the top talent. Being recognized as a star coach is an advantage in the recruiting market, which explains why universities are willing to spend what it takes to get a coach with this star power. Thus, these coaches can demand increasingly higher salaries as institutions bid against each other for their services. They know that athletic directors will pay what they believe the market demands to hire the star or highly promising coaches they expect or hope will make their programs successful.[21]

In this marketplace, former star coaches, whose success has waned in recent years, may no longer command the high salaries they once did, but they still may enjoy relatively high salaries in the marketplace of the mid-majors seeking to move up the college sports ladder. Mid-majors may lack the appeal needed to attract current star coaches, but they can hire fading star coaches or coaches with star potential who have been associated with established big-time programs as assistant coaches or as head coaches of less prominent big-time programs or rising mid-majors. Thus, at both the elite and subelite levels of major college sports, the star wars arms race keeps driving up the price of coaches and the perceived cost of doing business.

Part of the athletic trap related to the star wars arms race is the cost of replacing high-paid coaches before their contract has expired. High salaries are accompanied by high expectations, and when they are not met, coaches lose their jobs. Termination, however, involves buying out the remainder of coaching contracts, which can be very expensive. For example, over a period of just four years, Auburn University paid $12.28 million in buyouts to two fired coaches. Between 2010 and 2012, six of the fourteen members of the top football conference, the SEC, made coaching changes that had a total buyout cost of $26.5 million.[22] These expenditures demonstrate the intensity of the desire to be successful and the amount of money schools are willing to pay to try to achieve that success. Firing and hiring (more expensive) coaches in the star wars arms race can be risky business, though. Research has shown that losing teams that hire a new coach improve relatively little compared to teams with similar records that do not replace their coach. On the other hand, schools that win about half of their games and replace their coach tend to do relatively worse in subsequent years, compared to teams with similar records that do not make a coaching change.[23]

Despite these facts, schools continue to make these risky investments and perpetuate the star wars arms race. Largely as a result of Title IX pressures, the arms race has been extended to the most commercialized women's sport as well. Women's basketball coaches were the third-best-compensated employees in college athletics in

2010, with a median total compensation of $348,000 for a head coach and $331,000 for all their assistant coaches.[24] In 2011 the best-paid coaches of the elite women's basketball programs earned university-based salaries of $1.9 million (Tennessee), $1.6 million (Connecticut), $1.1 million (Baylor and Texas), and $985,000 (Rutgers).[25] Most coaches at top programs in women's college basketball appear to earn much less in supplemental income than their male counterparts, but there are some exceptions. Two coaches (at Tennessee and Rutgers) earned more than $100,000 in additional nonuniversity income,[26] such as money from shoe and apparel contracts, summer camps, and athletic foundations. One coach at a mid-major-level institution (Middle Tennessee) was able to supplement his university income with $88,000 in outside income.

The Tennessee and Connecticut women's basketball coaches were legendary for their success, and other major women's programs have had prominent coaches with long tenures and have achieved high rankings in the national polls for their sport. Paying these big salaries, though, is deepening the financial hole in which these elite women's basketball programs find themselves. These programs have the same problem balancing their budgets as most men's college sports have. The combination of inexpensive tickets, high salaries for coaches, and less interest from the IGT in the women's game has resulted in budget deficits for these elite women's programs. For example, the two most prestigious programs in women's college basketball lost money in this sport in fiscal 2010. The University of Connecticut lost approximately $725,000, and the University of Tennessee lost approximately $715,000 that year. The University of Oklahoma has lost even more, $1.1 million in fiscal 2007 and over $1.6 million in fiscal 2010. The university salary of the Oklahoma coach in fiscal 2011 was $920,000.[27] Overall, only one institution at the top level reported a surplus for its women's basketball team in fiscal 2010.[28]

More broadly, women's basketball at the fifty-three public universities in the six largest conferences had operating losses in fiscal 2010 of $109.7 million, whereas the men's teams in those conferences had operating surpluses of $240 million.[29] Thus, the formula of spending more to win more and make more money may be dubious in men's college sports,[30] but it definitely is not true in the biggest women's sport, where their star wars arms race is significantly contributing to its losing financial equation. Even though questions of gender equity complicate arguments about the justifications for major investments in women's sports, it is clear that universities are assuming large and growing deficits to achieve such sports equity.

Beth Bass, chief executive officer of the Women's Basketball Coaches Association, acknowledged the need to try to be more business savvy in her sport. However, she also argued that the highest salaries were being paid to coaches of the most successful programs and that these investments had valuable benefits for their institutions. For example, she cited the positive recognition for the institution gained from success on the court. She added that it was hard to assess the value of having the players in the community serving as role models and graduating at far higher rates than their male counterparts.[31]

The athletic director's salary may add to the difficulty of balancing the athletic budget. In 2011 the average annual compensation of athletic directors in the FBS was $450,000, and at five FBS institutions the athletic director was paid $1 million or more. Between 2010 and 2011, at least ten public universities increased the pay of their athletic director by at least $75,000.[32] Some observers proposed that with coaches' salaries propelled ever higher by the athletic marketplace, we could expect athletic directors' salaries to rise as well.[33] Star athletic directors are in demand because their job is complex and challenging and can be pivotal in shaping the future success of big-time athletic programs. Athletic directors may handle budgets of more than $100 million, oversee very lucrative licensing and media contracts, and manage athletic facilities valued in the billions of dollars. They are also expected to be rainmakers (bringing in large donations) and hire star coaches to guide their teams to success.

The Facilities Arms Race

The other arms race involves the construction and renovation of facilities, and it has resulted in very large long-term debt service burdens.[34] First-rate facilities attract star coaches and top athletic prospects, allow institutions to charge higher ticket prices, and generate significant revenue from major booster and corporate sponsors, who pay for luxury suites, premier seating, and other amenities in the arena or stadium. State-of-the-art facilities can be very expensive, costing hundreds of millions of dollars for stadium construction and improvements. The facilities arms race appears to have been unaffected by the recently dismal state of the economy.[35] There were many expensive athletic construction projects under way in 2012. The most expensive projects involved football stadiums. For example, the estimated cost of stadium construction or renovation projects was $378 million at Arizona; $321 million at California-Berkeley; $250 million at Baylor and at Washington; $164 million at TCU; and $100 million at LSU. Ohio State University reportedly had a facilities debt of $197 million in 2007 and has had to pay $17 million in debt service each year.[36] It was able to manage its debt with a football ticket surcharge, which meant that it could get the 105,000 spectators who attended each of its home football games to help pay the university's athletic facilities debt.

The football stadium is a key element in an athletic department's on-campus revenue budget. Top teams with big stadiums generate substantial revenue from the sale of tickets and especially from luxury suites and premium seating. In 2011 five football teams in Elite 6 conferences averaged more than 100,000 spectators.[37] At the top of the list was the University of Michigan, with average attendance of more than 112,000 at its stadium that it calls "The Big House," followed by Ohio State (105,231), Alabama (101,821), Penn State (101,427), and Texas (100,524). Michigan benefited from a stadium modernization that was completed in 2010 and cost $226 million.[38] With eighty-one suites generating $55,000 to $85,000 per year and nearly three thousand premium seats generating $1,500 to $4,000 each year, plus the ticket prices and more than 112,000 fans in attendance each game, the University of Michigan expected to earn approximately $12 million per year, which would cover its $9 million in annual debt service for the renovation and expansion costs.

Boise State University has had outstanding football teams in recent years, but it is not in the same financial league as the schools in the Elite 6 conferences. In 2010–2011, its athletic revenue was $27.9 million, which was 48 percent of Arizona's athletic revenue, 43 percent of Cal-Berkeley's athletic revenue, and less than 20 percent of the amount the University of Texas earned from athletics that year.[39] In 2012, however, Boise State was investing $22 million in a new football complex to house coaches' offices, meeting rooms, recruiting and players' lounges, an academic resource center, weight room, athletic training room, equipment room, and locker room for the football team. It was also involved in two other athletics-related construction projects costing more than $9 million.[40] All this spending was meant to overcome a deficit in football tradition that much more established programs in the Elite 6 conferences enjoy, but trying to buy brand recognition and a certain cachet can be difficult in a world steeped in status distinctions and long-established traditions.[41]

Sports economist Andrew Zimbalist,[42] an expert on stadium financing, suggested that Michigan might have overestimated how much new revenue would be produced in the context of the lingering severe effects of the recession in Michigan, but he acknowledged that with its "spectacular brand," Michigan football would nevertheless benefit financially from its renovation and expansion project. Most other big-time football programs cannot expect such a rosy forecast of returns from their ventures in the facilities arms race, especially with a significant number of short-term fluctuations in attendance and competitive success at the big-time level. My own analysis of the NCAA and institutional data cited earlier showed that twenty-one football programs had increases of more than one thousand in average attendance and twenty programs had decreases of more than one thousand between the 2009 and 2011 seasons. I suspect that attendance varies with success on the field, especially for programs with less established brands or traditions. Changes in the economy, such as the major economic downturn of recent years, add further uncertainty to estimates about covering the costs of facilities construction and renovation.

Despite the uncertainties, facilities spending in college sports was $15.2 billion between 1995 and 2005,[43] which reflected a huge and growing investment in athletic facilities. More than $6 billion of this amount was spent on football, mainly for enhancements such as luxury suites and club seats that were expected to generate millions in additional revenue. As at Boise State, large amounts were also spent on sophisticated training facilities, fancy locker rooms and coaches' offices, meeting rooms, academic support centers, player lounges, and high-tech playing surfaces, none of which directly produces revenue. Of course, all facilities have maintenance costs that can add a significant number of dollars to costs such as debt service. Thus, the facilities arms race in college athletics to some extent is an amenities arms race.

As in the case of the star wars arms race, an institution can never be satisfied that its facilities are good enough or big enough to attract the athletes and coaches they want, which propels the arms race upward. For the biggest and wealthiest institutions and athletic programs, investment in new or renovated facilities may be relatively affordable. For less elite institutions and programs, participating in the facilities arms race can create substantial budgetary pressures. Paying for a new stadium puts additional pressure on university financial officers and athletic fundraisers, who are already burdened with substantial budgetary and financial challenges on most campuses. Having to accommodate major donors could seriously compromise athletic directors and presidents who are pressured to make decisions about coaches, athletes, or program direction that they are opposed or reluctant to do. The need for more funds can have a corrupting influence on athletic programs and those responsible for them. In the preceding chapter, we saw the powerful influence of major athletic donors at Oregon and UConn.

Haves and Have-Nots in the Arms Race

Although the financial elite in the major athletic conferences may be able to afford the increasingly higher annual cost of competing at the big-time level, many of the schools at the big-time level but with more modest resources are finding that keeping up in the arms race is more and more challenging. As the stakes continue to escalate, many institutions find it increasingly difficult to keep up, and some end up virtually on the sideline in the competition for top coaches and athletes and in the quest for championships, money, and other rewards from the IGT. To be athletically and financially successful at the highest levels of the NCAA, athletic programs need to recruit more effectively, win more, sell more tickets, raise more money, and generally find more revenue to cover their relentlessly rising athletic costs.[44] We see the logic here, though. Spending more implies the need to make more money, and so the arms race continues, with its accumulating financial fallout for the less successful have-not programs.

Although the NCAA may be biased toward the interests of its most powerful members, it does not want to see a large number of its members produce ever-larger deficits that result in severe athletic budget cuts and the elimination of teams. Similarly, the conferences derive a significant portion of their revenue from having brand-name teams, but they also do not want to see their membership decimated by the departure of less successful teams. Thus, there are revenue-sharing mechanisms in the sport sector of the IGT to help the less successful teams compete. Still, the elite teams are not really interested in sharing the resources that their success has made possible. They aim to get the most in the NCAA and in the conferences for themselves and continue to make it difficult for other schools to compete with them on the field or in the IGT.

We see a substantial and growing gap between the elite and subelite athletic programs. The top ten revenue producers in college sports generated between $98.5 million and $143.6 million in income in 2009–2010, but the median net athletic-generated revenue for FBS institutions was $35.3 million; for FCS institutions it was $3.3 million; and for all of the Division I schools without football it was about $2 million. Expenses ranged from the largest total expenditure of $130.4 million to median total expenditures of $46.7 million at the FBS level, a median of $13.1 million at the FCS level, and a median of $11.6 million at Division I schools without football. The bottom line is that college athletics was generally a losing proposition throughout Division I (and the other divisions), if we exclude institutional subsidies. Net losses averaged $9.4 million at the FBS level, $9.2 million at the FCS level, and $8.6 million for schools without football in 2009–2010.

No program in the FCS or without a football team reported a budgetary surplus in 2010, and the median losses increased in these two realms of Division I between 2009 and 2010. Furthermore, 4 percent of FCS football teams, 5 percent of FCS men's basketball teams, and 1 percent of FCS women's basketball teams reported a surplus for 2010, and at Division I schools without football, 5 percent of the men's basketball teams and none of the women's basketball teams had a surplus.[45]

The thrust of all these numbers is that the rich were getting richer, and the gap was growing between them and everyone else. It is important to reiterate here the $18.7 million gap between the financial elite of the twenty-two programs that were self-sufficient and the ninety-eight others in the FBS that did not generate enough revenue on their own to cover their expenses. It is also important to remember that this figure was $3.1 million more than the previous year.

Status Seeking against the Odds

Most universities find it difficult to bridge the gap and penetrate the upper echelons of college sport. Athletic programs move to the top by winning regularly, developing a large and loyal following, and building their brand in the athletic marketplace. This process of moving up requires time, perseverance, and money—a lot of money. Staying in the top ranks requires even more money. Teams win at the highest levels of college sport by hiring star coaches, recruiting star athletes, having state-of-the-art facilities, creating a strong tradition of program loyalty, and generating an ample athletic endowment. It is easier to stay at the top as an established BTU than to get there and stay there as an aspirant to elite status. The composition of the elite in college football and men's basketball is relatively stable over time, with the top-ranked programs disproportionately coming from the top ranks of the richest and most prestigious conferences.[46]

For individual institutions, it is very difficult to achieve the funding levels needed to attain and sustain membership in the elite conferences; even with funding, spending money does not guarantee elite status; and even when more spending does lead to more wins, it can take years for a reputation to coincide with levels of spending and athletic success. The reputation associated with established elite status is obviously not achieved suddenly or from just a few years of success.[47] Enhanced status is a product of time as well as competitive success and increased spending in college sports. For example, twenty-first-century football powers such as Boise State, which have had some success since 2000, have found it very difficult to become part of the BCS elite in football.[48] As relative newcomers at the top competitive level of the sport, they have had to prove themselves year after year to the IGT as they seek to establish themselves as a marketable national brand. In addition, they have to gain the respect of the members of an elite conference, which would like to see highly competitive teams in other sports along with football.

Some of the most rapidly increasing athletic budgets were in public universities in the FCS. This is an often observed paradox, since these schools were spending more on athletics at the same time that they were being squeezed by financial and economic pressures throughout the rest of the university. The regional universities among these public institutions were facing serious cuts to general institutional budgets as their states tried to deal with the lingering economic downturn. These institutions typically had smaller budgets than their states' flagships and did not receive as much in state funding. Thus, state budget cuts often hit faculty salaries, student tuitions, and academic programs at the regional institutions relatively harder than at the flagships or major research universities. The paradox of spending more on athletics as overall budgetary pressures worsened can be explained as a manifestation of the arms race and the athletic trap. Athletic directors and coaches insist that spending less will put them behind competitors, and presidents often go along with this argument because they do not want to see their major athletic programs fall behind or fail. After all, the failure of highly visible sports programs is easier for the public to see than is a failure to provide adequate support for academics.

The financial strain of the arms race has created significant stress for presidents and athletic directors of schools outside the financial elite. This is quite different from the experience of the elite BTUs. According to a report from the Center for College Affordability and Productivity that analyzed institutional subsidies of athletic programs, "Rich, famous and athletically well-known schools have only been trivially impacted at the institutional level by the explosion in (intercollegiate athletics) costs, while a significant number of schools that are, on average, poorer, less prestigious, and athletically more marginal have been clobbered."[49]

The athletic revenue potential of subelite programs is limited by smaller institutional budgets, smaller facilities, weaker athletic traditions, and less investment from the IGT. For them, keeping up in the arms race creates significant budgetary pressures because they have less capacity than bigger, wealthier, and more athletically known institutions to spend their way to success without incurring an increasing deficit. For institutions with financially needy athletic programs that cannot pay their own way, an important part of the solution to keeping athletics solvent has been the student athletic fee. The Center for College Affordability and Productivity has called institutional subsidies of athletics a tax,[50] and it is a tax that nearly all schools with intercollegiate athletic programs have believed they had to levy to subsidize athletics. The imposition of this tax was characterized in the preceding chapter as a form of exploitation, and it is especially exploitative when it is imposed on less advantaged nonathlete students.

Case Studies of Struggles in the Arms Race

Athletic directors and coaches believe that they always need to spend more to keep ahead of or up with the competition. Rather than seeing institutional subsidies as draining university resources or student fees as exploiting students, they see these forms of support as essential tools to get the money they need to succeed. Getting more from existing athletic and institutional revenue streams or finding new ones can be challenging for all schools competing in big-time college sports. It can be especially challenging for schools with less established brands in the college sports business, such as Rutgers University, the University of Maryland, and Towson University, three institutions whose situation we consider as case studies in this section. Rutgers and Maryland are state flagship universities with major college sports programs that are trying to keep up with the costs of competing at the top level of college sports, and Towson is a comprehensive university seeking to elevate itself to the level of a nationally known mid-major. Thus, these three cases illustrate the struggles that a combination of aspirations and the arms race can fuel for big-time sports programs at the major and mid-major levels. They also show the turmoil that the arms race can produce on the ground on college campuses.

Rutgers University

Although its conference, the Big East, was the weakest Elite 6 football conference, Rutgers wanted to rise to the top ranks of football. Its enhancement efforts had plunged it into the fiercest of arms races, increasing its athletic spending from $41 million in 2006 to $64 million in 2010, a 56 percent increase.[51] During this period, revenue increased from $21 million to $37 million, which is a 76 percent increase but not nearly enough to keep pace with rising expenses.

The $115 million in athletic subsidies between 2006 and 2010 rankled faculty members, who had been enduring salary freezes. They were not pleased that Rutgers had the highest athletic subsidy in the country among BCS schools, and their union questioned the priorities of the administration. To further complicate matters, Rutgers saw a drop in football attendance from more than forty-nine thousand to fewer than forty-four thousand between 2009 and 2011, suggesting the problem of maintaining the popular and competitive success of less established programs at the big-time level of college sports. Its success in football seesawed between 2009 and 2011. It was 9–4 in 2009 and 2011 and won bowl games after those seasons, but it slipped to 4–8 in 2010. It was 9–4 in the 2012 season but lost its last three games. It can be difficult to maintain or expand a fan and donor base when competitive performance fluctuates unpredictably.

University leaders were sensitive to the perceived clash of academic and athletic priorities on campus. As a university spokesperson told a reporter, "While athletics opens a door to the university, it is our outstanding academic programs, world-class faculty and unique campus community that make Rutgers a premier institution of higher learning."[52] He noted that the university's direct athletic subsidy was only 1 percent of the overall university budget. However, even if athletics was the front door to the university and $27 million was only 1 percent of the university's overall budget, $27 million nevertheless was a lot of dollars at a time when Rutgers and the state of New Jersey were struggling to balance budgets. In 2007 Rutgers cut six sports to cover an athletics budget shortfall of $80 million. Nevertheless, athletic spending continued to increase in recent years as state subsidies for the university declined and the university froze faculty salaries and postponed infrastructure improvements in academic buildings.

Rutgers sought a sweeping solution to its financial problems in athletics when it decided to accept an offer to move from the Big East conference to the Big Ten in 2012.[53] Although Rutgers had been successful in football in the Big East, its success was not enough to avoid budget shortfalls. Part of the problem was the Big East media payout of $6 million. This was relatively paltry amount among Elite 6 conferences. The move to the Big Ten would increase its conference media payout to $24.6 million in return for the Big Ten's expansion of its geographic reach and its access to new and lucrative TV markets. Thus, this deal appeared to be a good business decision for both Rutgers and the Big Ten.

The Rutgers president hoped that joining the Big Ten would enable his university to reduce its athletic subsidy by $1 million per year and also increase the university's national exposure. He also noted that membership in the Big Ten would bring with it admission to a prestigious research consortium, the Committee on Institutional Cooperation. There was little doubt, though, that this move was driven by money and status in athletics and not by academics. While the move to the Big Ten was clearly a step up and at least a temporary remedy for its financial woes in athletics, new challenges awaited. Rutgers was likely to face stiffer competition against the many large and better-funded teams in its new conference. Thus, the move would not put an end to its participation in the arms race or lessen the hold of the athletic trap.[54]

University of Maryland at College Park

The University of Maryland at College Park, simply known as Maryland to sports fans, is part of the athletic elite as a founding member of the Atlantic Coast Conference. Its athletic budget of $54.7 million in operating expenses in 2009–2010 dwarfed the $20.1 million expense budget of fellow University System of Maryland (USM) member Towson University for that year.[55] Maryland balanced its budget, but did so by getting 17.2 percent ($9.4 million) of its revenue from student athletic fees and 7.9 percent ($4.3 million) from a direct institutional subsidy, which meant that more than 25 percent of its revenue came from athletic taxes.

Maryland's athletic financial picture had become quite ugly by the summer of 2012, when it cut seven of its sports programs.[56] Eight programs were originally on the chopping block, but men's outdoor track and field was temporarily saved because it was able to raise nearly $900,000 in donations to support the coming season. The program had to raise $1.9 million by the end of the year to be able to compete the next year and $3.76 million to be able to attain longer-term security. These cuts were prompted by an athletic deficit expected to reach $4 million for the current fiscal year and more than $17 million by 2017.[57] The president was upset by the pattern of increasing athletic subsidies and wanted the athletic program to move toward self-sufficiency. Of course, self-sufficiency is relatively rare in big-time college sports.

At Maryland, the athletic department had drained the athletic reserve fund it had amassed to deal with deficits. It had to cover buyouts and new contract costs as football and men's basketball added new head coaches, and it had to deal with a 20 percent decline in football attendance over five years, which complicated efforts to pay off a $35 million debt from stadium enhancements. In addition, it was experiencing significant declines in athletic donations and in membership in the Terrapin Club, which was its primary means of generating athletic contributions. Its budgetary prospects were not encouraging because ticket sales in football and basketball were not robust enough, donors were not numerous or generous enough, and its conference payouts were not big enough to reverse or offset deficits in the future.[58]

The disgruntlement of Maryland athletic supporters with this situation was evident in an op-ed piece in the *Baltimore Sun* by Todd Schoenenberger,[59] a former executive board member of the Terrapin Club. He argued that the university had made a "bad bet" a decade earlier when it decided to invest in an expensive new basketball arena at the expense of football at a time when both basketball and football were doing well. As a result, football did not have the resources to keep up in the arms race or to do well consistently in competition, which caused drops in ticket sales, support from boosters, and revenue.[60] When basketball declined competitively and financially as well, Maryland did not have the football revenue to cover the rising operating deficits in its athletic program.[61] Maryland's case suggests the kinds of decisions that institutions at all levels of the NCAA face when balancing the athletic budget with additional institutional funds becomes untenable.

When university officials face crises in the athletic budget, they rarely consider cutting the sports that are draining a disproportionate amount of resources from the athletic budget. They usually try to protect their revenue sports at the expense of lower-revenue and nonrevenue sports, even though the revenue sports are more costly and do not cover their costs. Cutting nonrevenue sports was a strategy employed by all three institutions in this section and has become a common practice throughout big-time college sports. While these kinds of program cuts in male sports have often been seen as a result of Title IX, we can see here how they actually result from the financial strains of the arms race for the top-tier revenue sports. These top-tier sports are protected by the athletic trap. The ties to these sports among alumni, boosters, and commercial partners in the IGT are often well established, strong, and reinforced by an array of compelling promises, expectations, and obligations. These ties are especially strong at the upper levels of the big-time college sports world but also exist at mid-majors such as Towson University.

There is a risk in cutting so-called minor sports, since they may have some influential alumni that follow and support them. Antagonizing these people could cost their loyalty to their alma mater. However, big-time sports attract a bigger following than do lower-revenue and nonrevenue sports. Presidents and athletic directors usually figure that the risks of cutting several nonrevenue sports are justified by the money saved, which can cover holes in the athletic budget and keep the athletic department and the big-time sports above water in the arms race.

Like Rutgers, Maryland was offered the perceived silver bullet of Big Ten membership. Like Rutgers, it leaped at the opportunity as a way to escape or minimize its chronic financial problems in athletics.[62] Maryland, though, would not get as big a boost in its conference payout as Rutgers would get. It would increase by approximately $7 million, versus the $18 million increase Rutgers expected to get. In addition, Maryland was faced with a $50 million penalty for leaving the ACC.

The decision to move to the Big Ten created hostile reactions from loyal Maryland and ACC fans. The decision-making process was also strongly criticized. One of its harshest critics was involved in it as a member of the Maryland Board of Regents. Tom McMillen was not a typical regent.[63] He was a former big-time sports insider, albeit an unusually articulate, well-educated, and politically conscious one. McMillen was a basketball star at Maryland, a Rhodes Scholar, a pro basketball player, and a member of the U.S. Congress. He was also a longtime advocate of reform in big-time college sports and served on the Knight Commission.[64] He opposed the board's vote to support Maryland's move from the ACC to the Big Ten. He especially took issue with the way the vote occurred—over a weekend, with little documentation, and no involvement of major stakeholders.

Students, faculty members, student-athletes, alumni, and the ACC were all kept in the dark by the terms of a nondisclosure agreement imposed by the Big Ten. Mc-

Millen wondered why Maryland was in such a rush to sign the agreement, since it would not be joining the conference until 2014. He suggested that Maryland did not fully appreciate the leverage it had, since the Big Ten was anxious to add a school in the Washington-Baltimore television market. The possibility that Penn State might leave, create a void in this valuable market, and reduce the size of the Big Ten's television package caused paranoia among Big Ten officials and made Maryland an attractive prospect.[65] With Maryland and Rutgers joining the conference, the Big Ten would be well represented in two of the biggest media markets in the United States and strengthen the market position of the Big Ten Network. Thus, the qualities that drew the Big Ten to Maryland and Rutgers had less to do with the academic reputation of these institutions or their athletic prowess than their locations.

The power of the Big Ten over Maryland prompted Tom McMillen to observe, "Right now, universities and their boards are captive to a process controlled by the commissioners of the various athletic conferences. Commissioners managing hundreds of millions of dollars are extorting what they need from the universities, and the schools are powerless to stand up to them."[66] The relative powerlessness of schools to resist the influence of the major conferences over the churning process is part of the athletic trap. McMillen concluded this was another case of the tail wagging the dog in college sports and, as a result, undermining institutional integrity and distorting the priorities of higher education.

Towson University

What makes it difficult for campus administrators trying to tighten their athletic belt is that decisions about athletics may be strongly influenced by powerful outside forces, such as wealthy alumni and boosters. It is easy to lose sight of the financial crunch on campus when you are on the outside looking in, want to see your alma mater enhance its institutional and athletic stature, and see spending more money in athletics as the primary vehicle for such enhancements. My own institution, Towson University, illustrates the frustrations, difficulties, and costs of trying to get better in athletics as a mid-major. Its story is probably similar to the stories of many other comprehensive universities with athletic aspirations.

Towson is a regional comprehensive university in the University System of Maryland (USM).[67] It is less than fifty miles up the road from the University of Maryland. It is the second largest institution in the USM, with approximately 21,500 students. As the university has grown from a relatively small teacher's college to a large master's level university,[68] it has moved up the ranks from Division III to II to I (FCS) and to a highly competitive athletic conference, the Colonial Athletic Association (CAA).

Towson has had success in the past in its major revenue programs of football, men's basketball, men's and women's lacrosse, and women's gymnastics. In recent years, though, it has struggled both athletically and financially. Its premier sports of football and men's basketball were uncompetitive in the CAA for many of these years, and another top-tier sport at the institution, men's lacrosse, had fallen from its pedestal as a regular NCAA tournament participant.

Despite a pattern of steady annual increases between 2006 and 2011 totaling more than $6 million (up 42 percent), Towson's athletic expenditures of $20.5 million in 2011 placed it seventh among the nine public university full members of the CAA that year.[69] The two schools behind it did not play football. Although all the public schools in the CAA had heavily subsidized athletic budgets, Towson was tied for the highest subsidy level at 84.7 percent. Its budgetary challenge should be evident.

When Towson's president left for the University of Massachusetts in 2011 after an eight-year tenure, he stated that his greatest disappointment was his failure to achieve a rise in prominence in athletics that paralleled the institution's rise in overall stature. However, he left behind hopeful boosters who believed that Towson's athletic fortunes would turn around.[70] Their optimism seemed to be rewarded, with the football and men's basketball teams showing great improvement after hiring new coaches. An ambitious new athletic director was also hired, and a $73 million basketball arena was under construction.

Even during the down times, two local businessmen and powerful Towson alumni who had served on the state's Board of Regents remained true believers. They were quoted as expressing both frustration and hope that Towson still had a chance to achieve the same level of national visibility in athletics as other institutions in their conference had achieved.[71] One of these Towson supporters said that he was "jealous that those schools have figured out a way to (be successful in sports)." He thought the "pieces are there for us to get it right this time, including the road map given to us by VCU, George Mason and Butler (in men's basketball)," but he also felt that this was their "last, best time to get it right." The other prominent alum asserted that the university was investing in the new basketball arena because "we believe that, with the combination of our (new) athletic director and coach, we may be a few years from being in the same place George Mason was in 2006 (in the Final Four)."[72]

One of the former regents expressed the institutional enhancement rationale as the basis of his belief in the importance of athletic success to the university. He said that "in this day and age, athletics leads the way in the marketing of a university. . . . It gets a school in the media much more and in a positive way. It gets the alumni interested and creates an esprit de corps among students and faculty that can't be achieved any other way."[73] These kinds of statements often are more fanciful and ideological than factual, but what is ironically true is that Towson had already achieved academic prominence. Under its recently departed president, it was highly ranked among similar types of universities in its region. Good students continued to apply to Towson, the institution continued to attract more applicants than it could accept, and donations continued to come in despite the disappointing performance of its major and most visible sports teams. The dramatic turn of fortune for the football and men's basketball teams was not necessary for these things to happen.

Even with dramatic improvements on the field and on the court and significant increases in its athletic budget, Towson continued to struggle to keep up in the arms race. Furthermore, it was not evident to the average student or faculty member that sports success had lessened the financial strain on students or made the lot of faculty members any better. Students still paid the mandatory athletic fee and higher tuition costs. Faculty members were looking forward to their first salary increase in many years, but that had to do with the economy and state politics and little or nothing to do with how the football team performed.

Some saw the construction of the new basketball arena as a symbol of Towson's promise in athletics. For at least one outspoken retired faculty member, though, it represented something very different. This former faculty member wrote a letter to the school newspaper to complain that the money could have been better spent on scholarships for students, academic departments, or the many Maryland citizens who were suffering in the weak economy."[74]

This criticism implies the opportunity costs that may be associated with athletic investment at public universities. Furthermore, Towson's heavy reliance on the athletics tax, and student athletic fees in particular, was a significant opportunity cost of trying to elevate athletics, since university fee revenue is money that could have been collected for various academic purposes. Revenue streams are not plentiful at the mid-major level, though, which is why athletic directors and presidents at this level rarely stop or reduce the flow of these funds to athletics. Even among the FBS schools that generate an athletics surplus, a majority continues to collect these fees. In the arms race, an institution can never have too much revenue. Towson certainly counted itself among those with less money than it thought it needed to compete successfully on a consistent basis in its top-tier sports.

The story of the struggles of athletic striving at Towson University has continued to evolve. In the fall of 2012, the athletic director followed a common pattern and recommended the termination two lower-tier men's sports, men's soccer and baseball. They were two of the oldest athletic programs on campus.[75] These recommendations were ostensibly meant to solve three problems: competitiveness, long-term financial viability, and compliance with Title IX. What distinguishes this case is that the new president did not immediately rubber stamp the recommendations. She had relatively little experience dealing with commercialized sports but wanted to make her own decision and sought more information to guide her decision. She asked the chair of the university's Board of Visitors to lead a task force charged with an external review of the recommendations, and she directed it to receive input from interested parties on and off campus.

After two months of public comment and study, the task force predictably accepted the athletic director's recommendations, albeit with the acknowledgment of some dissent in the group. I say "predictably" because it is the action predicted by the athletic trap argument. Evidence of the athletic trap included the hiring in recent years of a new athletic director and head coaches in football and men's basketball, investment in an expensive new basketball arena, and the upgrading several years earlier of the football stadium. Furthermore, the task force was chaired by a former regent and the current chair of her Board of Visitors, who was quoted earlier as a strong booster of Towson athletics.

The task force report recognized the seriousness of the financial deficit in athletics and the issue of heavily relying on student fees. Nevertheless, it did not consider eliminating or deemphasizing football as a major way of reducing the deficit problem and gender inequity, and it recommended pursuing a possible increase in student athletic fee revenue. The task force did not unanimously support the report's conclusions. A minority of the task force was concerned that the athletic director's recommendations were contrary to the reform philosophy and recommendations of the Knight Commission because the recommendations favored the most commercialized sports at the expense of broader male participation opportunities. These voices of dissent were not persuasive or numerous enough to challenge the views of the majority.

Although the task force seemed to be in the grip of the athletic trap, the president still seemed to want to resist its influence. As with the athletic director's recommendations, she did not immediately endorse the advice of the task force. She announced that she would take another two months to make a decision, as she struggled with trying to balance the budget, implement Title IX, and accommodate the student-athletes in the programs slated for cuts. She knew there were powerful forces at play here. She risked alienating the powerful chair of the task force and other influential boosters of big-time sports at her school. However, the recommendations had already antagonized parents and boosters in the baseball and men's soccer communities. We see how athletic decisions and the athletic trap can put presidents in very difficult situations.

Finally, in March 2013, after five months of review, the president made a decision—to discontinue baseball after the current season and men's soccer, effective immediately. Men's tennis would be restored to enable Towson to meet the minimum standard for men's programs to be able to compete in the NCAA. In her email to faculty, staff, and students, she expressed her sadness in making this decision but affirmed that it seemed the "optimal solution" to the budgetary, Title IX, and competitive challenges facing the athletic program. The student-athletes in the terminated programs would have their scholarships honored and could continue to access the support services available to student-athletes.

As with the task force decision, the president's decision was predictable, although the process and time it took to arrive at it were unusual. As a president inexperienced with big-time college sports, she learned the harsh realities of the athletic trap and could find no way out. She may have wanted to save baseball and men's soccer, but she ultimately was unwilling to consider the kind of reform in athletics that would have made it possible for these sports to survive. What she may not have realized was that the stated challenges in athletics that were supposed to be reasons for dropping the two sports were not solved by her decision.[76]

As a mid-major, Towson would continue to face financial challenges. Indeed, despite the recent success of its football and men's basketball programs, it still had to deal with a budget deficit, and it would still have to rely heavily on student fees. The star wars arms race was not going to disappear, and successful coaches are often courted by more elite programs. As a result, mid-majors often feel compelled to pay them more, which further exacerbates existing financial problems. Or they must let the coaches go and try to find replacements who are likely to cost as much or more if the school wants to continue to be compete successfully in these sports. The cost of trying to close the compliance gap with Title IX was that male students had fewer sports to play. Competitiveness would remain a challenge, despite recent successes in the two big sports, because success requires expensive coaches, facilities, and equipment.

College Presidents, the Arms Race, and the Athletic Trap

Brit Kirwan was a college president who saw the big picture in big-time college sports and was very worried about what he saw. He was chancellor of the University System of Maryland and previously had been president of the University of

Maryland at College Park and Ohio State University. He was also cochairman of the Knight Commission. When the Knight Commission published a survey of FBS college presidents in 2009,[77] Kirwan noted that three-quarters believed that college sports could not continue on the current path set by the arms race. Peter Likins, president emeritus of the University of Arizona, did not think that the current business model in big-time college sports was financially sustainable. He believed that the current system of big-time college sports would eventually break down.

Despite these dire warnings, the arms race continues. The NCAA and the presidents have criticized escalating spending but have done little to stop it. Furthermore, higher education leaders such as Brit Kirwan often have difficulty when they try to avoid getting swept up in the currents of commercialism in college sports that they decry. It was Kirwan who represented the University System of Maryland when the Board of Regents secretly voted on Maryland's move to the Big Ten.

The FBS presidents who responded to the Knight Commission survey said they recognized the serious negative implications of the arms race and wanted to rein in athletic spending on coaches' salaries, the expansion of the athletic department's administrative infrastructure and personnel, and facilities construction projects.[78] The perceived negative implications of the arms race included problems balancing the athletic budget and getting spending under control. This was especially problematic for presidents of institutions not in Elite 6 conferences, who expressed concern about how much of their institution's resources were being spent on athletics. Another adverse consequence that the presidents identified was the "insidious and growing cultural divide between academics and athletics" in which athletics had taken the upper hand. They were bothered by how much the commercial model distracted from the core institutional mission and values and how it negatively impacted student-athletes.

Presidents also said they recognized the growing gap between the haves and have-nots, and some presidents of the have-nots believed that they were being unfairly exploited by the elite programs. They had to make substantial investments to compete at the top level of college sports, but they were not receiving the same financial or other benefits as their counterparts in the more elite conferences. Presidents with lower-status programs worried about their ability to remain competitive and stay in Division I. Nearly half of the respondents were concerned that the rising cost of competing in big-time sports could lead to cutting the number of varsity sports they could offer in the future.

Almost three-fourths of the presidents thought that athletics posed "unique challenges" in trying to control costs when compared to other parts of the university. The unique challenges are encapsulated in the athletic trap. Boosters and the IGT have poured large amounts of money into big-time college sports. This money and the brand enhancement that can come from winning in the big-time sports arena have encouraged schools to participate in the star wars and facilities arms races. Getting entangled in the race to join the big-time elite has undermined presidents' sense of control over athletics. This is another manifestation of the athletic trap.

Thus, the Knight Commission survey showed that presidents of BTUs generally seemed to recognize the seriousness of the arms race, at least as an abstraction. Yet they expressed little confidence that they could stop it. Other evidence raises questions about how directly threatened by the arms race many of these presidents actually felt. In its second annual survey of college presidents in 2012, *Inside Higher Ed* found that 70 percent of Division I presidents thought that colleges and universities spent "way too much" on their sports programs.[79] However, this study also found that half as many believed that their own institution was spending too much on athletics. Only 19.8 percent of the presidents of public institutions and 14.2 percent of the presidents of private institutions said cuts in athletic budgets were "currently under discussion" at their schools. In contrast, 30.5 percent of the presidents of public schools and 48.2 percent of presidents of privates said athletic budget cuts were "appropriately off the table."

Presidents on many campuses had a full plate of challenges following the economic downturn of 2008. Cutting athletic budgets was not going to solve broader campus problems such as reductions in state support, shortfalls in the university budget, student and public unhappiness about tuition increases, faculty unhappiness about their stagnant salaries, inadequate academic preparation of students, and threats to academic quality. As a result, making significant cuts in the athletic budget was not at the top of the list of strategies when presidents were contemplating how to address the major challenges facing their campuses in recent years. This was especially true at private institutions.[80]

Some presidents nevertheless made athletic budget cuts. According to the first annual *Inside Higher Ed* survey of presidents in 2011, about 33.9 percent of the presidents of public doctoral universities, 25 percent of the presidents of public master's institutions, 17.2 percent of presidents of private doctoral universities, and 7.3 percent of the presidents of private master's universities indicated that they had made budget cuts in athletics as a strategy to address the financial consequences of the economic downturn. There seemed to be some reluctance in making these cuts. The survey also found that if there were no political consequences, only 8.5 percent of the presidents of large public doctoral universities and slightly more (8.7 percent) of their counterparts at public master's universities said they would make significant cuts to their athletic budget. None of the presidents of private doctoral institutions and 8.3 percent of their counterparts at private master's institutions said they would make significant cuts in the athletic budget if there were no political repercussions.

Thus, we see the effects of the perception of unique challenges in cutting the athletic budget that the Knight Commission found. College presidents may feel that they are in a trap that prevents them from reducing their commitment to these programs. They also may truly believe what they say about the value of their big-time sports programs. In either case, their perceived need or desire to support big-time athletics may explain why many presidents do not want to cut their athletic budget or do not think it is necessary. They make athletic cuts in many cases because they feel pressured by legislators looking for dollars to trim in order to balance the shaky state budget.

It is the nature of arms races that voluntary unilateral disarmament is seldom seen as an option. The athletic trap implies that presidents are likely to feel locked into their commitments and do not want to risk substantial resistance if they propose scaling back on their big-time sports. Thus, they deal with political pressures to reduce the university budget by cutting the lower-profile nonrevenue sports. They make these cuts reluctantly. University strategies for handling financial pressures often reflect distorted priorities of universities. Presidents have been more reluctant to cut big-time sports budgets than the budgets for the library, academic departments, or the addition of tenure-track faculty.

Barring outside intervention, the arms race will continue as long the media, private businesses, and boosters remain interested in investing increasing sums of money in big-time college sports. This interest is driven by the popularity of these sports as commercial entertainment. This popularity stimulates the investment of the IGT commercial players. Even in the depressed economy of the past few years, college sports have remained popular and have kept the media, commercial sponsors, vendors, merchandisers, and boosters interested in spending increasing sums of money on them. The college sports business may be largely recession proof,[81] but this does not mean that everyone who competes in big-time college sports is insulated from the financial pressures of bad economic times.

Universities invest in college sports because they want the spillover effects that Anderson found.[82] Winning in football seems to produce these institutional enhancements, but more elite programs enjoy more of these benefits. College presidents would be wise to keep in mind Anderson's conclusion that the benefits ultimately were not worth the financial investment. Winning can be expensive (especially at the highest level of big-time college sports), relatively few schools have consistently successful football programs, and the arms race can consume significant portions of the revenue universities generate when they are successful. Less successful programs get fewer benefits but still pay the price. The hope or expectation of big returns from their athletic investment propels institutions forward in the arms race and obscures the reality of smaller returns most should expect.

Competition in the college sports business can be frustrating or disappointing when assessed with clear eyes. Even the elite big-time programs have difficulty retaining their top ranking year after year [83] The ups and downs that individual big-time college sports teams experience over time do not bother the media, corporate sponsors, vendors, and merchandisers in the IGT. They will make money as long as the games they telecast and the branded clothing and equipment they sell continue to attract audiences and customers. Switching loyalties is part of their business model. If fan and customer interest no longer matches the projections and criteria of investors, they are likely to start backing away from their past levels of financial investment. When this happens, the financial foundation of big-time college sports will begin to crack, threatening the financial stability of the college sports business.

So far, investors have continued to invest increasing amounts in college sports.[84] This keeps adding fuel to the arms race. Institutions believe they need to spend more to have a better chance of competing successfully for the increasing rewards in the IGT. However, the arms race constitutes the ultimate financial athletic trap because the social psychology of ambition and the uncertainty associated with this competition do not encourage the sober reflection that could result in disarmament.

We see in the arms race in college sports the same kind of speculative mentality and emotionally driven decision making that characterized Wall Street before the dips and the big crash in the first decade of the twenty-first century. The rapture of irrational exuberance[85] about sports on college campuses has led many into the financial trap of the arms race and produced few of the anticipated or hoped-for financial returns for most of these schools. The financial threats to the big-time world of intercollegiate athletics are real and can be quite serious, at least for the less affluent members or the have-nots. However, along with these challenges to the stability of the college sports business, there are other threats.

The athletic trap can obscure or make it difficult to avoid problems representing the dark side of big-time college sports. Deviant behavior, corruption, and scandals repeatedly surface in big-time college sports. Irrational exuberance and the arms race may challenge the future financial viability of the college sports business as it currently exists, but publicity about social deviance can threaten the integrity and reputation of the institutions sponsoring these programs. College presidents can get caught up in these problems and even contribute to them. The problems they face when they venture into the dark side of college athletics are the focus of the next chapter.

CHAPTER FIVE

Deviance, Corruption, and Scandals in College Sports

Revelations about illegal payments, cheating, exploitation of student-athletes, fixing, the crimes of athletes and coaches, and other transgressions in college sports have damaged the reputations of the deviant individuals and universities. Damaged reputations and NCAA penalties may have hurt these people and institutions for a while, but the star athletes and star coaches involved in these scandals usually have gone on with their careers without suffering any permanent blemishes or harm. The big-time universities caught up in these scandals also typically have bounced back from these embarrassments without losing their fan or financial base, except for the lost championship revenue or recruitment opportunities for the year or two they served their NCAA probation.

There is a well-established pattern at the highest level of college sport. Teams break the rules to get a competitive advantage, get caught after a while but not very often, pay the penalties for a year or two, then resume competing as if nothing happened. The cycle of cheating may resume as well. This deviance is normal in college sports. According to an analysis by *Inside Higher Ed*, nearly half (53) of the 120 universities at the top FBS level committed major rule violations between 2001 and 2010.[1] The result was fairly consistent with the previous two decades, but the number of institutions committing serious academic violations almost doubled from 8 to 15 between the 1990s and the 2000s.[2] Many of the violations concerned improper recruitment practices and excessive financial benefits for recruited or competing athletes. The academic violations included misrepresentation of academic credentials and the submission of papers essentially written by others, including academic support staff in some cases. The list of violators is significant not only because of the number of institutions on it but also because many of the institutions are academically well respected.[3]

The public seems to be aware of the deviance in college sports, and even self-described sports fans appear somewhat cynical about it. In a national Marist poll conducted in March 2012, 56 percent of college football fans and 57 percent of college basketball fans said they believed that it was "a common practice" for college sports programs to break the rules in recruiting and training college athletes.[4] The date of the poll is significant because it followed a couple of years with a spate of highly publicized scandals in college sports, including the Ohio State and Penn State scandals. It is not clear how much these scandals dulled the enthusiasm of college sports fans.

Deviance in college sports is treated by the press and the NCAA as especially unethical or immoral when the actions are serious and repeated, when the intentions of those responsible are viewed as malevolent, when institutional or academic integrity is substantially undermined, when crimes are committed, or when people are hurt. In these cases, the terms *corruption* and *scandal* are often used. Yet even when the NCAA has shut down incorrigible programs with the "death penalty" or applied other severe sanctions, the schools and their reputations have eventually recovered. The Penn State sex abuse scandal seems different from normal deviance in college sports, though, as we discuss later in the chapter.

Although deviance in big-time college sports has different forms, all share a common root—the influence of the intercollegiate golden triangle. The IGT offers the possibility of big payoffs in money and prestige. The biggest rewards go to the biggest winners and the most respected brands at the top level of big-time college sports. It is very expensive to win consistently, build a school's brand, and get these rewards. There are other costs, too, when schools want to win too much or become too protective of their brand and too willing to do whatever it takes to become or remain successful. This can be a path to perdition.

Presidents caught in the athletic trap may believe that they have an obligation to facilitate the success of their big-time football or basketball program. This can mean providing enough financial resources, hiring top coaches and athletic directors, making academic exceptions to admit outstanding athletes, or kowtowing to big athletic donors. It can also mean looking the other way when rules are broken or participating in cover-ups to protect the reputation of the athletic program and institution. When presidents and trustees want to win too much or enjoy basking in the reflected glory of a winning program, they may effectively give up their control over athletics to the people running athletics. Or they may find themselves at the mercy of wayward or misguided boosters whose only interest is having exciting and successful teams to watch. These situations are ripe for deviance, corruption, and scandal.

Three cases serve to illustrate different contexts and types of deviance. The first involves the University of Miami and shows the vulnerability of athletic programs with a history of big-time success. The second involves Binghamton University and is an example of what happens when a school tries to move up the big-time sports hierarchy too quickly. Both of these cases are normal deviance in the sense that they have happened many times over the history of college sports. Sometimes the schools are repeat offenders, and sometimes schools are new at deviance. In either case, we have come to expect such behavior. An apparent escalation in the number and seriousness of rule-breaking cases in college sports in recent years has put substantial pressure on the understaffed NCAA enforcement division,[5] and it caused the NCAA president to warn of tough new rules and sanctions for the rule breakers.[6] His warning seemed hollow in the face of the University of Miami scandal, but an even more serious and entirely different type of scandal at Penn State posed a powerful and perhaps unprecedented challenge for the NCAA and big-time college sports. It is why I call this case exceptional deviance.

Wayward Boosters: The University of Miami Case

Universities and their athletic foundations actively court prospective boosters. They provide the money that fuels big-time college athletic machines. Nevin Shapiro had been a Miami Hurricanes football fan since his boyhood in Miami Beach and the glory days of the Miami program.[7] After making money in real estate as a young man, Shapiro was able to afford the $12,000 it cost to be an official University of Miami booster. This was in 2001, and in that year, he also became a "living scholar." This was a university program, which was approved by the NCAA, that matched athletes with living scholar boosters who were supposed to be paying for the athlete's scholarship. This was one of the few things that Nevin Shapiro did for Miami athletics that did not violate NCAA rules. What the university and the NCAA may not have realized at the time was that a Miami athlete was being paired with a convicted felon, who had pleaded guilty to felony assault in 1995.[8]

Among many violations, Shapiro reportedly provided thousands of illicit gifts to at least seventy-two Miami athletes from 2002 through 2010. His virtual crime wave in Miami athletics was not ended by a university or NCAA investigation, but instead by his arrest and incarceration for his involvement in a $930 million Ponzi scheme. Investors thought their money was going into Shapiro's grocery distribution business.[9] The primary source of information about his NCAA infractions was Shapiro himself. He reportedly felt angry and vindictive toward the once beloved University of Miami when the Miami players he had befriended and given so many gifts failed to support or even have contact with him after his conviction.

Charles Robinson, an investigative reporter for *Yahoo! Sports*, had received a tip about Shapiro's illicit involvement with Miami athletics while Shapiro was talking to federal prosecutors about a plea deal regarding his Ponzi conviction.[10] He heard that Shapiro was a partner in a Jacksonville firm of sports agents, Axcess Sports, at the same time he was a major Miami sports booster. This was a significant violation of NCAA rules. Shapiro was using his access to players to introduce them to partners in his firm. The reporter arranged a phone interview with Shapiro through his lawyer. At the time, Shapiro was being held in a county jail in New Jersey and had unlimited phone privileges. Robinson impressed Shapiro with his background knowledge and questions, which resulted in scores of phone calls and detailed information about what Shapiro did.

Shapiro estimated that the gifts he gave Miami athletes were worth millions of dollars; however, the gifts and other benefits were not limited to cash, and the beneficiaries were not just athletes. Athletic recruiters allegedly brought recruits to Shapiro's home or yacht so that he could promote the program and make their job easier. Many of his contacts with recruits violated NCAA rules. He claimed that he gave cash to athletes who needed the money, took high school prospects and Hurricane athletes to night clubs and strip clubs, paid for prostitutes for them, bought them meals and treated them to entertainment, let them stay on his yacht or in his home, and in one case even paid for an abortion for a dancer at a strip club whom a player had gotten pregnant. He gave the most talented athletes gifts of cash, jewelry, clothing, travel, and televisions as an inducement to get them to sign with his Axcess Sports agency.

The remarkable number of NCAA violations this one man perpetrated transgressed at least four NCAA bylaws, involving impermissible compensation to coaches, amateurism of athletes, improper recruiting, and extra benefits to athletes. While he was breaking NCAA rules, he was also making major donations to the Miami athletic program, including a $50,000 check that Miami president Donna Shalala happily accepted during half time of a basketball game. His explanation for his impropriety was that he "did it because (he) could . . . And because nobody stepped in to stop me."[11] He developed what he thought were strong friendships with the athletes on whom he was lavishing his gifts. Once word spread that he was providing benefits to players, they began flocking to him for a share of his generosity. In an environment where money flows freely to everyone except athletes, wealthy boosters are happy to confer gifts. Since athletes are often from lower-income families, it is not surprising that they are drawn to gift givers and accept what they are given. Shapiro empathized with them.

Shapiro said it would not have been difficult for officials at the university to discover what he was doing, but he believed that they did not want to know. Both university and athletic officials valued his hundreds of thousands of dollars in donations and did not want to bite the hand that was feeding their athletic program.

They instead allowed him to lead the football team out of the stadium tunnel and on to the field, to fly on the team plane to an away game, and watch games from the sideline. He was a highly valued asset in Miami athletics. Of course, the money he was donating was tainted, coming from his illegal Ponzi scheme.

Under pressure from the NCAA, eight Miami players who admitted to taking improper benefits were declared ineligible by the university and were expected by the NCAA to repay the benefits.[12] This was the deal the university worked out with the NCAA in the hope that the players would regain their eligibility in time for the upcoming season.[13] However, these penalties do not reflect the extent of the scandal or the number of people and amount of money involved in it. The University of Miami told the press it was fully cooperating in the NCAA investigation, and it claimed ignorance about Shapiro's assorted and numerous misdeeds. The university may have been reluctant to be totally transparent, though, because if the NCAA was able to corroborate all of Shapiro's allegations, it would place the university in jeopardy of more serious NCAA sanctions.

The ease with which this overzealous booster was able to engage in repeated NCAA violations for almost a decade demonstrates how vulnerable established big-time athletic programs are to outside interference and how limited NCAA enforcement efforts are. For the University of Miami, though, breaking NCAA rules was not new. It appears that its past experience had not made it more vigilant in its effort to prevent future transgressions. The NCAA sanctioned Miami in 1981 and 1995 for wrongdoing in football, including a Pell Grant scam in 1995. In 2003 it was again put on probation and lost scholarships for actions in baseball. *ESPN* writer Pat Forde compared the pattern of repeated scandals and at Miami in particular to a wheel that keeps turning around and returning to where it had been.[14] He called it a "wheel of scandal." Forde suggested that schools like Miami were caught in cultural cycle they did not seem able to escape. The driving force was a love of football coupled with high expectations among fans and people at the university tied to or depending on football success.

In 1995, the longtime Miami president Edward Foote declared, "If something is broken, we will fix it . . . I believe and predict that the difficulties [in our athletic program] that have plagued the [football] team in the past are history." In 2011 Foote's successor, Donna Shalala asserted that, "I have no tolerance for breaking rules."[15] Miami athletic director Paul Dee ironically criticized the University of Southern California in 2010 for its scandal involving illegal payments to players. As chairman of the NCAA committee on infractions, he pointed to "systematic failure" at USC, and said that "High-profile players demand high-profile compliance," as he announced the sanctions USC would face.[16]

It appears that public assertions by top university officials do not have much influence on the cycle of conventional corruption in big-time college sports. One might have thought that President Shalala's prior experience in higher education administration at a BTU (University of Wisconsin) and her years in Washington, D.C., guiding the Department of Health and Human Services through the turbulence of welfare reform would have inoculated her against scandals in college athletics. What her experience taught her was how to manage a crisis but not how to avoid it.[17] She resisted calls for her resignation and for punishing football more harshly and continued on with her agenda of elevating the status of the university and pursuing a billion dollar capital campaign. Although she said her university would cooperate with the NCAA investigation, she was careful not to supply too much fuel, since Miami hypothetically could face severe sanctions as a repeat offender, including the so-called death penalty—suspension of the program for one or more seasons.

The case of the University of Miami shows how the athletic trap can get universities involved in trouble. Presidents know that the cultivation, care, and feeding of wealthy donors is part of their job description. Turning their back on athletics is rarely an option at such schools as the University of Miami, with a history of being at the top of big-time college football, a legacy to protect, and rabid fans to satisfy. Because of the amount of money required, generous boosters are an important part of the equation of success. Presidents, like politicians, may be reluctant to look too closely at the character of their donors and risk losing their support.

Thus, the Miami case illustrates how the need for money can influence how big-time athletic programs conduct their business. They attract big-time donors who sometimes engage in big-time NCAA infractions. The fact that Nevin Shapiro was also a criminal shows that there are unsavory characters who love sports and want to get closer to the action. This implies the need for extra NCAA and institutional scrutiny when large sums of money come from individual donors. The dilemma is that schools are reluctant to question the character of donors willing to invest large sums of money in their athletic program and the NCAA does not have the staff to scrutinize every big-time donor in college sports.

Striving and Deviance in College Sports: The Binghamton Case

Lois DeFleur worked her way up the career ladder in higher education. She went from sociology professor to provost to president. When she became president of Binghamton University in 1990, she assumed leadership of a respected public doctoral research university with modest athletic aspirations that competed at the Division III level. Yet DeFleur was ambitious and wanted to increase the prestige of her institution. Elevating the status of athletics was part of her agenda. She wanted her school to be at the same level academically and athletically as its peer institutions in the SUNY system.[18] Many faculty members did not share DeFleur's enthusiasm about having a more competitive and commercialized sports program. She pushed on, though, ignoring opposition from the faculty senate. In 1998 the athletic program achieved Division II status, and in 2001 it was competing at the Division I level. Although not everyone was happy about it, Binghamton had achieved what the president wanted in its rapid rise up the ranks of the NCAA.[19]

There were several concerns. Along with the issue of compromised academic standards, there was the increased investment that a big-time athletic program would require. An example was the expenditure of $33.1 million to build an events center, which was completed in 2007 and served as the new home for the basketball program. Binghamton also hired a new and more expensive men's basketball coach with an excellent sports pedigree as an assistant coach at big-time Georgetown but with less stellar credentials in recruiting athletes who were serious students.

Questions were soon raised about the recruits he brought to Binghamton. They were very good basketball players, but they had problems in the classroom and with the law. An adjunct professor, Sally Dear, complained that pressure from the athletics department to change her grading policy for basketball players made her feel like she was being harassed. After she complained, she was not assigned classes for the following semester, ostensibly as a part of university cost cutting. She felt like she was being punished for telling the truth about a sacred cow on campus, much like whistle-blowers often are. In addition, the former faculty athletics representative (FAR) was worried that the university was watering down its academic admission standards to allow star basketball players to be admitted. The FAR had served in this position for ten years but was replaced after the basketball coach was hired. In fact, the admission standard for men's basketball appeared to be lower than for other sports. It seemed evident that the path was being cleared for the basketball coach to run his program in the way he thought it needed to be run.

A philosophy in basketball that focused single-mindedly on winning was very different for Binghamton and was out of sync with other members of its athletic conference, the America East. The FARs in this conference were more likely to aspire to be like Ivy League or Patriot League schools than schools in a higher-pressure big-time conference. However, the dream of the Binghamton president, athletic director, and basketball coach was to compete against big-time teams in the NCAA tournament and enjoy more visibility for its basketball team and the university.

There were obvious signs of danger for Binghamton in its rapid rise in the NCAA and in its lofty aspirations. In 2009 Binghamton's sports dreams turned into a nightmare. The 2009 season ended with the excitement of participating in the NCAA tournament for the first time, and coach Kevin Broadus was rewarded with a five-year contract extension. However, a few months afterward, things began to unravel for both the coach and his program.[20] As the fall semester was beginning, one of his star players was arrested and charged with selling cocaine. As a result, he was dropped from the team. Two days later, the university dismissed five other players (three returnees and two new members) for unspecified misconduct. The media also began to focus on Sally Dear's problems with the basketball team and her termination.

The combination of these events and questions about lowered academic standards prompted the Board of Trustees of the State University of New York (SUNY) to engage a law firm to gather facts about the case and to make recommendations to the board.[21] President DeFleur publicly supported this independent audit as a way to restore integrity to her institution and confidence in the athletic program. The report was written by Judith Kaye, former chief judge of the New York Court of Appeals and cost SUNY and Binghamton nearly $1 million.[22] It presented findings and made recommendations regarding admission standards, support services, responses to allegations of misbehavior, the Sally Dear allegation and aftermath, the oversight of the basketball program, and the role of a faculty committee and the athletic board in oversight and control of athletics. It was probably not a coincidence that Sally Dear was rehired on the day when the SUNY audit was announced, although she was assigned to a different department.

The findings of the Kaye Report suggest numerous questionable practices regarding the basketball program. Many were departures from established institutional standards and policies. In combination these practices led to corruption of the university's academic and athletic reputation. For example, many of the top basketball recruits were academically underqualified, and some had a history of behavioral problems at other institutions. When members of the admissions staff resisted efforts to bring in the least qualified of these athletes, they were strongly opposed by the coach and athletic director. In one case, university administrators reversed a rejection decision regarding a basketball player. Concerns expressed by the athletics compliance director about irregularities in admission procedures were ignored. Binghamton officials said that accepting minority athletes was part of their effort to add diversity to the student body. However, the university had an inadequate support structure to help academically at-risk student-athletes to succeed. Furthermore, it appeared that Coach Broadus had much less interest in giving minority athletes a chance for a college education than in getting highly talented minority athletes to play for his team.

The Kaye Report also pointed to a culture created by the coaching staff and athletic administration at Binghamton that emphasized damage control at the expense of "constructive discipline and personal responsibility." That is, the university seemed much more concerned about reducing public relations fallout than about articulating and enforcing a code of appropriate conduct in athletics. This culture may be part of the explanation of the treatment of Sally Dear. Judge Kaye also suggested that the problem in the Dear case was less about whether her allegations were true than about how the university responded to her. It did not seem to take her allegations very seriously and tried to dismiss them and then her. The judge was concerned that this process of handling such complaints could make other faculty members with grievances reluctant to express them. In fact, the culture of big-time college sports is not about due process or fairness in handling complaints or grievances. It is about unqualified support for the success of the big-time sports teams. This is an implication of the athletic trap, which involves real and perceived obligations for presidents and other administrators to try to help big-time athletic programs to be as successful as possible.

Once the Binghamton administrators decided to make the move to the big-time in athletics, they were trapped. They made the promises, investments, and other commitments to compete and succeed at this higher level of sport. Then they had to try to fulfill them. The Binghamton case became a scandal because, over and over again, the university administration gave in to the wishes of the athletic department and basketball coach and was unintentionally or intentionally blind to indications of possible problems in basketball. As a result, institutional integrity and the integrity of the athletic program were seriously undermined. The president, trustees, and athletic director wanted too much to join the athletic big time and enhance the university's brand through sport. This motivation explains the willingness to allow the basketball coach to do what he thought he needed to do to succeed. Ceding this control along with a general lack of oversight of the basketball program allowed the basketball program to spin out of control and get into trouble. For these reasons, the Kaye Report recommended creating bigger roles for the faculty senate athletic committee and the athletic department's athletic board in oversight of athletics and having SUNY consider appointing an athletic oversight officer for the more competitive athletic programs in the system.

The obvious implication of this recommendation is that Binghamton was responsible for its athletic program, but another implication is that the SUNY system should have some accountability for the things that happen in athletics among its member institutions. This broader concept of the scope of accountability in higher education systems is especially interesting when we think of it in relation to the public universities that play at the highest level of college sports. We could expect much resistance from individual institutions in the name of protecting institutional autonomy. However, when things get out of control, as they too frequently do in college sports, the normal rules no longer seem to apply.

At the level of the strivers in big-time college sports, such as Binghamton, the risk of deviance seems especially acute. These institutions need to win and win relatively quickly to quiet the critics and justify the significant financial and administrative commitments required to succeed at the Division I level. Among the twenty-four schools that moved up to Division I between 2000 and 2009, five were sanctioned for major NCAA violations in various sports.[23] There was evidence from text messages to prospective recruits that were reviewed by the NCAA infractions committee that these institutions were not ready to participate in big-time sports.

A common theme found by the committee in these cases was that these schools were small and had inadequate staffing and funding to play at a higher level. Such is the lure of big-time college sports, though. Highly educated and intelligent decision makers forsake their usual rationality and make decisions guided by hopes and dreams. They make bad financial and administrative decisions and academic compromises to fulfill these hopes and dreams. In this process, they seem to forget that their primary mission is to educate. The commissioner of the mid-major Colonial Athletic Association commented that strivers may be impulsive in allowing aspirations to get ahead of reason. In a desperate effort to succeed, schools admit student-athletes that are not good academic or social fits for the institution, and ultimately "it all crashes and burns."[24] Thus, what happened at Binghamton was part of a pattern. This is normal deviance at the level of new and striving big-time athletic programs.

It happens among strivers at higher levels of big-time college sports, too. Boise State had been piling up wins in its football program and knocking on the door of the football elite. It kept making its case for a chance to play in the BCS championship game and considered conference churning as a strategy to join the elite. Apparently, it also stretched the rules in pursuing its ambitions, since it was penalized in 2011 for NCAA violations in five sports, including football.[25]

The president, provost, athletic director, and basketball coach at the center of the Binghamton scandal have all been replaced, leaving a tainted university and athletic brand in their wake. A striking consequence of the scandal is that the basketball program went from a first-ever appearance in the NCAA tournament just before the scandal was uncovered to declining success over the next three seasons and the futility of struggling to win a single game less than two years after the coach resigned.[26] Thus, coaches who recruit star athletes with dubious academic credentials and criminal histories can win big. However, the gains in exposure and prestige for striving institutions are quickly undone when the publicity turns negative, as it did at Binghamton.

An irony of this case is that after causing serious damage to their institution and costing it money as well as embarrassment, all of the major players who lost their jobs had a very soft landing. The president enjoyed a substantial pension after twenty years in her position. The athletic director, Joel Thirer, reportedly made over $195,000 as a tenured professor the year after his resignation, more than he earned as athletic director. He was installed in the Binghamton Hall of Fame in 2011. The coach did even better. After an extended suspension, he received a $1.2 million buyout of his contract.[27]

Exceptional Deviance in Big-Time College Sports: The Penn State Case

Even though the details of cases of deviance like those at the University of Miami and Binghamton University may be very troubling and taint the reputations of these institutions, these kinds of cases have become predictable as normal deviance and thus, somewhat muted in their effects on college sports. The critics express outrage and call for radical reforms or even the end of big-time college sports. The public, fans, and alumni may for a while feel some disappointment or disillusionment with the schools involved. The NCAA applies sanctions to punish the wrongdoers and to demonstrate they still have big-time college sports under control. University and athletic officials promise they will make changes to assure these kinds of acts will not happen again under their watch. The faces may change at the guilty institutions, but the IGT does not go away, and big-time college sports live to play another day with little permanent scarring to show from these scandals. As normal deviance, this is business as usual in big-time college sports.

The same cannot be said for the Penn State case. It is exceptional deviance. Many of the details of this sordid case are widely known because they were revealed in the highly publicized 267-page report of the Special Investigative Counsel (SIC) commissioned by the Penn State Board of Trustees.[28] The independent investigative team was led by former FBI director Louis Freeh, whose name is associated with the report. The SIC was asked by the Penn State trustees to uncover the facts, explain what happened, and help the university avoid these kinds of problems in the future. The university trustees who asked for an independent investigation might have hoped that its report would enable Penn State to restore its reputation after their own and the university's serious mishandling of this matter resulted in a lot of negative publicity. However, the report itself and the NCAA's use of it ultimately had a very different result.

Before the Sandusky scandal, football coach Joe Paterno's regime was known for its integrity as well as for its success on the field. His moral creed was "Success with Honor."[29] The story about Penn State football was that players went to class, graduated, and a number played pro football. Furthermore, the coach donated substantial sums of money to the library and other academic facilities and purposes. Penn State had a clean program, free of NCAA scrutiny. All of this was undone by the failure of the coach and the university to report alleged incidents of child sexual abuse on campus by an assistant coach who had gained a great deal of respect as the architect of the renowned Penn State defense. The failure to report the alleged abuse was not just a lapse of judgment or "mistake" as Paterno referred to it. It was a crime under the Clery Act. The assistant coach, Jerry Sandusky, was eventually arrested and convicted as a child sexual predator on forty-five counts of child sexual abuse.[30]

The Jerry Sandusky–Penn State scandal is not the usual story of cheating to win in big-time college sports.[31] There are some elements found in other cases of deviance in big-time college sports, but the deviance itself is seamier, and the responses are more troubling in the Penn State case. This case is about sexual abuse of children by a respected football coach, but it is also about how the athletic department and university administration colluded and effectively allowed the abuse to go unreported and keep happening. This story demonstrates what can happen when an athletic program and its coach are treated as sacred and omnipotent and when, as a result, protecting their legacy becomes more important than doing the right thing. The Freeh Report called this a "culture of reverence."

Louis Freeh held a press conference on the day of the release of the report prepared by his independent investigative team. He said the evidence showed "active agreement to conceal."[32] He went on to say that a culture called "the Penn State Way" put athletics and the university's reputation ahead of even the welfare of the child victims in this case.[33] In a culture of reverence, they showed more reverence for the reputation of Penn State football and the university than for the young victims of the abuse. Although Freeh did not explicitly use the word cover-up to describe the collusion of Penn State officials, the press has had no reluctance to refer to a cover-up in this scandal. Concealment is really just a synonym for cover-up. It revealed what Freeh called "a total disregard for the safety and welfare of children" by the most powerful men at Penn State.[34] It also showed how big-time college sports can distort moral values and priorities.

This culture of reverence developed because Penn State football under coach Joe Paterno made a lot of money for the university, attracted huge crowds and a large and dedicated following, and allowed Coach Paterno to wield a tremendous amount of power on campus. The success of the football team and the idyllic and isolated location of the campus led many to refer to Penn State as "Happy Valley." The residents of Happy Valley were very proud of their football team and coach. In this culture, few publicly challenged the coach or his program. This was true of university and athletic officials. Thus, no university administrator acted on the allegations he heard about Sandusky, and the athletic director, a senior vice president, and Joe Paterno reportedly lied to a grand jury when they were asked about what they knew about allegations of Sandusky's sexual deviance on campus. As a result of their inaction, Sandusky was allowed to continue his serial abuse.

My aim here is not to focus on all the details of the report or its recommendations. It is instead to consider what it tells us about where big-time sports programs can lead when they achieve the prominence and commercial success that presidents, trustees, athletic directors, coaches, alumni, and boosters dream about. The problem is that achieving prominence and commercial success in the athletic arena gives big-time college coaches and athletic directors a great deal of power, and this power is not always used responsibly. I am reminded here of Lord Acton's dictum that power corrupts and absolute power corrupts absolutely. Even initially well-intentioned leaders are corrupted by the capacity to do and get what they want without being accountable to anyone else.

Joe Paterno's long tenure as a successful football coach gave him a deified status on campus. He was able to use it to assure that his program could be run the way he wanted it run and that he would not have to deal with any interference from university or athletic officials. Paterno knew the importance of protecting his program's reputation from bad publicity, and university officials knew that public perceptions of the university were significantly tied to the success of the football team under Paterno. Recall how much Binghamton was willing to defer to a relatively novice head coach with one successful season at a mid-major level and how committed it was to damage control to protect the institution's reputation. Then consider the empire that Joe Paterno's football teams had created at Penn State and how closely intertwined the reputations of the university, football team, and its head coach were. The deference to the coach and the willingness to do whatever it took to protect the image of Penn State football become more understandable in this context.

In the culture of reverence at Penn State, Joe Paterno reigned supreme. His power is illustrated by the attempt by the president and athletic director to fire him in 2004. He was seventy-seven years old, and his team had a 3–9 record the previous season. Coaches of big-time programs that do as poorly often are asked for their resignation. Because Paterno did not want to step down, his "bosses" decided not to argue with him. He continued to coach and build his legacy, and in 2011 he was the winningest coach in big-time college football history. When his teams began to win again, his status and power were further reinforced.

Joe Paterno was not exactly the man he appeared to be, and the football program was not what it appeared to be. His authority allowed him to circumvent normal campus disciplinary processes and mete out whatever punishments he thought were appropriate when his players transgressed. While they were never caught violating NCAA rules, they were not angels. An ESPN report revealed that forty-six of his players had been charged with a total of 163 crimes from public urination to murder between 2002 and 2008, and *Sports Illustrated* reported in 2011 that among its top twenty-five teams, Penn State tied for the fourth-highest number of arrests, with sixteen players on the 2010 opening-game roster having been charged with a crime.[35] Paterno and Penn State publicists worked hard to shield the football program from adverse publicity for this kind of behavior. Protecting the reputation of its coach and his cash cow of a program was paramount.

At the end of his life, which came relatively shortly after he was fired, Paterno continued to defend his team and its legacy. In a letter to ex-players he wrote after the exposure of the scandal, he said, "This is not a football scandal and should not be treated as one." He argued that the history of his program belied the idea that this was a Penn State football scandal and asserted that the critics were "unfairly besmirching both a great university and the players and alumni of the football program who have given of themselves to help make it great."[36] The letter entirely misses the point that this was a Penn State scandal because he and other campus leaders failed to act responsibly in addressing the seriousness of Sandusky's abusive behavior.

The irony of the Penn State case is that the football program did exactly what presidents and trustees promise big-time sports will do. Football success bumped up the university's prestige and helped turn it into a world-class university by making it more visible and inspiring more alumni and financial support. In the end, however, the football program and its head coach became self-serving, unaccountable, and morally corrupt in protecting what had been wrought from sports success. Thus, it fell farther and harder than programs that had not achieved its level of success.

The Aftermath of the Penn State Scandal

With less provocation than in the Penn State case, critics have called for the elimination of programs that have engaged in serious or repeated normal deviance.[37] The exceptional deviance at Penn State was arguably more serious and outrageous than these other cases, but it did not bring an end to Penn State football, as some critics demanded. Although the NCAA did not impose its death penalty and take the team off the field for a season or more, it applied unprecedented sanctions. The NCAA response was prompted by the powerful indictment of the program presented in the Freeh Report. It condemned the university's leadership, its culture of reverence, and the actions and inactions of Joe Paterno.

The coconspirators were fired or forced to resign. President Graham Spanier and Coach Paterno were fired, and Gary Schultz, the senior vice president of finance and business, and the athletic director Tim Curley resigned. Spanier, Schultz, and Curley all faced criminal charges for lying to a grand jury, obstruction of justice, endangering the welfare of children, and criminal conspiracy.[38] Paterno might have been indicted as well, but he died before any action could be taken. Still, his legacy and good name were severely tarnished.[39] Sandusky was sentenced to thirty to sixty years for his crimes.[40] The victims of Sandusky's abuse paid a much higher price, though.

While many of the Penn State faithful rallied around their coach and school even after the release of the Freeh Report,[41] public reaction was generally much more negative outside the Penn State family. In one national poll by *USA Today* and Gallup about a week after the story got into the press,[42] two-thirds of those following this scandal agreed with Penn State's decision to fire Joe Paterno. In addition, 59 percent of the respondents said the Penn State football program "had become too powerful," while 24 percent thought it had kept the program within appropriate limits. Although only 14 percent thought the university should cancel the remainder of its season, one-third indicated that the scandal had given them a more negative view of the university as a whole.

Another national poll conducted by Widmeyer Communications around the same time revealed widespread negative opinions about Penn State as a result of the scandal.[43] It also revealed questions about big-time college sports in general. One finding was that 67 percent of the respondents said that Penn State's handling of the "child sexual abuse controversy" was very or somewhat similar to the way that the Catholic Church had handled previous child sexual abuse cases. Another finding was that 83 percent of respondents believed the culture of big money in Division I college sports in the past two decades was a large or moderate factor in the delayed response of Penn State officials to the Sandusky case. Sixty percent said it was a large factor. In addition, 72 percent thought that Division I college athletic programs had too much influence over college life. There was an even split among those who would discourage and those who would not discourage their child from attending a Division I school that placed a strong emphasis on sports. Forty percent said they were very or somewhat likely to discourage their child from attending a BTU, while 41 percent said they were very or somewhat unlikely to discourage such attendance.

The Widmeyer poll also asked respondents to indicate the advice they would give to the NCAA for handling this case: 15 percent said the NCAA should bar the football team from conference play in the next season; 15 percent said the football program should be shut down in the upcoming season; 18 percent said Penn State should be banned from postseason bowl games for the current 2011 season; 14 percent said the team should not be allowed to play in the postseason in 2012; 13 percent said Penn State should be banned from postseason bowls for five years; and 37 percent said no NCAA sanctions were needed. The pollsters did not ask how the NCAA should treat the institution if it were the one the respondent rooted for.

Whether or not the NCAA took the public pulse in weighing its options, NCAA president Mark Emmert was surely aware that there were many people in the public, the press, big-time college sports, and especially at Penn State anxiously awaiting his organization's response. After facing much criticism over the previous two years for a spate of high-profile scandals at institutions including the University of Southern California, Ohio State University, the University of Miami, and the University of North Carolina, the NCAA might have felt it was facing a trial of leadership. Its hold over college sports and football in particular had been undermined by the rising power of the conferences and the BCS. Some questioned its future role in big-time college sports and whether it could keep it under control.

In a Public Broadcasting System (PBS) interview with Tavis Smiley after the release of the Freeh Report, NCAA president Emmert said that this case was unlike any other in the history of college sports.[44] It went to the core values of college sport, he asserted. He then affirmed the NCAA's commitment to the values of the collegiate model and lamented how far Penn State had strayed from it. College sports scandals often seem to produce ironies, and Emmert's comments suggest at least two. First, Penn State had not violated any NCAA rules in this case or in the past under the leadership of Coach Joe Paterno. Second, Penn State under Paterno's leadership had long been viewed as the embodiment of all that was good about big-time college sports.

Emmert nevertheless was determined to hold Penn State accountable to the

NCAA. With the blessing of the NCAA executive committee, he acted quickly and decisively. He used the Freeh Report as the basis for his decisions. The death penalty had been on the table, but the new Penn State president argued strongly against it and convinced the NCAA to impose lesser punishments. It is not clear, however, how much less severe these punishments were. There were five major sanctions: (1) a $60 million fine, with the money to be used for an endowment for victims of child sexual abuse; (2) a four-year ban on postseason competition; (3) a five-year probation for the athletic department; (4) a reduction of ten grants-in-aid per year over four years; and (5) the vacating of 111 football victories since 1998, when Joe Paterno first became aware of allegations against Sandusky.[45] The $60 million was estimated to be the approximate amount of money Penn State earned from football in a year. Penn State's conference, the Big Ten, added its own financial penalty, withholding $13 million in conference revenue over four years. This money was to be used to help victims of abuse. Current members of the football team would be allowed to transfer without sitting out a year. Penn State president Rodney Erickson accepted the consent decree stipulating these conditions because it kept his football team on the field.

The $60 million fine was widely seen as the harshest of the penalties. It went beyond the corrective and punitive sanctions the NCAA customarily imposed. In effect, it represented a form of community restitution, according to *Sports Illustrated* writer Alexander Wolff.[46] Although this is a big number, it should be put in perspective. First, Penn State ranked third, behind Texas and Notre Dame, in *Forbes* Magazine's 2011 rankings of college football's most valuable teams.[47] Equity in Athletics Data generated for the U.S. Department of Education indicated that in the 2010–2011 academic year, Penn State football produced $72.7 million in revenue and cost the university $19.5 million, which resulted in a surplus of more than $53 million. Total revenue for Penn State athletics that year was $116.1 million and the overall surplus was $31.6 million. No university subsidy was provided for athletics at Penn State. These figures show how important Penn State football was to the athletic program and university. It subsidized other programs and still produced a "profit" for the university. Thus, the fine and the other penalties suffered by football promised to cut significantly into athletic revenue and cost the university a great deal of money.

Despite the harsh NCAA sanctions, Penn State retained its place in the elite of college football. Although some of its players departed in the aftermath of the scandal and the team struggled in its first two games of the 2012 season under its new coach, it ended its season with a record of 8 wins and 4 losses and a second-place finish in its division of the Big Ten. Parenthetically, it finished behind undefeated Ohio State, which was also ineligible for postseason play as a result of NCAA sanctions. As a university, Penn State was less damaged by the Sandusky scandal and the NCAA penalties than some observers had predicted. In the ensuing year, enrollments increased, donations remained strong, and the university made substantial progress in the governance and oversight changes that had been called for by the Freeh Report.[48] Its image may have been initially tarnished for many people, but its athletic and institutional "recovery" after the scandal demonstrates the resilience of big-time college sports in the face of even the most horrible kind of scandal.

Penn State's lawyers presented arguments in its defense to help mitigate NCAA sanctions and avoid the death penalty. These arguments included the university's commissioning of the Freeh Report; waiving attorney-client privilege; trustees' acceptance of responsibility for its lack of oversight; severed ties with Paterno, Spanier, Curley, and Schultz; Penn State's clean prior record with the NCAA infractions committee; the huge financial cost of penalties Penn State would be paying to the NCAA, the Big Ten, and civil litigants; the university's commitment to implement all or nearly all of the 119 reform recommendations of the Free Report; and the additional harm a death penalty would cause for many innocent people not involved in the scandal.[49] The innocents included current players, the new coaching staff, and the residents of central Pennsylvania who lived and worked in the shadow of Penn State and depended on it for their business and entertainment. The hundreds of thousands of Penn State alumni could also be added to this list, since their pride in their alma mater could have become shame for many.

The NCAA might have decided against the death penalty for other reasons as well. It might have been concerned about the loss of TV and other revenue Penn State opponents would have experienced if they did not get to play Penn State. Mark Emmert surely was appalled by Penn State's behavior in this scandal, but his job still required him to protect the commercial interests of the NCAA and its other member institutions in the IGT. Thus, talk about the preeminence of the values of the collegiate model was at odds with the fundamental reality of big-time college sports that the commercial model and ties to the IGT are paramount. Without them, big-time college sports cannot exist. This is notwithstanding the many years that Penn State appeared to contradict this assertion.

The Penn State case reveals the bizarre way in which the athletic trap can make BTUs vulnerable to deviance but also protect them from the worst consequences that could result from being caught. The deeply embedded and powerful culture of football and its athletic and financial status explained the unwillingness of university officials to acknowledge Sandusky's behavior. They seemed to see this case only in terms of protecting the brand of the football program and the university. The athletic trap shaped their perceptions. On the other hand, the athletic trap also involved long-established football traditions and enduring and entrenched relation-ships and commitments at Penn State that bred a deep loyalty in the Penn State community and among fans.

The Penn State case also involved a web of financially remunerative relationships in the IGT and for the NCAA that seemed to insulate it from the worst sanctions. The NCAA president believed he had to act decisively in this case, but he also did not want to act in a way that damaged the NCAA brand or its lucrative relation-ships in the IGT. The athletic trap created a tightrope that Mark Emmert had to walk carefully to protect the image of the NCAA and big-time college sports but also allow Penn State to survive as a big-time power in college football. Thus, it ap-pears that the athletic trap may help the biggest of the BTUs to endure egregious moral lapses and serious sanctions. They may be too established to fail, much like the big banks on Wall Street after the financial collapse of the past decade. The full story of the Penn State scandal will take many years to write. As the aftermath of the scandal continued to play itself out, the university had to deal with legal and financial repercussions and had to persuade its accrediting body that it should not lose its accreditation.[50]

The Athletic Trap and Corrupted Values

Even though the Penn State scandal is not a typical case of deviance in big-time college sports, its lessons are important for those participating at this level of college sports or wanting to become part of it. It constitutes immorality as well as crimi-nality and shows how infatuation with big-time sports success and its heroes can lead otherwise responsible people to make some very irresponsible decisions. Once in the athletic trap, presidents, athletic administrators, coaches, athletes and their families, and boosters who decide to go down the path of deviance find it difficult or impossible to acknowledge their wrongdoing without some negative repercussions.

When the reputation of a big-time sports program is threatened by possible rev-elations of wrongdoing, a culture of reverence can morph into a culture of damage control. The culture of reverence tightens the grip of the athletic trap and can sub-vert the procedures that universities are supposed to follow to handle institutional problems. At Miami, Binghamton, and Penn State, university officials used various strategies to minimize the damage to their institutions' public images. These three cases collectively suggest that damage control is a typical part of the dynamics of handling both normal and exceptional deviance in big-time college sports. Evidence from other institutional spheres beyond athletics and higher education indicates that this strategy is widely used whenever preserving the organization's reputation is more important than redressing harm caused by the organization. Concerns about reputation, liability, and the bottom line overshadow concerns about victims. The Penn State case showed that administrators who orchestrate damage control efforts for their institution may be unable to protect their own jobs. They are blamed and cast out by trustees or other higher authorities as part of a purge to purify the institution and restore its good name.

There are some cases of presidents and trustees who have tried to resist the corrupting influence of the athletic trap and stand up for the integrity of their institution. For example, they have tried to rein in successful coaches who have gotten out of control or shut down out-of-control programs. In taking these actions, they have outraged alumni and fans and received hate mail and some death threats. One case involved the late NCAA president Myles Brand when he was president of Indiana University. He fired basketball coaching legend Bobby Knight. It was 2000 and after Knight had crossed the line one time too many in a series of abusive actions toward players, the media, and Indiana students. Although Myles Brand accomplished many things in academe and gained a lot of notoriety as NCAA president, this one act may be what the public most remembers about him.[51]

A case at the University of Cincinnati involved trustees pushing the president to get a successful but wayward coach under control. When Nancy Zimpher was hired by the University of Cincinnati, she was instructed by the trustees to do three major things: improve the school's image, get the budget under control, and get the basketball coach under control.[52] The coach, Bob Huggins, was very successful and popular with fans, but he had a reputation for having players who got into trouble with the law, for not caring about their academic shortcomings, and for outbursts on the sideline. His arrest for drunken driving, which was recorded on videotape, shortly after Zimpher arrived on campus resulted in a forced leave and a warning from the new president. Unsatisfactory contract negotiations over the next year led to an ultimatum from the president: resign or be fired. He left in 2005. An interesting postscript to this case is that Nancy Zimpher went from Cincinnati to the position of SUNY chancellor, where she faced the Binghamton scandal and commissioned the independent audit of it.

Tulane president Eamon Kelly shut down the Tulane basketball program in 1985 in a point-shaving case.[53] The case involved five players, and money and cocaine were allegedly at the heart of the scandal. For the Tulane president, it was more important to uphold the academic reputation of the university than to allow its basketball team to tarnish it. In a familiar story, the players did not meet the usual high academic standards of the university. They were there to win basketball games and enhance their career prospects. Despite the gravity of this case, there were still some angry alumni who did not want to see the basketball team eliminated.

The rest of these stories is that Bobby Knight and Bob Huggins got lucrative jobs elsewhere, and Tulane eventually restarted its basketball program. Although Joe Paterno and the presidents of Penn State and Binghamton lost their jobs following the scandals on their campuses, the Miami president hung on to hers, and the new football coach is trying to run a successful and clean program.

The Descent into Deviance and the IGT

Many scandals develop in college sports because presidents and trustees become unwitting, and sometimes calculating, coconspirators in the processes of deviance and corruption that enable scandals to arise and fester. They do not pay enough attention to what is happening in their athletic program. They defer to the judgment of self-serving athletic directors and coaches and approve the admission of athletes with histories of academic and disciplinary problems and brushes with the law. They gladly accept the involvement and contributions of boosters who may not have the best interests of the university at heart. Boosters and athletic foundations may influence the recruitment and admission of athletic prospects, the selection of coaches and athletic directors, and the amount invested in athletic programs and facilities. Allowing boosters to have these kinds of influence undermines normal governance processes and can result in significant breaches of institutional integrity. The apologies that presidents sometimes make to boosters who feel ignored or underappreciated can be embarrassing for university leaders when they are reported in the press. However, these stories reveal the grip of the athletic trap.

The athletic trap can also influence hiring decisions in athletics. In their zeal to get basketball coaches who promise to make big-time teams big winners, presidents and athletic directors hire coaches with checkered ethical records. They pay big money for star coaches and coaches on the ascent. John Calipari, the basketball coach at the University of Kentucky, is an example of one the biggest winners in the star wars arms race. Kentucky has a rich tradition in men's basketball, and its boosters expect national championships. They had won seven before Calipari's arrival, the second-highest number in Division I behind UCLA. When his team won the national championship in 2012, he was rewarded with a salary boost. His estimated total contract of $5.4 million was only slightly less than the salary of the Alabama football coach, who was best-paid coach in college sports in 2012.[54]

In hiring Calipari, though, Kentucky overlooked some significant blemishes on his record. He had been the basketball coach at Massachusetts and Memphis before moving to Kentucky, and both schools had their Final Four appearances during Calipari's tenure vacated as a result of NCAA rule violations. Furthermore, he allegedly has had recruiting help from a questionable figure who was believed to befriend players and point them toward specific schools and agents.[55] Both Memphis and Kentucky defended their choice of Calipari because he eluded NCAA censure for his own actions, despite the trail of corruption he left behind each time he moved up the coaching ladder. However, he did not escape the reproach of his coaching peers, who voted him the "biggest cheater" in their sport in a 2012 CBSSports.com survey.[56]

Even if Calipari was not as guilty of cheating as many of his peers assumed, he gave critics additional fuel with his "one and done" approach to recruiting. His star recruits had a history of playing one year of big-time college basketball and leaving school to pursue professional basketball careers. NCAA president Emmert did not like this practice because he said it created "the wrong type of environment for us. If you're coming to us to be a collegiate athlete, we want you to be a collegiate athlete."[57]

Calipari has criticized the NCAA president for suggesting that athletes not interested in being serious students should not play college sports. Calipari said it sent the wrong message to young and aspiring athletes who would pay even less attention to their studies if they could skip college and go into the pros. Calipari's comments seem more self-serving than altruistic, though, because it is more important to him as a coach to have access to a pool of talented players, even for a year, than to have his players complete their college education.[58] For all the criticism he has received, though, his approach is totally consistent with the philosophy of big-time sports in the IGT, highlighting entertainment, winning, and making money from sports success.

This philosophy of big-time college sports reflects the commercial model. Its ascendancy over the collegiate model is a fundamental reality of big-time college sports that the NCAA and college presidents rarely acknowledge. By embracing the commercial model even as they extol the collegiate model, presidents of BTUs put their institutions and themselves at risk of getting caught up in the arms race and being involved in various forms of deviance. They hire coaches such as John Calipari and pay them huge salaries despite questions about their character and values. BTUs want winners, and winners are rewarded, even when they put their schools at risk of NCAA sanctions.

The lack of genuine commitment to the collegiate model is why college presidents and the president of the NCAA are accused of hypocrisy. The potent influences of the commercial model and the athletic trap can make it seem difficult or impossible to follow through on commitments to the collegiate model. By failing to follow through on these commitments, presidents allow athletics to take over the academy. In such cases, the athletic trap exerts a powerful grip over decision making about athletics, and at the same time a culture of reverence reinforces athletic commitments. Athletics takes down the academy when university officials seem powerless to stop corruption and scandals and even take an active part in them. When this happens, we read about the "shame of college sports." This is the title of a controversial article in the October 2011 *Atlantic Monthly* by respected historian and Pulitzer Prize–winning author Taylor Branch,[59] and it appeared *before* revelations about Penn State surfaced.

The descent into deviance often begins with the lure of the IGT and its promised rewards, which can weaken commitments to the collegiate model, core academic values, and institutional integrity. This process of corruption is difficult to escape once it becomes embedded in the athletic trap as normal deviance. Doing whatever it takes to win and succeed in the IGT can lead to overlooking the rules in recruiting, tampering with student records, giving improper academic assistance to marginal student-athletes, and hiding the misdeeds of coaches and athletes. In addition, with more money and attention attracting more disreputable characters, athletes may be tempted by under-the-table cash and other gifts or even get involved with gamblers and fixers and alter their performance to beat the betting line. As long as no one is caught, this behavior is likely to continue.

When wrongdoing is discovered and publicized, penalties are imposed, reputations of individuals and institutions are tarnished, and the course of athletics, at least for a while, can change dramatically. Institutions at the top of the college sports hierarchy generally have reserves of tradition and a loyal fan base that enable them to pick themselves up and try to return to their former prominence. Institutions such as Binghamton with less established athletic programs and fewer resources tend to find it more difficult to engage in successful damage control after plunging into corruption and scandal.

Scandals, Blind Spots, and Corrupted Decisions

When deviance happens, the athletic trap can make it difficult for university and athletic administrators to address it directly, especially when there is a powerful culture of reverence for athletics on campus. At Penn State, the reservations that the president, vice president, and athletic director had about not reporting the allegations of child abuse were effectively muted when the powerful figure of Joe Paterno did not want the allegations to be reported. Cognitive dissonance theory tells us that once people commit themselves to a decision, they begin rationalizing it as the right decision. This appears to be what happened at Penn State, and it may be a common practice at other schools where university officials have not done the right, appropriate, wise, or legal thing in the midst of scandals.

Bazerman and Tenbrunsel used their idea of "blind spots" to explain why the leaders of the Catholic Church failed to do the right thing in their decisions about the child abuse scandal they faced.[60] They suggested that church leaders and leaders in other institutional spheres often underestimate the influence of their self-interest and expect to act more ethically than they actually do. That is, leaders often have blind spots in their ethical thinking. In an interview about the Penn State scandal, Ann Tenbrunsel suggested that the concept of "motivated blindness" helps explain why university leaders, church officials, corporate CEOs, and other decision makers act unethically.[61] They are motivated by their extreme loyalty to their organization, which blinds them to certain ethical implications of their decisions. She characterized such excessive commitment to the organization as the "dark side of loyalty" in which too much loyalty corrupts ethical thinking.

In big-time college sports, blind spots are mainly the product of structural influences embedded in the athletic trap and cultural forces such as a culture of reverence. These structural and cultural influences can create excessive and uncritical loyalty to athletic programs, coaches, and athletes, and bias decisions about them. At Penn State, for example, officials wanted to be compassionate toward Sandusky, warn him about the risks of bringing children to campus, and get him professional help. However, they paid little or no attention to the welfare of his abuse victims. They saw Sandusky as a potential victim, while ignoring the actual victims. This was their blind spot. At the same time, though, they were well aware that if the allegations they were hearing were true, they could, in the words of vice president Gary Schultz, open a "Pandora's box." They worried how many other children might be victims.[62] Their worries were not about the harm the children suffered but about the damage the revelations could cause for the university and athletic program.

It turns out that the NCAA's poster child for the collegiate model and good citizenship was actually an object lesson in what can happen when athletics takes over the academy and corrupts its core values. Penn State was corrupted by a football team that became too successful, too rich, and too powerful. Power corrupts and too much power led to absolute corruption in this case. Penn State and the other scandals described in this chapter show that rhetoric about the collegiate model is just window dressing to cover up less commendable realities of the excesses associated with implementing the commercial entertainment model. These two models are fundamentally at odds with one another, and this is never more evident than in cases where presidents and trustees have to monitor and make decisions about allegations of dubious practices in athletics.

The issue is whether college presidents, trustees, and the NCAA are committed to real reform in college sports. Real reform would mean elevating the collegiate model to the prominent place they often say it occupies in college sports. Are they willing to dismantle some of the athletic trap and remake elements of the athletic culture to emphasize a serious commitment to student-athletes and academic values and restrict the influences of fans, boosters, and the IGT? By failing to make a commitment to genuine reform, they will continue to foster the arms race and feed the cycle of deviance in big-time college sports. These issues of control and reform are the main focus of the next two chapters.

CHAPTER SIX

Control and Reform
in Big-Time College Sports

The way governance is supposed to work in traditional universities is that the governing board is the final authority and is accountable in all matters relating to the general interest, well-being, and reputation of the institution it serves.[1] Boards delegate responsibility for the daily operation of the university to presidents and administrators and usually permit various forms of shared governance involving faculty, staff, and students. Because they have the last word, board members are supposed to be familiar with their institution, at least from the forty-thousand-foot level. Board members may be appointed or elected, but they are laypeople and are a buffer meant to protect institutions of higher education in the United States from government control and political influence commonly found in other countries. While trustees of private institutions generally see themselves as stewards protecting the interests of the institution, trustees of public universities often see themselves as guardians of the public interest.

Actual boards often depart from this idealized conception of their role. In athletic matters, boards have often taken an aloof or passive role. On some boards, though, a few members have assumed an activist role in pushing their pro-athletics agenda. The stance of the board toward athletics affects the amount of latitude presidents, athletic directors, and coaches have in running athletic programs. Presidents know they must report to their board, but they generally expect a certain amount of freedom in making decisions in athletics as in other realms of campus life. When they face resistance from the athletic department or boosters, they hope the board will back up their decisions. Presidents can run afoul of their board when they are perceived as being either too tough or too lenient in cases of uncooperativeness, defiance, or alleged rule breaking in athletics.

Knowing exactly how to handle athletics can be difficult for presidents. Research by the *Chronicle of Education* regarding the authority of presidents with the twenty-five biggest athletic departments revealed that none had contract language about oversight of athletics.[2] These contracts, which typically did not spell out any specific job responsibilities, were more likely to stipulate goals in areas such as fundraising and financial management. Athletics was mentioned only in relation to perks, such as athletic tickets that presidents could use for entertainment and fundraising. Following the governance issues raised by the Penn State scandal, presidents at top BTUs were beginning to discuss how to make their authority over athletics more specific.

Penn State was unusual among public universities in that the president had a seat with voting rights on his board.[3] Combined with vagueness about his authority in athletics and the board's specific role in athletic oversight, the president was able to build strong support among board members and avoid questions when news about the scandal began to surface. On other BTU campuses, presidents often lack this kind of formal or informal power on the board. When they also lack a clear scope of authority over athletics, they are likely to worry about upsetting trustees, state regents, and powerful alumni and boosters in taking decisive or bold actions in athletics. This uncertainty about authority tightens the grip of the athletic trap.

When the athletic trap is in place, presidents generally believe they are expected to devote a significant and sometimes disproportionate amount of time promoting and supporting athletics. This task is likely to conflict at times with other demands they must meet. For example, boards also want the president to balance the budget while keeping costs under control, manage a successful capital campaign, recruit and graduate good students, hire outstanding faculty members, enhance the brand and ranking of the institution, and keep the campus quiet and happy. At public universities, presidents have the added responsibility of having to lobby the legislature for support for major programs and state funding, which has been substantially diminishing for a number of years. Duderstadt and Womack have asserted that it is nearly impossible for presidents to do all they are expected to do and that public university presidents typically must deal with a basic mismatch between their responsibilities and their authority.[4] Their job is made more difficult by meddling, incompetent, and unsupportive board members and by a board's expectation that the president support athletics.

Presidents may face tough decisions about their athletic programs, such as hiring and firing athletic directors and coaches and adding and cutting athletic programs. When presidents make decisions more on the basis of the commercial model than the collegiate model, these decisions could create serious concerns about whether the institution's academic integrity, educational mission, or Title IX compliance is at risk. Furthermore, presidents invite criticism for their irresponsibility or hypocrisy as academic leaders in these cases. On the other hand, when presidents try to honor their public commitment to the collegiate model, they may find that they antagonize powerful constituents of their institution and complicate relationships in the intercollegiate golden triangle.

Thus, presidents can have a challenging balancing act as they try to satisfy a wide range of expectations about athletics. Efforts to keep athletics under control are often complicated at BTUs by external stakeholders, such as boosters, politicians, and the many powerful entities in the IGT. They are hard to keep in check because they do not report to the president and they do not share the president's concerns about balancing athletic commitments with the educational mission of the university. Both internal and external pressures pushing presidents and their institutions toward more big-time athletic success have contributed to the kinds of issues and problems examined in the preceding two chapters.

The NCAA has gathered college presidents on more than one occasion in recent years for summits to address the most serious problems of college athletics. These summits usually end with assertions about how the NCAA and the presidents will be taking strong steps to get big-time college athletics on track and in harmony with the collegiate model. Yet no one has seemed to back away from the commercial model or the commercial opportunities presented by the IGT.

In recent years, presidents have been wrestling with many other problems outside of athletics that are more directly related to the central mission and operations of their institutions. They have faced strong criticism that higher education has been falling short of its promise and that things have been getting worse.[5] According to the high-profile Spellings Commission,[6] major problems in contemporary higher education prominently included access, cost and affordability, educational quality, transparency and accountability, and innovation. Critics of higher education have added the investment in big-time sports programs to this list of problems.[7] In light of these criticisms, presidents sometimes become defensive when they are arguing in favor of practices such as mandatory student fees for athletics, admission of academically underqualified student-athletes, and large expense budgets in athletics or when they try to explain rule breaking in their campus sports programs. They face additional criticism for a lack of transparency and accountability when scandals hit the news.

At a time when these kinds of problems demand the full attention of presidents, trustees, and their universities, athletics can seem to be a distraction—a claim that critics have always made about big-time college sports. In fact, athletics took over the academy almost from the outset of big-time college sport in the sense that presidents and trustees allowed athletics to consume significant amounts of university resources and sidetrack students from their studies. They also permitted sports programs to continue after major scandals tarnished the university's reputation. It is a testimony to the entrenched place of big-time athletics at BTUs that presidents and trustees rarely consider discontinuing athletic programs after experiencing serious and repeated cases of deviance, corruption, and scandals. They instead lament and sometimes apologize for the excesses, mistakes, and misdeeds and declare that they will not let these things happen in the future. They may be reluctant to take responsibility if their job or reputation is on the line or they could face serious sanctions or legal prosecution. They keep kicking down the road the questions about how to maintain integrity and solvency in an environment shaped by the commercial model and the temptations of the IGT. This chapter focuses on these questions as issues of control.

The Athletic Trap and Presidential Perceptions of Control

The athletic trap imposes real and perceived constraints on presidential decisions and actions in athletics. Big-time athletic programs nurture a culture of reverence that can lead to motivated blindness, which can keep presidents from seeing athletic problems fully or realistically. Presidents who want to rein in their big-time athletic programs realize it can be difficult. The Knight Commission and *Inside Higher Ed* survey data cited in chapter 4 indicated that most university presidents acknowledged that there was an arms race in athletics but also that many fewer thought they were spending too much on athletics. This same confidence in their own decision-making abilities was expressed in the 2012 *Inside Higher Ed* survey about the scandals of the past year,[8] in which 81 percent of the presidents of public doctoral institutions and 76.2 percent of the presidents of public master's institutions agreed that these scandals damaged the reputations of all higher education, not just the institutions involved. Sharing this view were 58 percent of the presidents of private doctoral universities and 67 percent of the presidents of private master's institutions. Furthermore, about half of the presidents of public doctoral (53.5 percent), public master's (49.5 percent), and private master's (50 percent) institutions believed that scandals were "inevitable in big-time college athletics." Approximately 42 percent of the presidents of private doctoral universities expressed this opinion. However, more than 70 percent of the presidents of private universities were "confident" that the kinds of athletic scandals that had happened at Penn State, Miami, and other universities in the past year "could not happen at my institution." Public university presidents were not quite as confident, with 46.8 percent of those at public doctoral universities and 64 percent at public master's universities expressing confidence that their institutions were immune from such major scandals.

Presidents of all kinds of universities involved in big-time sports generally seemed to think that they would handle scandals and the arms race better than their peers. This unusual confidence in themselves was implied by the relatively few presidents who thought that their peers were in control of their big-time athletic programs. Only 12.3 percent of the presidents of private master's institutions, 13.8 percent of their counterparts at public master's institutions, 19.4 percent of those who led private doctoral universities, and 29.3 percent of those at public doctoral universities held this opinion.

One of the features of the athletic trap is that presidents often do not realize when they are in it. They can see it elsewhere but not on their own campus. This helps explain why presidents frequently flounder when they have to deal with their own serious financial problems, rule violations, and scandals in athletics. Motivated blindness can prevent them from seeing the seriousness of problems as they arise, which results in their exacerbation and escalation.

The issue of control is both a matter for individual institutions and a systemic matter concerning all of big-time college sports. Thus, while presidents see a systemic problem, they do not see it at the level of their own institution. Nevertheless, they seem to recognize that the system may be spiraling out of control with its arms race and the series of scandals. The sense of powerlessness many have expressed may relate more to the system than to their own campus.[9]

The 2009 Knight Commission survey focusing on financial issues indicated that presidents with elite FBS programs were more confident than their counterparts with nonelite FBS programs about their institution's ability to continue supporting their big-time programs in the arms race.[10] Having vastly different amounts of athletic success and revenue explains this difference in perceptions. However, there were many presidents who were confident they could sustain big-time programs on their own campus but were not so confident that other schools in their conference or at the FBS level nationally could sustain their programs. Of these presidents, 80 percent said that major systemic changes were needed. They had deep concerns about the long-term sustainability of big-time college athletics in its present form. Thus, the presidents with the most competitive and commercially successful programs generally wanted to see significant systemic changes, but they did not think they and their presidential colleagues could bring about these changes. Furthermore, they were not sure who could be an effective change agent, implying that they were not placing their faith in the NCAA. The tough and decisive actions taken by the NCAA in the Penn State case might have changed their minds a few years later, but these actions did little to change the basic structure of commercialized sports or the commercial model on which it rested.

Challenges to Presidential Control of Big-Time Athletics

Prestige, competitive and commercial success, and confidence do not inoculate presidents against financial crises, ethical transgressions, academic corruption, or embarrassing scandals in athletics. Perhaps because they think they are in control of athletics, presidents are likely to find it a jarring experience when these problems surface on their campus. Whether they were aware of these problems or could have prevented them, they will be held responsible by trustees, alumni, the NCAA, and outside reviewers. Responsibility for athletics may not be spelled out in their contract, but when things go wrong, presidents are held accountable. These problems are frequently seen as failures of leadership.

The Kaye Report about the Binghamton scandal and the Freeh Report about Penn State are highly publicized examples of such indictments of leadership. The trustees and the governance processes were also criticized, but the presidents are likely to feel the sting of this criticism most sharply. While most trustees can walk away from such scandals with their anonymity intact, the president's name is often featured in the headlines and stories. Presidents typically receive more media coverage for a scandal than for all the good things they may have done for their institution. This tarnishes their reputation, but they also can be forced to resign or be fired, as the Binghamton and Penn State presidents were.

Presidents need to feel confident and optimistic to be effective leaders. However, there are reasons for a sense of powerlessness or fatalism in regard to sports. Duderstadt and Womack suggested presidents generally face the dilemma of having a lot more responsibility than authority or power. This is especially true at public universities and in athletics. Various challenges make it difficult for presidents to be in full control of their athletic department. The athletic trap is a combination of responsibilities, commitments, expectations, and obligations that place substantial constraints on the president's capacity to lead in athletics. According to one president interviewed in the 2009 Knight Commission survey, "The real power doesn't lie with the presidents. Presidents have lost their jobs over athletics. Presidents and chancellors are afraid to rock the boat with boards, benefactors, and political supporters who want to win, so they turn their focus elsewhere."[11]

Presidents recognize that rapidly escalating salaries for coaches and athletic directors are a major factor in the arms race that is threatening the long-term financial viability of big-time college sports. Nearly all of the presidents in the Knight Commission survey believed that the salaries of big-time football and men's basketball coaches were "excessive." Yet the psychosocial dynamics of the arms race keep driving up these salaries and athletic spending in general. Alumni and boosters want winners, and coaches are seen as a key to getting the star players needed to win. Thus, proven and promising coaches dictate their price in the free market of big-time college sports hiring. Presidents face the constraints of courts that have shown an inclination to punish schools for antitrust violations if they unite in an effort to try to cap coaches' salaries. There seems to be little chance presidents will be able to intervene in other ways to constrain the free market for coaches. The effects of the star wars arms race are exacerbated by the companion arms race in facilities construction and renovation.

Another challenge for presidents is exercising significant power over the conferences, the NCAA, and their media and business partners in the IGT. Indeed, presidents invite the scorn of college sports insiders whenever they try to exercise their influence in these domains. Presidents have been portrayed as sports novices with little insight about how a big-time sports program actually works and whose influence was seen as unhealthy for big-time college sports. For example, a sports writer for CBSSports.com expressed skepticism about the presidents' ability to make the best decision in 2012 about the college football playoff system to replace the controversial BCS arrangement. He wrote that football was "not the presidents' specialty," and added, "Judging from recent scandals, neither is running a major university."[12]

If presidents want to be taken seriously in athletics by the college sports establishment and by their trustees and campus community, they will need to do their homework to make themselves knowledgeable.[13] If they lack a sophisticated understanding of athletics and athletics administration, they may find themselves ceding control to more savvy coaches and athletic directors, to partners in the IGT, and to boosters, benefactors, and fans who are all needed to make the financial model for their athletic program work. Taking the job of president at a BTU without adequate prior experience dealing with big-time athletics could be a recipe for failure when a president is pressed to make tough decisions or is facing a crisis.[14]

Higher-education experts and officials have argued for a new financial model in big-time college sports to resolve financial problems that have intensified for many universities as a result of the economic hard times of the past several years. The most powerful players in the college sports establishment and the IGT, though, are unlikely to back away from a financial model that continues to generate big rewards for them. They may have some concerns about the future, but they tend to be optimistic about their prospects in the short term, even if many nonelite athletic programs are struggling and some schools are getting caught up in scandals. University System of Maryland chancellor and Knight Commission member Brit Kirwan observed that the 2012 *Inside Higher Ed* survey of presidents indicated both the need for major reforms and the reason why they were not likely to happen. He suggested that presidents of the most powerful schools in the NCAA were unlikely to initiate any major changes as long as they thought their own institution was an exception to the bad things happening elsewhere in big-time college sports.[15] Thus, the presidents with struggling athletic programs are not getting a lot of sympathy or assistance from peers at more successful BTUs.

The job of presidents is further complicated by resentment on campus. Public institutions of higher education have been seriously hurt by budget shortfalls and program cuts resulting from the extended underperformance of the national and state economies. Pressures to spend more in athletics have highlighted the differential treatment of athletics and academics on campus. As athletic budgets and salaries have risen in recent years, academic budgets and salaries have remained stagnant or declined. Many faculty members resent the attention and money that go to athletics when they have to keep tightening their belts. Furthermore, the glaring imbalance between spending on athletes and ordinary students cited at the beginning of the book reinforces the perception of distorted values for critics of big-time athletics. Thus, the gap between athletics and academics on campus is both cultural and a matter of economics and stratification.

The athletic trap and a culture of reverence have given some star coaches and athletic directors more power than presidents over athletics.[16] Still, we have seen that college presidents sometimes show real courage in using the authority of their position to face down powerful coaches, athletic directors, and boosters. In some cases, the president has dropped the football program to remedy financial issues in athletics and to protect the institution against possible threats to its academic integrity. Perhaps the most famous example of this kind of action involved the legendary University of Chicago president Robert Maynard Hutchins. When he dropped football and deemphasized athletics in 1939, the University of Chicago boasted football All-Americans and national champion teams under the legendary coach Amos Alonzo Stagg.

More typically, presidents feel that their hands are tied in the athletic arena by the athletic trap, by a culture of reverence, and by the pressures, constraints, and promise of the IGT. Motivated blindness and a sense of powerlessness can impair their judgment and lead to their mishandling of simmering or newly emergent crises in athletics. The evidence has predictably shown that many presidents of BTUs feel confident in their own and the institution's ability to ward off threats and problems in athletics. However, even the most experienced college presidents of elite universities can be vulnerable to the trap of big-time college athletics, as shown by the recent cases of Penn State University, the University of Miami, the University of Southern California, the University of North Carolina, and Ohio State University.

A Profile of a President and His Athletic Trap

Sam Wickersham, a senior writer for *ESPN The Magazine*, wrote a profile of Gordon Gee in 2011 when Gee was in the midst of a highly publicized scandal in athletics at Ohio State University.[17] This profile reveals a great deal about the athletic trap and how highly experienced and politically savvy presidents survive scandals, despite their limited capacity to prevent them. Gee had been a college president for thirty-one of his sixty-seven years and was known for his churning. After being a law professor and law school dean, he became president of West Virginia University in 1981. From there, he moved on to the presidencies of Colorado, Ohio State, Brown, Vanderbilt, and Ohio State for a second time in 2007. He became very familiar with big-time college sports during his travels.

Gee developed a reputation as a colorful figure with his bow tie and his outspoken and charming manner. He was a master fundraiser, and he came to see athletics as a valuable tool for raising money for the universities he served. It was only at Brown where his corporate marketing style did not mesh with the Ivy League ambience of the university. He acknowledged that he struggled during his first turn at Ohio State in the 1990s. He created controversy by ending open admissions, and he had trouble dealing with a "separate and isolated" athletic department that had created its own culture of reverence in a state that loved its big-time sports teams and especially football. Although he had previously helped build Colorado into a football power, the intensity of support for athletics and especially football was a bit intimidating. He tried to gain credibility in dealing with athletics at Ohio State by admittedly pandering to the coaches. He was afraid he would lose his job if relations with athletics did not go well.

After leaving Ohio State for the presidencies of Brown and Vanderbilt, he returned to Ohio State in 2007. Ohio State trustees recognized that his controversial policies in admissions and other areas established during his first presidency there had benefited the university. He had also cemented his reputation in the ensuing years as one of the most respected and sought-after university presidents in the United States. They wanted him back so badly that they were willing to make him one of the best-paid university presidents in the United States. In the FY2010–2011, his total compensation of nearly $2 million put him at the top of the pay list for public university presidents. Only three public university presidents made more than $1 million in fiscal year 2011, and somewhat ironically, Graham Spanier, the ousted Penn State president, was third on the list, earning approximately $1.1 million.[18]

Despite all his presidential experience, two stints at Ohio State, and his presumed acumen, Gee was not able to stop a scandal in his own backyard. It involved football coach Jim Tressel. Like Joe Paterno, he was lionized for his success on the football field and was viewed as a model citizen among coaches. He also earned almost twice as much as Gordon Gee. Ultimately, though, he lost control of his football program and his job as coach. Players took illegal cash payments, and Tressel failed to report what he knew when he became aware of the rule violations. This failure to disclose possible violations by the coach was a major NCAA infraction, which nearly always resulted in the firing or forced resignation of the responsible coach.[19]

Like other presidents, Gee was at least outwardly confident he could control athletics, and he was supportive of his coach when the scandal began to gain public attention. He praised the coach for his "superb integrity." In response to a question about whether he planned to fire Tressel, he said, "Let me be clear. I'm just hoping the coach doesn't dismiss me."[20] Uttered in a joking manner, his remark nevertheless captured the essence of the athletic trap at Ohio State, and Gee was aware of its grip.

Gee ultimately fired the coach, but not before the embarrassing press conference at which the president defended his coach. He had wanted to show the public he was in control of his athletic department, but his unwisely uttered remark revealed the truth. He had promised that he would have a zero-tolerance policy for those who violated NCAA rules. He instead buckled when initially faced with the news of possible violations. His normally confident and savvy demeanor evaporated in the grip of the athletic trap. He knew how important it was to stand up for his football program and its coach. It was a significant part of his job, even though football revenue was only 1 percent of his nearly $5 billion university budget. The surplus from football and basketball funded other athletic programs, but more importantly, sports success was a critical part of the university's identity and reputation.

Gee tied his fate to the fate of his athletic teams because he identified so publicly with them. In fact, spectators could see his image on the JumboTron in the stadium urging them root harder for their team. He knew that, in Ohio State's culture of reverence, people loved Ohio State football and also its typically highly ranked men's basketball team. He used sideline credentials, locker room visits, chances to meet the football and men's basketball coaches, and his presidential suite to entertain donors and politicians and get their support. People responded generously because they loved him and what he was selling. His greatest success was getting a $100 million gift from the billionaire who chaired the Ohio State board of trustees.[21] However, Gee realized that he would lose much of his capital and political support if he failed to support athletics. He had to handle scandals effectively to protect the reputation of his university and to keep his job.

Gordon Gee's deference to athletics at Ohio State contrasts with his work with other presidents in the 1980s following the SMU death penalty case. He led a group of presidents who were committed to getting athletics under control. Their work influenced the reformers in the early years of the Knight Commission, whose 1991 plan for reform made presidential control its centerpiece.[22] Presidents used this idea of presidential control as the rationale for establishing the NCAA Division I Board of Directors as its primary policy-making body. Then they hired college presidents to lead the organization. Yet even the most respected and experienced presidents continue to struggle to run athletics on their own campus. As Sam Wickersham observed in his piece on Gordon Gee, "He's always tried to control athletics by amassing political capital, spending it on sports and living with the glory or fallout."[23]

Having to accept the vicissitudes of big-time college sports is part of the athletic trap. For Gee, part of his accommodation was to look the other way. He did not meet regularly with the NCAA compliance officer in athletics, and he backed away from his zero-tolerance policy. When other Ohio State administrators advised him to let Tressel go, he resisted. He subscribed to what he called his "three-bullet theory." He believed that he could apologize to the trustees and ask for their forgiveness only three times before risking termination. Thus, he leveraged his capital, first supporting and then firing the football coach when public revelations became too difficult to ignore. Unlike former Penn State president Graham Spanier, though, Gee kept his board fully informed of the facts of the case and his handling of it. Since Tressel had friends on the board, Gee was very cautious in using one of his bullets and taking the risk of antagonizing trustees by prematurely firing him. He took this action only after it became apparent to the board that the rule violations were more numerous than originally thought, and the board unanimously supported him.

Presidents seem to survive athletic scandals when they skillfully manage to protect the images of the university and athletics, avoid getting caught up in the scandal or a cover-up, and retain the support of their bosses, the trustees. Surviving scandals and keeping their job, though, is not the same thing as controlling athletics. Gordon Gee knew this, but he recognized that the athletic trap was too entrenched at institutions such as Ohio State for even the president to be able to lessen the influence of big-time athletics on campus. When presidents virtually throw up their hands and accept that they are more of a captive than in control of the athletic department, athletics has taken over the academy.

Gordon Gee's experience at Ohio State needs to be framed in a broader context including his immediately prior presidency of Vanderbilt University. He gained a lot of publicity for his restructuring of Vanderbilt athletics by eliminating the position of athletic director and absorbing athletics into the Division of Student Life. His invited contribution to the *Forum* of the academic honor society Phi Kappa Phi in the fall of 2005 explaining the philosophical rationale for this reorganization now seems ironic. This was about two years before his move back to Ohio State. In this article, Gee emphasized the importance of placing students and academics at the center of the university and of integrating athletics into student life and the academic enterprise. He asserted, "Most importantly, colleges and universities have to, in good conscience, reconcile big-time athletics with our educational mission. We have to believe in our students, above all else."[24]

He went on to say that it was time to pursue an agenda of reform in college athletics. He proposed ideas such as tying television and conference revenue to graduation rates to change the amount of commitment to academic performance in the athletic culture. He also argued that integrating the athletic budget into the university's central budget would help keep athletics in proper alignment with other university priorities. Then he went on to say, "Presidential oversight ensures that athletics does not detract from but supports an institution's strategic goals. For although athletics success for its own sake may bring revenue . . . , that success is ultimately a waste of resources if success in athletics does not support the university's academic life in the longer term."[25] He believed that genuine reform should be grounded in a shared desire on campus to do what was right and based on real institutional leadership.

These are lofty sentiments, which Gee could not or did not want to apply to Ohio State. The athletic trap and culture of reverence were much too entrenched, and opportunities for presidential control over athletics much more limited. Vanderbilt is the rare case in the big-time college sports world where a serious effort has been made to elevate the collegiate model.[26] Ohio State is more typical with its predominant emphasis on the commercial model, which is the model most aspiring BTUs try to emulate, despite the risk of serious missteps.

Board Responsibilities and Challenges in Athletics

Presidents may think they are running the university and are in charge of athletics, and trustees may think that the president is doing what they want. Tough decisions and crises can seriously challenge these beliefs. When presidents and trustees fail to do their job and do not provide the leadership expected of them, the consequences can be spectacularly bad for their university and the students and the public whose interests are supposed to be their primary concern.

The president is the visible public face of university governance, but the trustees hold the ultimate authority. Apart from the chair or board spokesperson, we seldom see much of trustees, until they get embroiled in controversies or scandals. When things go wrong, they often find themselves in the public eye along with the president, and they are likely to feel the same sting of criticism the president feels. This can be a jarring experience for board members, since they do not expect it and were not prepared for it. Board service is supposed to be an honor, a chance to serve a university they truly care about, or an opportunity to build a resume. It can also be a chance to get closer to the athletic program, coaches, and athletes they have followed so faithfully. It is not supposed to be a nightmare of accusations, criticisms, and perceived failure.

Although the governing boards of individual institutions vary in their membership, recent surveys have shown that these boards are likely to be dominated by affluent older white and politically conservative businessmen.[27] The increasing influence of the marketplace and of corporate business models in higher education explains why a business background is seen as a valuable asset by board selection committees. A background or prior special interest in higher education is relatively rare among board members, which may be why less than 15 percent of board members in a *Chronicle of Higher Education* survey responded that they saw themselves as "very well prepared" for their board service when they became members,[28] and 40 percent said they were "slightly" or "not at all" prepared. The typical characteristics of board members suggest that their understanding of universities is rooted in a period when institutions of higher education were very different from what they are now. Universities today are more diverse than they were in the past, and public universities generally are more concerned than in the past about rising tuitions and affordability, accountability, public support, and educational quality.

Board members typically meet two to four times in a year.[29] With all the pressing university issues they must address, they are unlikely to spend much time on athletics at a typical meeting. According to the *Chronicle* survey, 45 percent of trustees said they addressed issues concerning athletics once or twice a year, and 13 percent said they never addressed athletic issues. Only 5.8 percent said they considered athletic issues once or more a month. This is why trustees may be very unprepared when a major athletic decision or a crisis in athletics faces them.

Some of these trustees may face these issues with a degree of hostility. The *Chronicle* survey showed that 22 percent of the trustees at public universities and 43 percent at private nonsectarian institutions said big-time athletic programs were more of a liability than an asset. The survey also found that trustees generally were much less likely than presidents to see athletics as a liability. There seems to be little likelihood that presidents of BTUs would voice this opinion publicly.

At BTUs, the hoopla surrounding big-time athletic teams and events may mitigate reservations some board members have about athletics and excite others. Their business background and conservative politics may make most board members comfortable with the commercialism in athletics and make it easy for them to accept the justifications for investing in big-time programs. Some board members may be athletic boosters as well. Thus, as long as the president seems to be promoting or at least supporting athletics, they will probably be satisfied to stay out of athletic issues and decisions. Boards generally are more reactive than proactive, and they tend to let presidents do their job with minimal interference from them.[30] They realize that getting along with and trusting the president will make their job easier and give the president a chance to act more decisively and be more efficient. They will get upset, though, if they think the president has not been keeping them informed about important matters that could make athletics a serious board matter. They do not like to be blindsided.[31]

Part of the reason that boards are not well prepared to deal with athletic issues is that presidents do not communicate much to them about athletics, even when serious problems arise. Trustees have been warned to pay attention to athletics. For example, experts on college sports have talked to trustees at the annual meeting of the Association of Governing Boards of Universities and Colleges (AGB).[32] The NCAA president, college presidents, and a member of the Knight Commission have encouraged them to try to integrate athletics more fully into the academic mission of the university and to be wary of "rogue trustees" who tried to get involved in athletics in unhelpful ways. They also spoke about measures to protect academic integrity in athletics, the dangers of profligate athletic spending, and the need to allow the president to exercise his or her legitimate authority in overseeing the daily operations of athletics on campus.

The advice given to trustees at the AGB gathering by NCAA and university officials may seem ironic or even hypocritical in light of the realities of the sports world they oversee. Most trustees are unlikely to notice, though, since relatively few spend enough time on campus or talking to the president to be fully up-to-date about what is happening in athletics. Presidents withhold information from trustees for various reasons. They may want to avoid overburdening trustees with unnecessary details. They may think there is nothing the trustees can do. They may want to avoid trustee interference. Or they may want to try to fix problems before they escalate and become an embarrassment to the institution and a threat to the president's job. However, withholding important information can prevent trustees from doing their job. Poor communication between the president and board not only undermines their relationship but can make it more difficult to handle serious problems effectively in athletics and elsewhere in the university.

Nancy Zimpher did what her board at Cincinnati instructed her to do about the basketball coach, and she weathered the storm of adverse criticism when she fired him. By working closely with her board, she maintained its trust and full support throughout this episode. Gordon Gee survived a major scandal at Ohio State in part because he kept his board fully informed as he managed the crisis. On the other hand, Graham Spanier kept his board in the dark about the long-brewing Sandusky affair, and as a result the board became angry and fired him. It also acted awkwardly in the way it fired Joe Paterno. Board members were not prepared to handle this crisis, and they handled it poorly. They were not happy to become one of the culprits in the Freeh Report about Penn State scandal, but their flawed relationship with their president set them up for failure.

Speaking about the Penn State board in the Sandusky scandal, James Duderstadt said that the trustees needed "to take strong, demonstrable action" in this case to assert their control. He added that they needed to treat it like any other "renegade" program in the university. It could even involve imposing their own death penalty for football to show they were in control. However, he recognized that football at Penn State was not like other campus programs. He acknowledged that such strong action would "run afoul of the many existing contractual commitments and likely trigger an avalanche of lawsuits. ([These could come] from television networks, others in the Big Ten conference, and brands that sponsor the team, to name a few.)"[33]

These commitments are the athletic trap. The athletic trap effectively tied the hands of the Penn State trustees if they had any inclination to act more dramatically to try to redeem themselves and rectify the wrong that had been done. Thus, athletic traps constrain trustees as well as presidents. The structural nature of the athletic trap means it is not tied to specific individuals or practices. It is part of a broader and more entrenched pattern that is reinforced by complex and long-term relationships, commitments, and obligations. Individual trustees and boards have limited terms and time to spend on athletic matters and thus rarely have the opportunity to do much to alter the broad structure of the athletic trap during their tenure.

The AGB has recognized the intensifying pressures on boards created by the growing commercialization and importance of big-time athletics on college campuses.[34] It promulgated three major policy statements regarding board accountability in athletics in 2004, 2007, and 2009.[35] Its 2009 statement was a joint effort of the AGB board and staff members, college presidents, and NCAA representatives. It addressed areas of board involvement in athletics and made recommendations addressing major concerns in these areas.[36] The primary goals of these policies and recommendations were to protect the welfare of student-athletes and integrate intercollegiate athletics into the academic enterprise. That is to say they wanted to achieve an appropriate balance between the collegiate and commercial models of college sports.

A central theme of the 2009 AGB document was restoring the balance between athletics and education through greater institutional accountability. This is also the theme of a 2010 Knight Commission report about reforming college sports.[37] This state of balance arguably has never really existed since the emergence of big-time college sports more than a century ago. The relationship between the academy and athletics has mostly been upside down during the history of big-time college athletics. Thus, the AGB was actually pushing for a new rather than restored balance between academics and athletics.

The AGB advised boards to have a healthy skepticism about big-time athletics and be vigilant in their oversight role.[38] Boards also were advised to be sure that compliance processes were in place and operating effectively. Board members needed to ask presidents to provide them with access to information about all important aspects of athletics, including admissions, academic performance, graduation rates, budgets, and conference business. However, they were reminded that this information was not very useful unless board members used it to ask probing and insightful questions. Board members were advised against developing close personal relationships with coaches and the athletic director, which could bias their decisions about them and their programs. The same could be said about the relationship with the president. It needed to be professional and respectful, but not personal. This is likely to be difficult for those board members who were attracted to the board because it gave them a chance to rub shoulders and fraternize with powerful and prominent figures on campus.

The AGB followed up its 2009 statement on board responsibilities with a project that surveyed presidents and board chairs of Division I institutions and systems. The project was funded by the Knight Commission and focused on gaps between the principles of effective oversight articulated in its 2009 statement and actual practices. This gap analysis was meant to show how well boards understood and acted on their fiduciary responsibility in athletics. The report presented findings regarding five major areas of the 2009 AGB statement—board policy on athletics, delegation of authority and responsibility in athletics to the president, financial responsibility, student well-being, and compensation of athletics personnel—and proposed three main recommendations to governing boards.[39]

The results are striking in what they reveal about the ability of presidents and boards to oversee and control athletics on their campus. Many findings show a significant gap between AGB recommendations and the reality on Division I campuses. For example, one-quarter of the presidents who responded said the governing board at their institution did not have an explicit policy about board responsibilities in athletics. Only 47 percent of those with a policy had one that generally conformed to the AGB model. Only two-thirds of respondents had a formal board policy that delegated responsibility for athletics to the president. While 86 percent conducted annual assessments of the president's performance, only 71 percent of these institutions looked at the president's role in athletics in their assessment.

More than 25 percent of the respondents said that their boards did not receive enough information to monitor revenue flows from TV contracts, booster clubs, affiliated foundations, corporate sponsorships, and athletics conferences. In addition, about 26 percent said their boards were not adequately informed about revenues and expenditures for the revenue-generating sports or about institutional subsidies. While boards were generally well informed about the academic progress of teams, only one-third were thought to be sufficiently informed about the declared majors of student-athletes or how much time student-athletes devoted to athletics.

The findings also showed that the presidents assumed a direct responsibility for the star wars arms race. Eighty-six percent of the respondents said that the president approved all coaches' and athletic directors' contracts. Their willingness to sign off on the huge and increasing salaries of star and would-be star coaches reflects either presidents' perceived need or desire to inflate the athletic budget or their sense of pressure from the athletic trap to agree to these inflated salaries. We might wonder about how much control the president can exercise over athletics in the 14 percent of cases where these contracts did not require the presidents' signature. This is just one of the many troubling questions this survey raises about athletics oversight and control.

The body of findings from this study was the basis for three general recommendations:[40]

1. The governing board is ultimately accountable for athletics policy and oversight and should fulfill this fiduciary responsibility.
2. The board should act decisively to uphold the integrity of the athletics program and its alignment with the academic mission of the institution. Policies that define the administration of athletics programs should be consistent with those for other academic and administrative units of the institution or system.
3. The board must educate itself about its policy role and oversight of intercollegiate athletics.

Like the Knight Commission, the AGB was ultimately interested in seeing an "appropriate balance" between athletics and academics in higher education. Its report warned that if institutions did not accept this responsibility, policy makers or others "will do it for us."[41] The "others" could be legislators, members of Congress, or the courts. The college sports establishment and higher education in general are usually averse to such intervention and often feel that it threatens their interests.

Many boards need to figure out how to close gaps between the AGB's recommended policies and practices and the reality on their campuses. This may involve walking a tightrope between sufficient and excessive oversight. They need to be specific about the duties and authority of the president in relation to athletics; exercise oversight without micromanaging (i.e., give presidents sufficient authority, flexibility, trust, and support, but still demand a regular flow of key information so that they can exercise their authority responsibly); and have policies that restrict individual trustees from forcing their will about athletics on the board or the president.[42] The AGB specified clear lines of authority and accountability in athletics from boards to presidents, presidents to athletic directors, athletic directors to coaches, and back up to boards.

The AGB wanted to create a structure in which the academic accomplishments of student-athletes were valued at least as much as the number of wins their teams produce or the amount of media coverage, publicity, or money they get. It placed trustees, along with presidents, in the middle of efforts to reform big-time college athletics to achieve this vision. It put an ambitious agenda before boards and presidents. Then it increased the pressure on them when it conducted and published its gap analysis related to its 2009 statement on board responsibilities.

The directors of the AGB project observed that the Penn State scandal was a "painful reminder" of the need for boards to be informed, to exercise effective and responsible athletic oversight, and to be in a position to hold presidents and their institution accountable.[43] Although their survey occurred before the revelations about Penn State, it is evident that their prior policy statements and recommendations in this vein had little influence in this case or in many others. The arms race was still very much alive, and scandals seemed to be reaching another peak. On some campuses, presidents were not confiding in trustees about serious problems in athletics. On others, presidents and boards seemed to be at odds with each other how to run the university and where it should be headed.

A highly publicized and politicized dispute in 2012 between the University of Virginia trustees and the president resulted in the firing and rehiring of the president.[44] The case did not involve athletics, but it showed that more turbulence than constructive change is likely to result when boards and presidents are not aligned in their views about change. In this case, the board showed an unusual amount of activism in pushing for change. It got into trouble by ignoring the input of the president and misjudging faculty opposition to the board's plans and faculty support for the president. The applicable lesson for athletic reform is that trustees and presidents need to respect one another, share a similar conception of where the university needs to go, have an effective working relationship, and be united in how they will handle campus and booster sentiment about change.

Trustees typically show little initiative on athletic issues because they spend little time at board meetings discussing athletics. Some individual trustees may want to micromanage certain budget or hiring decisions in athletics, but they usually seem happy about the state of sports on their campus. This changes when problems are brought to their attention. The fallout from these problems might prompt some board members to vow to make significant changes to prevent these problems from occurring in the future. Change is not an easy matter, though, even for the people with ultimate authority over the institution. It may be especially difficult in athletics.

Role of Faculty Members in Big-Time College Sports

Faculty members are not likely to have a prominent role in athletic reform. Notwithstanding the case at the University of Virginia, faculty members generally have very little clout in the university governance processes.[45] According to a 2007 nationwide Knight Commission faculty survey, many respondents had a broad understanding of how commercialization skewed decisions about athletics.[46] The survey found that nearly 50 percent of the faculty respondents believed that athletic decisions on their campus were "driven by the priorities of an entertainment industry that is not interested in their university's academic mission." This belief is at the core of some of the harshest criticisms of big-time college sports.[47] Respondents were generally satisfied with the academic performance of student-athletes, but they were less satisfied with how well football and basketball players did in the classroom. Some faculty members seemed to understand why big-time athletes might have academic problems. Approximately one-third of those in the survey believed that some compromises of academic standards were necessary to be successful in football and basketball.

Faculty members may be skeptical when their president invokes the collegiate model or articulates the standard set of justifications for big-time athletics on campus, and they are often unhappy about the amount of money their university spends on big-time athletics. In general, though, faculty members in the Knight Commission survey expressed satisfaction about their president's oversight of athletics. This may be due to the limited salience of athletics in their everyday lives as faculty members. Respondents generally ranked intercollegiate athletics near the bottom of their list of priorities for faculty governance groups on campus. Faculty members may know the names of star coaches or a few star athletes, but they probably do not follow specific issues or developments in athletics on their campus. Athletics may move up their priority list only when a team wins a major championship or when a scandal on their campus makes the news.

The faculty members in the survey who were involved in athletics governance were more positive about all aspects of athletics than were those not involved in governance. Faculty athletics representatives (FARs) are responsible for overseeing the academic integrity of the athletic program and protecting the welfare of student-athletes. FARs and other faculty members involved in athletics may generally be positive and supportive because they were drawn to these roles by their love of sports. This would create motivated blindness for them. If they are troubled by the realities they discover in sports, they may be reluctant to express their concern because they feel intimidated. In either case, they are not going to be much help in the oversight process. In fact, they have been criticized for doing more to help the athletic department do what it wants than to help assure its compliance with the rules.[48] In general, presidents and trustees probably will not be able to count on strong and informed faculty support in efforts at reform. According to the main finding of the Knight Commission's faculty survey, "A striking number of professors say they don't know about and are disconnected from issues facing college sports." Being closer to athletics seemed to make faculty members less rather than more objective or critical.

Leadership and Reform in Big-Time College Sports

Even when presidents and trustees agree that serious reforms are needed in athletics, their influence tends to be diluted by the athletic trap and powerful forces in the IGT. These forces reinforce the rhythms, rituals, and traditions of big-time college sports and the commercial model on which they are built. They represent a powerful and alluring commercial entertainment complex that attracts big investments from the media and business, captivates fans, and tempts and traps universities with its rewards and promises. The influence of the IGT is often greater than the influence of the presidents, trustees, and regulatory bodies that try to control it. Thus, the issue of control in big-time college sports persists and reform remains elusive.

The average tenure of college presidents today is about ten years,[49] which is enough time to forge and begin to implement a plan for change to reform the athletic department. Factors that could affect their chances of success include the amount of support they get from their board and the faculty, their skill in renegotiating relationships in the IGT, and their ability to convince alumni and boosters that the proposed changes are good for the university. They also need to reassure their loyal sports fans that they will not be deprived of their entertainment. This last part is especially challenging because genuine reform could scale back athletics in a way that affects its commercialization and makes it more difficult to compete successfully at the same level as it once did. Unilateral disarmament in the arms race, for example, could leave an institution standing still while its opponents breeze by and continue to pour more money into sports.

The entrenched structures and culture of the athletic trap explain why college sports experts tend to be pessimistic about real change in big-time college sports.[50] Longtime college sports observers have seen or read about prior reform efforts, which have not altered the commercial foundation of big-time college sports or its reliance on the commercial model. Some reforms have strengthened academic eligibility standards, increased penalties for NCAA violations, and increased athletic scholarship amounts. These kinds of reforms have not affected the commercial model or underlying structure of big-time college sports. Proposals for structural reforms that would change the commercial landscape of college sports will require strong, informed, and dedicated leadership. This leadership will mainly have to come from presidents, but they will need the support of their trustees. The presidents will also need to deflect or redirect resistance from powerful opponents in the college sports establishment and from their own boosters.

The commercial foundation of big-time college sports has endured all kinds of criticisms and attempts at reform. Even the harsh treatment of Penn State by the NCAA did not significantly alter this foundation. The reason may be, as some critics observed, that the NCAA was more concerned about showing it was in control than about getting to the root of the scandal or bringing righteous order to big-time college sports.[51] The NCAA's actions in this case were dramatic because they happened so quickly, were so severe for Penn State, and were technically beyond its ordinary scope of authority. Yet they also demonstrated the NCAA's reluctance to put big-time programs completely out of business for even one season. Perhaps more importantly, the NCAA also did not want its punishment of an individual big-time program to hurt the other "innocent" schools in the big-time realm.

If reform is to happen in big-time college sports, the role of the NCAA will have to change. As its commercial influence has been eroded by court decisions, the rise of the conferences, and the BCS, it has tried to reassert its role as the dominant governing body in college athletics. Ironically, the Penn State case gave it another chance to do this. However, its primary role has been to preserve the ascendance of the commercial model and the financial basis of its own influence. It has made some changes in academic standards, but it has been wary of upsetting its commercial partners in the IGT because NCAA officials, like BTU presidents, know that the college sports enterprise that gives them and BTUs money, prestige, and power relies on commercialism.

What kind of reform can we realistically expect the leaders in big-time college sports to pursue? Dismantling the relationships in the athletic trap is difficult and can take time. Reducing the influence of the big-time college sports culture on college campuses and across the United States where football and men's basketball are king is likely to be challenging. Presidents and trustees may not even see the need for reform on their campus because they have blind spots created by the athletic trap and cultures of reverence. We know that most presidents think these problems are elsewhere and could not happen to them or their institution.

In the next chapter, I propose a model of reform that is meant to provide a blueprint for change that builds on the patterns and trends in college sports that have been identified in this book. I hope it will challenge presidents, trustees, the NCAA, and other major figures in the college sports establishment to think in new ways about the landscape of college sports and how to achieve an appropriate balance between athletics and academics. As sports writer John Feinstein observed, we have reached the point where "fixing college sports requires less talk, more action."[52]

CHAPTER SEVEN

Reforming College Sports

Significant change in big-time college sports is difficult because its organizational structures, the athletic trap, and the culture of reverence that spawn and sustain them are deeply entrenched. We know, for example, how intractable the financial arms race has become, despite the fact that NCAA leaders and college presidents recognize it as a serious problem and would like it to end. The Knight Commission has made progress in working with the NCAA to introduce academic reforms into college sports,[1] but it has had less success convincing the college sports establishment to reform the underlying commercial structure of big-time college sports programs and reduce their dependence on the intercollegiate golden triangle.[2]

After a serious scandal, presidents may have a chance to build support from faculty members, some trustees, and some alumni for major changes in big-time athletic programs on campus. Sometimes, they have little choice. At Penn State, the new president accepted the harsh NCAA penalties because he realized that his institution would face the death penalty if he did not. Trustees supported him because they wanted to redeem themselves and restore the reputation of their university. The NCAA imposed the penalties because it knew its credibility was on the line. Yet even in this case of exceptional deviance, a seriously damaged institutional image, and a black eye for the college sports establishment, there were many students and faculty members who were unhappy about their president's acceptance of the NCAA's stiff penalties.[3]

At Penn State and other institutions with powerful sports traditions, a combination of pride, loyalty, motivated blindness, and a love of big-time sports may contribute to resistance to change, even when the circumstances seem most propitious. These factors tighten the hold of the athletic trap, which is why presidents often find it difficult to free themselves and their institutions from it. It appears that extraordinary circumstances are needed for some on these campuses to accept accountability for wrongdoing and recognize the need for some changes. The rewards of the IGT tighten the grip of the athletic trap even more. They also make it more difficult for presidents, trustees, and people associated with big-time athletic programs to contemplate genuine reform.

Although presidents and trustees of BTUs have rarely pushed for major athletic reforms on their campus, this time could be different. This might be one of those times in the history of college sports when conditions are ripe for university officials to engage in a serious dialog about change. The willingness of presidents to talk seriously about reform would be a necessary condition. The Knight Commission has frequently pointed to presidents as the pivotal players in the governance and reform of college sports, so any reform would require their active leadership, which begins by getting their campuses, trustees, and influential alumni on board.

Data from presidential surveys cited in the preceding chapter show that presidents generally are not happy about the current state of big-time college athletics and say that colleges and universities spend "way too much" on their sports programs.[4] They want change in the system, though not necessarily on their own campuses. Furthermore, a majority at all but private doctoral institutions believes that scandals are inevitable in big-time sports programs. Most think these scandals damage the reputation of individual institutions and higher education in general. Relatively few think that NCAA reform proposals will achieve meaningful results and end these scandals.

The challenge is to convince these presidents that college sports and their institutions will benefit from their bold leadership on these issues. They have to be convinced that they hold the key to genuine reform. Although few boards of trustees appear to be activist enough to take the lead in spearheading athletic reforms on their campus, their support for presidential reform initiatives will propel these initiatives forward.

Allen Sack made a strong argument in the *Christian Science Monitor* that the aftermath of the Penn State scandal was an especially opportune time for the NCAA and college presidents to pursue serious athletic reforms.[5] He was not a voice in the wilderness nor was he an intellectual who never played the game. He played football at Notre Dame, earned his Ph.D. in sociology at Penn State, and was a professor in the business college at the University of New Haven. He was also president of the Drake Group, a national organization of faculty and staff members that defined its mission as "defend(ing) academic integrity in the face of the burgeoning college sport industry."[6]

Sack contended that the only "cure" for the problems and scandals bred by commercialism in big-time college sports was for the NCAA to "follow its stated mission." This mission was for athletes to be "an integral part of the student body" and for the NCAA to maintain a clear line of demarcation between collegiate and professional sports. Although he did not want college sports to lose its tax exemption, he said it was time for the House Ways and Means Committee "to closely examine whether the NCAA is running a not-for-profit enterprise or an unrelated business." He identified this unrelated business as commercial entertainment.

Presidents of BTUs recognize, without publicly acknowledging it, that their big-time sports programs put them in the commercial entertainment business. They seem to like being in this business or, once in, believe there is no way to get out it. When they and NCAA officials are criticized for too much commercialism in athletics, they use the rhetoric of the collegiate model in the NCAA mission statement to fend off criticisms. Thus, they seem to want people to believe they are serious about academic integrity and the welfare of student-athletes, but the compromises they make to support the commercial model convey a different message.

In fact, with the commercial model often overwhelming the collegiate model in big-time college sports, the NCAA and the presidents have been unable to maintain a clear line of demarcation between the amateur model they extol and the realities of the commercial model.[7] The athletic trap reinforces their commitment to the commercial model and also restricts their options of reform. This may be why presidents tend to be skeptical about the chances for real reform. They have been successful in raising academic eligibility standards and have put more emphasis on graduation rates. These kinds of changes are important, but they are not a serious threat to the underlying commercial structure that continues to undermine academic integrity at BTUs.

It is not surprising that powerful figures in the college sports establishment who have benefited from the status quo in college sports have done little to try to change it. It would be ironic, though, if change happened despite the absence of serious reform efforts in the college sports establishment. One would think that demands for major reform would be taken more seriously after the kind of exceptional deviance that happened in the Penn State scandal. This case led to unprecedented action by the NCAA and calls for the university to add a self-imposed death penalty. Yet the system of big-time college sports seemed to survive largely intact even after this egregious case of deviance. Sack and others proposed that this case should be a springboard for real change. The NCAA recognized the seriousness of this case and acted accordingly. Yet, on individual campuses, the business of big-time college sports went on as usual. This is the "not in my backyard" perspective that presidents typically express about the need for reform on their campuses.

Significant change could still happen. Scholar Charles Clotfelter and former Ivy League executive Jeff Orleans separately suggested the "asteroid theory" of change.[8]

The theory assumes that only a cataclysmic external event or immensely powerful outside influence is likely to alter the well-established patterns in big-time college sports. This theory implies that the people who are in charge of big-time college sports will not be the drivers of major change. It assumes that the forces of change are much more likely to come from outside events or influences that the people who run college sports cannot control.

Clotfelter suggested, for example, that a court decision against the NCAA regarding its use of athletes' likenesses could threaten the financial foundation of big-time college sports by challenging the idea that college athletes are amateurs.[9] Congress also could intervene in college sports by taking away the federal tax-exempt status of athletic programs, which they have enjoyed because they supposedly involve amateur athletes and are part of nonprofit educational institutions.[10] Or, he added, evidence about the effects of concussions and other potentially disabling injuries could lead to costly lawsuits that would also threaten the financial structure of college sports. Orleans proposed that a major threat could be sex discrimination lawsuits. They could force additional program cuts and ultimately a redirection of financial resources away from the major men's programs that are at the center of the IGT.

In addition, demographic changes and persisting problems in the economy have begun to curtail or reverse enrollment growth and force many institutions to consider tuition discounts or reductions for financially strapped prospective students.[11] Along with budget-conscious legislators, these demographic and economic factors have intensified budget challenges for many public universities. If budget-cutting pressures continue to mount, athletics will be unlikely to escape the budget ax that has chopped academic and administrative budgets. These budget pressures will progressively affect institutions, from those with the least established and financially endowed athletic programs to those with more established and endowed programs. The first casualties in the athletic department are usually less commercialized and nonrevenue men's sports, but eventually the most prominent big-time programs where a disproportionate amount of the athletic budget is invested would be affected as well.

The arms race also creates budgetary pressures for all big-time and aspiring sports programs, and it seems to be beyond the control of the BTU presidents, who are unwilling to try to control it. The continuing failure to control the arms race could lead to a gradual process of attrition in big-time college sports, leaving only a relatively few schools with major investments in such programs. Big-time college sports would not disappear, but their face would dramatically change. The IGT would be focused only on those schools and conferences left standing after this financial shakedown has its full effect. We are moving in this direction, as conferences fight with each other to rule football and get the lion's share of its media coverage and revenue. Many observers see a super conference on the horizon. As for the rest, conferences and schools seem likely to keep trying to sustain themselves at more modest levels of IGT investment, further expanding the gap between the haves and have-nots.

Thus, change could happen as a result of outside forces or trends now underway and without the leadership or voluntary cooperation of the most powerful people in the college sports establishment. There never seems to be much appetite for serious reform, even though NCAA officials and college presidents often say it is needed when scandals erupt. In the aftermath of scandals, university and NCAA officials seem more interested in reasserting control and restoring their reputation than in changing the commercialism that breeds scandals. The rewards of the IGT keep enticing schools to compete at the most commercialized level of college sports, and the athletic trap locks schools into extended, recurring, and sometimes damaging commitments in big-time college sports.

Intentional, widespread, and lasting reform will happen only if the people with the most power in the college sports establishment as well as important players on the fringes want it to happen. If this is indeed one of those times ripe for genuine reform, a compelling plan will be needed to guide it, and this plan must be palatable to the people who run college sports. Thus, a successful plan for reform must be rooted in the current realities and offer the promise of beneficial outcomes for both the haves and have-nots in big-time college sports. My reform proposal should meet these requirements.

Basic Assumptions about Reform

While my proposal is not a complete or detailed blueprint for change, it is specific and concrete enough to provide a clear vision of a new structure and direction for college sports. It is also open enough to stimulate a discussion of exactly what college sports should look like after real reform. Of course, real reform will never happen if the ideas are seriously discussed only by academics, talking heads, and others outside the inner circles where decisions are made in higher education and big-time athletics. Thus, this discussion needs to happen among college presidents, trustees, leaders in the NCAA, and reform-minded members of organizations such as the Knight Commission and the Drake Group. I am not naïve. The history of college sports has a towering scrap heap of reform proposals. Yet the escalating arms race and the recent wave of normal and exceptional deviance present another of those opportunities in this history to construct the kinds of changes presidents, trustees, and the NCAA president say are needed. Furthermore, significant and unwanted changes could be propelled by an asteroid of powerful outside forces or cumulative fallout from the unrestrained pursuit of success in the IGT.

If the conversation about change is to result in actual change, there will ultimately have to be seats around the table for the conferences, boosters, the IGT, and perhaps professional sports league commissioners as well. These are the biggest players outside the campuses and the NCAA influencing big-time college sports. In addition, representatives of student-athletes should have a place at the table. They are not part of the current athletic governance structure of the NCAA and have minimal power in athletics on the campuses where they compete. However, it is difficult to justify their absence when all the high-minded rhetoric about college sports is about them. Their voice also needs to be part of the conversation about change. By including athletes in their governance structure, college sports would be following the example of the Olympics.

In 1981 the International Olympic Committee (IOC) created the IOC Athletes' Commission.[12] Most of the members of this commission are athletes elected by fellow competitors in the Olympic Games. The commission is a consultative body that makes recommendations to the IOC's executive bodies, and its chair sits on the IOC Executive Board. It is probably not a coincidence that five years after incorporating athletes in its governance structure, the IOC changed its charter to allow professionals to compete in the Olympics. Professionalism is an important element of my proposal and would be the biggest change in the structure of commercialized college sports.

If presidents are to have clout on their own campuses in trying to introduce significant athletic reforms, trustees will need to begin specifying the authority and oversight responsibilities of presidents regarding athletics in their contracts. Presidents cannot be worried about offending trustees and powerful stakeholders in athletics or be concerned they will lose their job every time they make a tough or controversial decision about athletics. Even though accountability for athletics is part of their own responsibilities, trustees must make it clear that presidents are expected to be in control of athletics and are not supposed to defer to powerful coaches, athletic directors, or boosters.

An effective reform proposal must address the pattern of increasing stratification between the haves and have-nots. Members of the elite have been increasingly condescending and greedy in their attitudes toward the strivers in big-time college sports. They have taken more and more of the rewards from the IGT and have wanted even more. They have resented the influence of the strivers in "their" world. They have shown little sympathy toward those who want to get more status, money, and power from playing in the big-time. Many of these strivers have felt left out or blocked in their aspirations. The reality is that relatively few have or will have the resources or commitment to compete in this very expensive game of elite big-time college sports. Since they are not likely to become part of the college sports establishment, I am proposing that most of them find a home in a different place in college sports. It is a world that largely reflects the principles, practices, and aspirations of the NCAA Division III.

Universities will not readily give up their place in the big-time, even though they know that competing at this level can produce significant financial, educational, legal, and ethical fallout. Big-time sports programs have become deeply entrenched in the structure and culture of the big-time universities that sponsor them. The athletic trap has reinforced this commitment, making it undesirable or difficult to change direction in athletics. For many universities, the athletic trap has meant they have had to keep scrambling to find the resources to meet contractual obligations and fulfill promises. They have had to make excuses for not winning enough and for getting embroiled in controversies and scandals. They know they have to win, and this drive to win and make a name for themselves through sports distracts universities from their educational mission and the collegiate model of athletics.

Realists and pragmatists might say that the history of big-time college athletics has demonstrated that serious calls for reform are unlikely to change much in the college sports business. Universities occasionally decide to drop expensive football programs to reduce the deficits in athletic budgets; however, others are ready to take their place. Perhaps unaware of the athletic trap in which they are becoming entangled, universities decide to try to compete at a higher level and make a bigger investment in athletics to become a member of the big-time. They believe their expected success in athletics will bring them more prominence and other benefits as an institution. They are likely to find that success is elusive and more costly than anticipated. They also may find that the athletic trap leads to commitments that distract from more basic institutional purposes and can blemish the university's reputation.

According to Suzanne Estler and Laurie Nelson, a common challenge for presidents and trustees with big-time athletic programs is "how to reap educational, social, and economic benefits from a strong athletics program without cost to the institution's academic and moral integrity."[13] They suggested that powerful outside influences create value conflicts for higher-education leaders, making it more difficult to solve this challenge. This is the challenge I have been addressing in this book. I have framed it in terms of the seemingly irreconcilable tensions between the collegiate and commercial models and between academic and athletic priorities. My reform proposal is an attempt to reconcile the irreconcilable at both system and institutional levels and to establish an appropriate balance between athletics and academics on individual campuses.

Although most of the elements in my proposal have been discussed before, some many times, my model is a more systemic approach than most prior proposals. It gets at the commercial foundation of big-time college sports, which has widely been seen as the source of its most egregious problems and scandals. It addresses the athletic trap that has flipped university priorities on their head. This trap has entangled universities and their officials in a complex and powerful web of commitments and promises that have distracted them from the central academic purposes of their institutions and undermined institutional integrity as well as their own. My model presents a new way of structuring and controlling the current distractions and excesses in big-time college sports.

Reform by Partition

The ongoing issues of academic integrity, the persistence of the arms race, and the recent wave of deviance, corruption, and scandals are not necessarily harbingers of the death of big-time college sports, as some critics proclaim. In contrast, I see their confluence as an opportunity to build a new, more realistic, and more stable structure that incorporates both the collegiate and commercial model. I do not see the solution to the current excesses and problems in big-time college sports as the clearer or sharper demarcation of college sports from commercial entertainment and professional sport that Sack wanted. Alternatively, I would draw this line of demarcation within college sports itself.

My proposal is reform by partition. It incorporates many of the elements of big-time college sports but confines them to a smaller partition of college sports than the big-time realm currently represents. My model of reform by partition restructures college sports into two distinct domains, one for relatively uncommercialized and nonrevenue sports and one for the most highly commercialized big-time revenue sports. This partition roughly parallels the current division between the have-nots and haves in college sports.

Perhaps surprisingly, this partition idea reflects the thinking of one of the major figures in the college sports establishment, Duke basketball coach Mike Krzyzewski. He has proposed three distinct organizations in college sports for football, men's basketball, and nonrevenue sports. His justification was that these domains of college sports needed different structures because they faced different demands and concerns. He recommended a different commissioner for each domain. Each commissioner needed the authority and determination to enforce the rules governing his or her domain. He also suggested rules that made sense and could be enforced. Sports writer John Feinstein also asserted in this vein that the rulebook should be ten pages instead of five hundred and that both the rules and the penalties needed to be clear. In addition, he commented, "If you want to pay players, fine; but if you don't, then those who do must be punished severely."[14] The implication is that integrity does not mean anything if rules are violated with impunity. In the absence of tough and consistent penalties for rule breakers, they will feel no compunction about breaking the rules.

Journalist and college sports expert Doug Lederman proposed that there were two ways to "fix" college athletics: make it fully amateur or more openly professionalize it.[15] The partition model does both by building on Krzyzewski's ideas for change. The big-time domain I propose preserves the most commercialized realm of big-time college sports in the form of super conferences for each of the most commercialized sports in the IGT. Super conferences admittedly do little to alter the influence of the commercial model. However, the big-time college sports world I envision would be more clearly defined and have sharper boundaries than the elite realm of big-time college sports currently has. This domain would also distance itself from the rhetoric of amateurism and the collegiate model that the NCAA currently expresses to describe all of college sports.

The super conferences would be overseen and controlled by presidential commissions in each big-time sport. I would envision football and men's basketball as the first super conferences because they are the most commercialized college sports with the highest standing in the IGT. Each super conference would be advised by its own athlete advisory council of current and former athlete-students. Super and regional commissioners would report to the presidential commission and administer and regulate the regional conferences they have created in their sport. Regional conferences would coordinate competition and other sports-related activities among members. Presidents, super commissioners, regional commissioners, and professional staff members in each super conference sport would engage in external relations with the major players in the environment of this big-time college sports domain. Their responsibility would be to form and sustain the relationships and secure the contracts that provide essential media exposure and revenue for their sport. These major players include the IGT, boosters, fans, the government, and pro sports leagues. They also would respond to major influences on their sports domain from the economy.

The second partition would be a nonrevenue domain, which would be organized by the principles of the collegiate model. Programs in this domain would not be prevented from generating external revenue, but they would function essentially as nonrevenue sports currently operate. The expectation would be that they would be largely or entirely funded from general institutional funds. This domain would be regulated and run by a revamped NCAA, the "New NCAA."[16] In effect, the New NCAA would put the old NCAA out of the business of running a system that has operated as a virtual cartel. This cartel has historically exploited student-athletes and restricted their economic rights.

The New NCAA would be overseen and controlled by a presidential council, which would be advised by an athlete advisory council representing a cross section of current and former student-athletes in a variety of sports. The New NCAA commissioner would report to the presidential council and administer and regulate the sports programs in its domain. Different New NCAA divisions would reflect differences in factors such as enrollment, institutional mission, and athletic resources, so that programs in a division can be competitive with each other.[17] Institutions could be members of different divisions for different sports. Divisions coordinate regional conferences, which coordinate competition and other sports-related activities of member programs. The major elements in the models of these two domains are listed in figures 1 and 2 on the next two pages.

Organization, Governance, and Rules in the Partition Model

Although the first two super conferences would logically be for football and men's basketball, others could follow. Modified versions of full-blown super conferences could be established for other sports with a significant commercial potential. I assume, though, that organizing a super conference on any scale would be financially prohibitive for most other college sports, even if they currently have ties to the IGT. This means that the New NCAA would be the regulatory body for most athletic programs in this new world of college sports. It also means that the new BTUs under this plan would be members of one or more super conferences for their highly commercialized sports and members of the New NCAA for all of the other sports. This is not unlike the current situation where a school can belong to different conferences for different sports and even compete at different NCAA levels in different sports. However, the governance and rules will be vastly different in the new organizational structure I am proposing. Universities will have different athletic administrative structures for New NCAA programs and for each of their "super" sport programs.

The institutional membership of the New NCAA would include all schools in the existing NCAA, since schools with programs at the super conference level would also have other athletic programs competing in the New NCAA. Thus, many of the universities competing at the NCAA Division I level today, as well as those

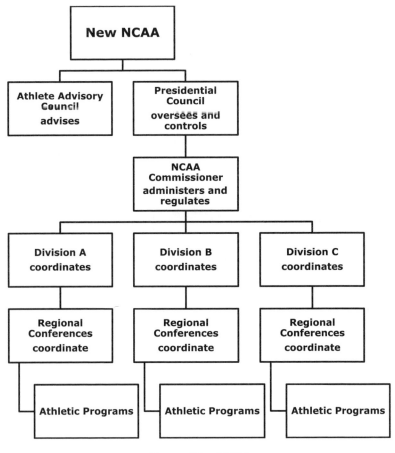

Figure 1. New NCAA

competing at the Division II level, will compete at a less athletically and financially demanding level that has many of the features of Division III today. Competing in a super conference will be too expensive for the have-nots and most of the strivers in big-time college sports today. Yet the upside of this ostensible downward mobility is that institutions competing in the New NCAA would eventually be able to back out of the athletic trap, stop making academic compromises, and reshape their campus culture so that athletics and education are more fully integrated.

New NCAA programs would be integrated into the administrative structure and culture of the university. The prototype for this integration is the Vanderbilt model conceived by Gordon Gee. Athletic staff would be part of the academic or student affairs division. The centerpiece of this sector of college sports would be a collegiate model truly emphasizing the student-athlete and a commitment to in-

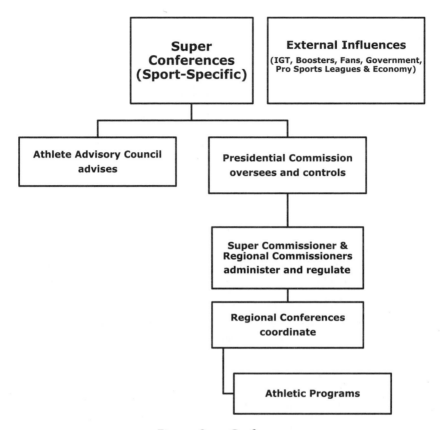

Figure 2. Super Conferences

stitutional academic integrity in athletics. Athletes would not receive merit-based athletic scholarships but instead be eligible for need-based financial aid, like their nonathlete classmates. Their academic support would be integrated into the general student support structure of the institution.

Despite possible competitive, organizational, and financial differences, the different divisions of the New NCAA would be expected to embrace the same broad philosophy shaped by the collegiate model. This philosophy values athletic competition but balances athletic commitment with a strong commitment to academics among genuine student-athletes. This is an idealized version of the philosophy of athletics for many Division III programs. A core assumption of this philosophy is educational enhancement through athletics, in which student-athletes get an opportunity to develop and use their bodies along with their minds in a physically demanding and vigorous extracurricular activity.[18]

There is no way to legislate the competitiveness or desire for status that schools, teams, and athletes might pursue at any level or in any domain of college sports. These influences can be found in college athletics in the world of elite small colleges and the Ivy League as well as in bigger universities at higher and more commercialized levels of the NCAA.[19] Thus, we might expect varying degrees of competitive intensity and status seeking in the New NCAA. However, for presidents and campuses in this realm, the hold of the athletic trap and the influence of a culture of reverence would be substantially diminished.

Super conferences would embody the basic assumptions of the commercial model that currently predominates in big-time college sports. Thus, they would be intimately tied to the IGT and place a strong emphasis on winning and commercial success. As in big-time college sports today, the commercial model would continue to drive the programs in this domain in an intense pursuit of competitive and commercial success. With talented athletes and coaches and intense competition, super conferences would function as developmental leagues or feeder systems for the professional leagues. This is essentially how elite football and basketball programs function now.

The BTUs competing in this domain could stop pretending they are not in the sports entertainment business and formally acknowledge it as part of their mission, as Clotfelter has been advocating.[20] In addition, BTUs competing in super conferences would abandon the myth of amateurism. They would formally and openly include athletes among all the other professionals in the athletic department. They would become *athlete-students*, in contrast to the *student-athletes* participating in intercollegiate athletics in the New NCAA.

Presidential commissions must be willing to grant their super commissioners the scope and amount of authority typically enjoyed by commissioners of successful professional sports leagues. They must be able to govern with a firm hand to keep their highly ambitious members' programs in line. Programs and their personnel would be responsible for strict adherence to organizational and competitive rules approved by their presidential commission, and deviants would be severely punished. Expulsion from a super conference would be the severest punishment for programs, and its counterpart for personnel would be a lengthy suspension or lifetime ban.

Presidential commissions would base decisions about regional conference affiliation mainly on geographic location, which would sustain or create new natural rivalries. While super conferences would risk antitrust action if they prevented schools from switching conferences, they could limit churning by restricting their size and making the cost of leaving the conference very expensive for member schools. On the other hand, if super conferences operate in a free-enterprise environment, the well-managed super conferences would retain their members by attracting enough IGT media and business investment to satisfy members. The job of super commissioners would be to assure as much equity as possible in distributing their super conference resources. Poorly managed super conferences could fail and break up, and their members could move to another super conference or gravitate to the New NCAA. Individual schools would be able to spend as much as they wished and be free to negotiate their own contracts in the IGT.

There currently are six to eight elite or almost-elite conferences. One conception of super conference configuration is four sixteen-member conferences. The online clipping service *College Athletics Clips* surveyed 400 of its subscribers in prominent positions in college athletics about their opinion concerning super conferences.[21] They were asked to respond yes or no to the question, "Within the next 5–10 years, do you think that there will be four super conferences of 16 schools each?" A significant majority (67.5 percent) of the 171 respondents answered yes. The survey's director suggested that those who answered no did not necessarily reject the possibility of super conferences, but instead might have thought there would be more super conferences or more or fewer members in each conference. In one four-by-sixteen configuration envisioned by *College Athletics Clips*, the Big Ten, SEC, and Pac-12 conferences would each be expanded to sixteen members, and the ACC, Big East, and Big 12 would be combined into one super conference with sixteen members.

In my conception, there would be a different super conference for each big-time sport. The financial data about college sports suggest that whatever the configuration of the super conferences or the number of member programs in each, each super conference would represent a small subset of the total number of college programs in its sport. With football expenses exceeding men's basketball expenses, I envision a separate super conference configuration for football and basketball. The super conference configuration of regional conferences might approximate the four-by-sixteen model for football, whereas the configuration for basketball might be at least four regional conferences and would likely have at least sixty-four members.[22]

Unlike athletic programs in the New NCAA that are fully integrated into the administrative structure of the university, super conference programs would be outside the general administrative structure of the university. They would have some autonomy in their operations, but super sport programs would remain connected to their university and its governance structure. They would employ the university name, utilize university-owned facilities, and rely on athlete-students admitted by the university and subject to student academic and conduct rules. In addition, the super sport program directors would be hired by the president, be university employees, and be accountable to the president and trustees.

Fewer Regulations and Less Deviance

College presidents and the NCAA have long been frustrated by the recurrence of normal deviance and scandals. The tiny NCAA enforcement staff has often been overwhelmed in its effort to keep this deviance under control.[23] There is a simple truism about deviance. There will be less of it with fewer regulations. Order does not require a lot of rules. It requires rules that reflect core values and enforcement that is consistent, fair, and firm. Thus, both the New NCAA and the super conferences should follow John Feinstein's suggestion and try to be relevant and pithy in formulating regulations for their respective domains. It will save them unnecessary negative publicity and make enforcement easier.[24]

Rule makers in the New NCAA should concentrate on upholding the core elements of the collegiate model: academic integrity, the welfare of student-athletes, and following the rules of sport. Thus, they should prohibit special subsidies for student-athletes for participating in athletics; expect student-athletes to follow the academic rules and rules of conduct that apply to all students on campus; and try to assure that the competition itself is fair, with no illegal performance-enhancing drugs or other special aids.

Probably the biggest difference between the New NCAA and super conference rule books will concern the status and compensation of athletes. Like student-athletes in the New NCAA, athlete-students in super sports would have to meet customary academic expectations for classroom performance, abide by student conduct codes, and compete fairly on the field with no illegal performance-enhancement aids. Unlike student-athletes, athlete-students would be paid employees or professionals. Current NCAA restrictions on the amount and types of money and other material compensation athletes can earn from their sports participation would be dropped. The NCAA athletic grant-in-aid would be replaced by a compensation package negotiated by athlete-students, their parents, or their agents. Compensation packages could include salaries, endorsement contracts, licensing agreements, and gifts from boosters and others. The new professionalized or employee status of athlete-students would not preclude receiving tuition and fee remission during or beyond their years of competitive eligibility. This would be part of the compensation package they negotiate with schools during recruitment.

Athletic directors for super sports will have to wrestle with issues of equity and practicality in figuring out the compensation packages for coaches and athlete-students, but the elimination of compensation restrictions for athlete-students would make issues of illegal cash payments and gifts to athletes largely irrelevant. These financial benefits have accounted for a significant number of rule violations under the current NCAA rules. Reducing deviance in this area does not mean that all the problems concerning outside compensation will be gone. In allowing gifts from boosters and endorsement contracts, the new policies will create some challenges for athletic directors and coaches who want to restrain the influence of boosters and the IGT on athlete-students. Restrictions may be difficult to enforce, though, since boosters and the IGT will expect substantial access as part of their quid pro quo or contract.

Athlete-students would have to meet academic admission standards that are comparable to current NCAA initial eligibility rules, and they would be required to take the equivalent of one term of academic courses each year from the school for which they compete. However, they would not be permitted to matriculate during the academic term of their primary season. This provision should alleviate many of the current concerns about distractions from academics, since big-time athletes would not be in class during the main part of their sports season.

The period of recruitment of athletes for super sports may have to be restricted, for example, to the last three semesters of high school. Communication rules during this open recruitment period would largely be dropped, which is essentially what happened at the 2013 NCAA convention. However, parents would have to accompany minor children on recruiting visits to the campus, be present for home visits, and sign all contracts. Athlete-students would be allowed to change schools without penalty after one or two years at a particular school. This is comparable to the free agency rules in professional sports.

Economics in the Partition Model

Another important difference between the proposed New NCAA and the super conferences involves funding and external relationships. New NCAA athletic programs would be funded entirely from the general university budget as a line item along with other educational or student programs. Thus, special institutional subsidies for athletics would be eliminated. Admission to athletic events would be free to all students, faculty, and staff. Rental of athletic facilities could also produce revenue to help subsidize these facilities. If student athletic fees are retained, they could be reduced and used to fund club and intramural sports programs as well as New NCAA intercollegiate programs. Club, intramural, and recreational programs could share athletic facilities with intercollegiate teams at schools with no super sport teams. Earmarked athletic donations would not be permitted for programs in the New NCAA, which would eliminate the need for special athletic fundraising staff and foundations.

On the other hand, athletic programs competing in the super conferences would be required to be fully self-supporting, with no institutional subsidies. Super sport program directors would have the authority to hire and negotiate contracts for coaches, athletic administrators, and other athletic personnel, including athlete-students, in their program. The super sport program directors could be paid from the university budget, but they could alternatively be paid the same way all other personnel in each super sport program would be paid—that is, from its self-support budget. This funding structure would parallel funding of other types of campus self-support enterprises, including continuing education, business incubators, research institutes, and medical centers. These enterprises generally utilize university facilities and generate overhead and prestige for their university. Super sport programs would not produce the same kind of overhead but would presumably bolster the university brand and prestige. This is presumably what big-time college sports programs currently do, which is an important part of the justification for investing in big-time sports. In the super conference model, universities would get the prestige of their affiliation with a successful big-time team without the direct costs they currently incur.

Super sport programs would have the authority and responsibility to manage their own finances. This decentralized budgeting strategy has been called "every tub on its own bottom" (ETOB).[25] These programs would be permitted to retain the revenue generated from their sports operations and be expected to cover all operational expenses and all or nearly all of their personnel expenses. The leasing of university facilities would be among their expenses. Major revenue sources would be essentially the same as they are now for big-time college sports programs. They include ticket sales, concessions, licensing agreements, other IGT contracts, sponsorships, donations, and conference and championship distributions. Athletic foundations would continue to be an important source of donations and other revenue. Separate athletic foundations would be affiliated with different super sport programs on a campus. These foundations would be accountable to their specific sport program director. Presidents and trustees would remain responsible for general financial and administrative accounting oversight and control for all intercollegiate athletic programs, including super sports. Donor involvement and athletic foundations would be strictly regulated to assure financial accountability and prevent excessive interference in program operations.

Merit-based athletic scholarships would be eliminated for both New NCAA and super conference programs. The elimination of athletic scholarships should produce a net cost reduction in athletics for most schools shifting from Division I or II to the New NCAA. They would be able to reduce funding for student-athletes who can afford to pay all or part of their educational costs. In contrast, eliminating university-funded athletic scholarships for super sport programs could increase costs for these programs but not for the institution. Since they will be self-supporting, the programs will have to use money from noninstitutional sources to compensate athlete-students. This new or reallocated money would be part of a restructured salary pool including athlete-students as well as coaches, athletic directors, and other athletic administrators and staff members. The amount in this salary pool might not be enough to meet the escalating salary demands of star coaches and athletic directors and also meet the new salary demands of star athlete-students. Thus, this salary structure could ratchet down salaries of coaches and athletic directors in the star wars arms race, while also increasing overall personnel costs in the new big-time world of college athletics. Whether or not salary costs continue to escalate in an arms race in big-time athletics, universities would not have to shoulder this financial burden. Expenditure budgets would be the responsibility of the super conference programs and would not be a responsibility of the larger institution. This is what self-support and ETOB budgeting imply.

Super conference programs could get more revenue from conference distributions, since they no longer would be sharing outside revenue with nonelite programs. They also would have less competition for IGT exposure and money from nonelite programs that moved to the New NCAA. Nevertheless, competing at this level would continue to be costly, and relatively few programs are likely to have enough revenue or be able to meet the other resource requirements for membership in a super conference.

The current NCAA would experience a substantial change in its budget as well as in the scope of its authority over highly commercialized athletic programs. Its loss of control over big-time football to elite conferences, postseason bowls, the BCS, and a new playoff system would be duplicated in men's basketball and other possible super conference sports. The administration of the New NCAA would be funded largely from membership dues and a portion of IGT revenue tied to its sponsorship role in national and regional championships. It would not generate even a fraction of the hundreds of millions of dollars it has been able to earn each year from its March Madness media contracts. This means that former NCAA Division I programs in football and men's basketball that relocate to the New NCAA could expect much more modest revenue shares from NCAA-negotiated media contracts than they formerly enjoyed.

Although the New NCAA domain would be viewed essentially in terms of the current model for nonrevenue sports, schools and conferences would have a chance to generate external revenue to support athletic programs. They would be permitted to negotiate their own contracts with IGT partners, but revenue from these contracts would be relatively limited for the more modestly funded and less commercialized athletic programs in the New NCAA. The IGT could be expected to invest most of its college sports money in the super conferences and the smaller number of high-profile, big-time programs in these conferences. The super conference members would be high-profile programs because media and business partners in the IGT will make them prominent.

Important aspects of the role of super conference commissioners would be managing the everyday operations and regulatory business of their conferences, assuring integrity and order in competition and member behavior, and organizing major championships. In addition, they would have to devote time to negotiating lucrative media rights contracts, corporate sponsorships, and licensing agreements. Revenue from these IGT partnerships would be essential in paying for the operation and staffing of the super conferences. The financial viability and long-term survival of the super conferences will depend on a variety of factors. The most prominent one may the ability of super conference teams to retain or build their fan base. Big-time sports will remain big-time only as long as they continue to generate substantial revenue. Their revenue potential will ultimately depend on their capacity to keep people interested and entertained.

The fans and consumers of big-time college athletics ultimately determine its success. The equation is pretty straightforward. The NCAA, the conferences, and schools make money from gate receipts, media money, business sponsors and investors, and vendors. When fans lose interest, fewer people pay to see live events, fewer people watch or listen to sports programming and ads on TV, radio, and the Internet, and fewer people buy licensed college sports gear. These consequences of declining fan interest hurt the bottom line of the media and other businesses in the IGT. When they see their profits drop, they take their business and money elsewhere. In addition, less public interest in college sports undermines many of the arguments that presidents make to justify their investment in college sports. Thus, the direct and indirect effects of declining fan interest could seriously erode the foundation of commercialized college sports.

In the reconstituted world of college sports created by the partition model, justifying athletics will be different for New NCAA and super conference programs. I would expect athletic programs to be in the New NCAA either because their schools have enthusiastically embraced the collegiate model or because financial strains or shifting campus priorities gave them little choice about scaling down their competitive and commercial aspirations. Colleges and universities will expect to pay all or nearly all of the costs of New NCAA programs from general institutional funds. They will do this because these programs are part of the educational experience of student-athletes and because the organization for these athletic programs will be embedded in the budgetary, administrative, and governance structure of the institution. Universities will sponsor big-time programs in super conferences because they think they can pay for themselves. These programs serve an entertainment and branding function for them. Universities will not expect to make money from them, but neither will they bear their financial costs. If these programs fail to balance their budgets or embarrass the university in a significant way, their institutional sponsor can move them to the New NCAA level or shut them down entirely.

Transitions

To be sure, there will be much resistance to implementing my reform by partition proposal. However, a major insider in the college sports establishment, Mike Krzyzewski, also thinks that college sports would benefit from a partition. Following Krzyzewski's lead, I have begun with the idea of separating big-time football and men's basketball from the nonrevenue or deficit-producing domain of college sports. We may have different reasons for advancing our partition ideas. By articulating the broad concept of a partition, however, Krzyzewski should give this idea some credibility in the college sports establishment. I have no illusions, though, about the difficulty of convincing presidents, trustees, and others in the college sports establishment about the need for this kind of change. The fact that Krzyzewski's argument has not yet caught on reflects the resistance to change characterizing big-time college sports, but this initial lack of interest does not make the partition idea less relevant or timely. My model gives some flesh to the outline he suggested, and it also specifically addresses serious problems in big-time college sports at a time of heightened concern about them.

I agree with those who say the current financial model of big-time college sports is unsustainable for nearly all schools that compete at the Division I level in football and men's basketball and expect to break even or make money from them. Very few programs in these sports or other sports come close to breaking even. My model is a pragmatic response to this reality. It is also a pragmatic response to the pattern of ongoing deviance and corruption in big-time college sports.

Highly commercialized programs would remain at the schools where these programs are the most popular, the most established, and the most financially successful. At this level, the accommodation of the collegiate model to the commercial model would no longer be seen as corrupt. Super conferences would be openly and aggressively oriented to making money and building brands from entertaining high-level competition. The biggest jolts for big-time programs competing in super conferences would probably come from being entirely financially self-supporting and from accepting the new legal and economic rights given to athlete-students. Presidents, trustees, and conference officials also might have to lobby and negotiate with legislators to find ways to protect this openly commercial enterprise from congressional intervention and new taxes. Keeping the finances of super sports separate from university finances should protect universities.

Finding new or reallocated money for athlete-student compensation under this model represents a major challenge. Super conference programs would be more dependent on exposure and money from the major media and corporate partners in the IGT, which would give these IGT players even more power than they currently have in big-time college sports. Super conference programs may have to do more to accommodate the cameras, coverage, scheduling, and product placement of IGT partners. They also might have to give up more control over the use of their university and team brand by these partners.

It can be daunting and disruptive to give up what we know and plunge into something new. This might explain some of the anticipated resistance to change. In addition, the IGT feeds dreams, which is why those with no realistic chance of moving up this hierarchy keep spending money to try to get there. This is also why those who are the most appropriate candidates to move from Division I to the New NCAA are likely to resist. The New NCAA is not a domain where coaches, athletes, athletic programs, and schools become as well known or make as much money as they currently could in the existing NCAA Divisions I and II. Dampening aspirations in a school's glamour sports is not easily accepted. Yet moving to the New NCAA is both realistic and pragmatic for most schools currently losing money by competing in Division I and aspiring to big-time status.

Universities might not want to move their big-time programs to the New NCAA; however, with ETOB budgeting and no institutional bailouts, some attrition in the super conferences seems inevitable. There are important benefits from making this move. Being in the New NCAA would loosen the hold of the athletic trap, make rational athletic decisions easier, and elevate the collegiate model to a place where these schools have usually falsely claimed it was. Like Division III programs now, these programs would provide challenging competitive opportunities for fun and personal growth for student-athletes. This is similar to the philosophy of the Association for Intercollegiate Athletics for Women (AIAW). This relatively short-lived organization was formed to coordinate competition among the many women's athletic programs that were spawned by Title IX in the 1970s. It died after a decade because it could not hang on to programs that were lured to the more established NCAA by its prestige, money, and ties to the IGT.[26] The AIAW philosophy lives on in the NCAA Division III and would also have a new life in the New NCAA with its serious commitment to the collegiate model.

Football is a very expensive sport, especially at the big-time level. This is why financially struggling football programs in super conferences may be prime candidates to move to the New NCAA, especially since they will not be able to depend on institutional subsidies to bail them out. Colleges and universities could also decide that football is too expensive at the New NCAA level and drop it entirely, so that athletic resources in the university budget could be distributed to a wider array of sports. Some advocates of Title IX have argued for reduced funding in football or the elimination of football as a way to achieve gender equity.[27]

It could be seen as a victory for the reformers if any of these forms of downsizing or migration occurs. Of course, asteroids also could drop, causing a significant restructuring of big-time college sports, which would not be orchestrated or wanted by presidents or trustees at BTUs. My model provides a plan that allows schools that can afford big-time sports programs to pursue them in a rational, deliberate, and intentional way that insulates the institution from much of the fallout big-time sports currently produce. The model also challenges presidents and trustees to loosen the grip of the athletic trap, face reality, and organize and fund athletics in a way that is both financially sound and academically justifiable. This means for many that they reduce their investment in big-time athletics, make athletics more a part of the university, and join schools with more modest athletic programs to form something like the New NCAA.

There will be bumps on the transition road. There are at least two major hurdles to overcome in trying to transform the NCAA into the New NCAA and at least two major obstacles to establishing super conferences. The first hurdle is convincing university and NCAA officials that the NCAA needs to give up its control over big-time sports and become the administrative and regulatory body for programs with more modest competitive and commercial aspirations. However, since the NCAA is empowered by its members and depends on their support, it would have to follow the dictates of college presidents and member institutions if they decided to move in the direction I have proposed. The second major hurdle is convincing presidents and trustees of schools with precarious big-time programs that they need to move them into the New NCAA. This is a hurdle because these university leaders may have a difficult time accepting that their dreams are unrealistic and harmful. In addition, they may have a difficult time seeing that they should and can free themselves from the long-term commitments of the athletic trap. It will take patience and determination to dismantle the athletic trap, though.

The super conferences are arguably a logical extension of current trends in the college sports realm. One major obstacle to the formation of super conferences is getting presidents and trustees at BTUs to recognize and accept this logic. It may be difficult for them to accept the administrative and budgetary changes in their major sports that would be necessary to compete in super conferences. These sports would be given relative administrative and budgetary autonomy, while the president and trustees would continue to have oversight responsibilities. In effect, though, at some BTUs with the biggest programs, athletic directors and star coaches currently have a great deal of power and autonomy. In addition, the university currently absorbs significant financial costs and assumes other risks, such as the effects of normal deviance and scandals.

The second major obstacle to forming the super conferences in my model is getting presidents, trustees, and the college sports establishment to acknowledge that big-time college athletes deserve many of the same employment rights that their coaches have long enjoyed. Even though this change in status would change the financial equation in big-time college sports, it should alleviate many of the concerns about exploitation and illegal payments.

Big-time college sports have significant costs as well as benefits for the universities involved in this realm. For many, though, the financial costs seem to exceed the less tangible benefits. I believe that the cost-benefit equation would be more favorable in the super conferences than it currently is in big-time college sports. This is because eventually the programs left standing in these conferences would be ones that have proved they can afford to compete at this level and can also avoid the scandals that regularly occur in big-time college sports. It should be easier to convince BTU presidents and trustees of the merits of super conferences if they have programs that are able to survive the competitive and financial pressures at this level. It will be more difficult to sell presidents and trustees at the other BTUs that they will be better off in the New NCAA.

This analysis may seem quixotic, as most visions of significant reform have in the past. After all, the big-time structure of college sports has resisted efforts to rein it in or place limits on it. It has continued to lure schools into it. Its trajectory has been in the direction of growth and more off-campus influence over athletics. However, real reforms do not come from realists. They come from unrealistic visionaries who see a different future and then become pragmatic when they find a way to act on their vision. Even if those who envision a different future for college sports do not have the courage, strength, or persistence to carry on in the face of severe criticisms and failure, college sports might change anyway. There might be an asteroid, as Clotfelter and Orleans suggest, that could break up college sports in ways that no one fully anticipates and few want. Despite resistance from NCAA officials, the college sports establishment in general, and some segments of the IGT, the college sports landscape could be significantly changed by presidents and trustees with a viable plan and the will to change. I have tried to provide an outline for this planning.

Epilogue

The athletic trap is part reality and part illusion. Being involved in big-time college sports and having to pay its rising costs may seem very real to college presidents. After all, there are annual budgets to balance, star coaches, administrators, and other staff members in the athletic department to pay, facilities to pay for and maintain, and boosters and fans to keep happy. In addition, there are negotiations with the media and various other business transactions with partners in the intercollegiate golden triangle that are needed to make big-time college sports viable. All of these things create the enduring obligations and expectations that define the athletic trap. At the same time, though, the idea that being involved in big-time college sports is a trap with no escape is an illusion. The trap has been constructed by a series of past decisions and is sustained by new decisions. Many of these decisions may seem perfunctory. Indeed, the senses of obligation and resignation associated with the trap are reinforced by the belief that discontinuing past athletic commitments is not a choice. However, presidents and trustees have choices but generally avoid or ignore facing this fact.

Dampening athletic aspirations and deemphasizing commercialized college sports are real choices for college presidents and trustees. Presidents could gradually loosen the grip of the athletic trap and free themselves and their institution from it by giving up their illusions about athletics and accepting a vision of it more in tune with reality and their educational mission. They will need the support of their trustees. Trustees usually follow the lead of presidents. In these tough economic times for most of the have-nots in athletics, saving money on nonacademic activities should be appealing.

I am not advocating the elimination of big-time athletics from all college campuses. I am arguing instead for a structure that allows students to compete in a variety of intercollegiate athletics at all types of institutions, and one that confines the highly commercialized version to a relatively small subset of these institutions. I am also arguing for a commercial model in super conferences that openly acknowledges the entertainment value, commercial opportunities, and professionalism in this realm. This would be a world in which less would need to be hidden and problems could be attacked before they turn into scandals.

When scandals occur, there are excuses and then mea culpas. Presidents and trustees say "never again on my watch." The NCAA convenes another presidential summit and vows to put in place new and tougher rules to prevent similar scandals in the future. However, if they do nothing to restructure the commercial foundation of the big-time sports realm that underlies these scandals, their assertions and vows will be meaningless. My proposal may not be the panacea that the most radical reformers want. It will not solve every problem, and there will be presidents, trustees, and boosters fighting it at every step if it were implemented. As a model for restructuring big-time college athletics, however, it addresses the underlying causes of its biggest problems and still preserves the media show that the most serious sports fans and the most powerful players in the IGT want to see. It is a proposal that bows to the power of these forces in big-time college sports but also pushes them to become more open about the kind of commercial product they produce. This is a product made by paid and unpaid professionals,[1] both of whom happen to be affiliated with higher education institutions. My proposal would treat star athletes in super conferences as the professionals they virtually are now, despite their official status as amateurs.

For those who think it is unseemly to be more open about commercial motives in athletics in big-time college sports, consider the case of private for-profit universities. They make no apologies for being in the business of selling education to consumers. Acknowledging commercial motives in big-time athletics is both honest and consistent with the increasingly commercialized nature of higher education in general. Super-level BTUs could try to emulate the honesty of for-profits in acknowledging basic truths about what big-time sports are. They could begin by acknowledging that they are in the entertainment business and want to make money and build their brand through sports. They also could tout the fact that they give promising athletes a chance to develop their sports career resumes. This is consistent with the value that most students put on jobs and careers in explaining why they attend colleges and the unabashed advertising by most universities that promises practical majors with real employment prospects.[2]

It is difficult to keep up with the elite in big-time college sports, and it is becoming more difficult as the gap between the haves and have-nots grows. The athletic trap mires schools in the arms race, which strains the budgets of all but the most successful athletic programs. However, even BTUs with elite programs are ultimately going to feel the pinch of constantly increasing expenditures. They cannot keep building bigger and fancier facilities or pay coaches ever-higher salaries, and they cannot all succeed in the recruiting game year after year to attract the best athletic talent. When the most talented athletes leave early for professional sports careers, the pressure on coaches to restock their talent and rebuild their team intensifies every year. When academic eligibility standards increase, it becomes more difficult to recruit and retain academically qualified star athletes. Academic reforms have made life more difficult for athletic programs that have relied on academically underqualified transfer students to be successful. Schools have learned that they pay a cost in NCAA penalties if they fail to keep student-athletes on track to graduate.

The greater commitment to the commercial than collegiate model has been necessary or inevitable when universities are involved the college sports business in the IGT. The super conference model acknowledges this. However, it offers a pragmatic option that avoids much of the corruption and hypocrisy now characterizing big-time college sports. The New NCAA model elevates the collegiate model and makes the commercial model relatively meaningless. Division I and even Division II schools with big-time aspirations for their top athletic programs will not like the idea of moving "down" to the New NCAA. For many, though, it might eventually be necessary as a result of economics, a major scandal, or power moves by elite schools pushing them away. In the end, those who make this move will benefit from a reordering of budgets and priorities that takes back the academy from the excessive and misplaced emphasis on big-time sports. The balance between academics and athletics assumed by the collegiate model would become a reality. This reality would not need the apologetics, myths, or false promises currently defending or justifying big-time college sports programs.

Scaling back commercialism in big-time college sports and moving to the New NCAA would take time, as the athletic trap is dismantled. They would require convincing the people who care most about the institution that a more modest athletic program would be in the best interests of the institution and student-athletes. They would require getting the support of trustees, some of whom may be major big-time sports boosters. Thus, presidents seeking genuine athletic reform might upset some trustees and also lose the support of powerful athletic boosters and alumni. They might even face threats and reprisals from them and many fans. They will surely get less attention from the media and corporate sponsors. Since their investments and support were largely or entirely directed toward athletics, losing them would not hurt the institution as a whole.

Reorganizing big-time sports programs to compete under the new rules of super conferences would also take some time. Planning will keep financial consultants, accountants, and lawyers busy. Those schools that decide they can afford to compete at the super conference level will be creating a firewall that insulates them from the financial ravages of the arms race. Presidents will still have to be involved in the governance of big-time programs at the institutional and systemic levels. Their universities will have their name in print, but it should less often be for the wrong reasons. Super sport programs will have to balance their budgets on their own, and when they do not, their universities will have the authority to shut them down or move them to the New NCAA.

The two partitioned domains I envision for college sports offer a blueprint for change that could alleviate, reduce, or concentrate the problems that are widely seen as needing fixing in the big-time realm. They will not change everything we have known about college sports or eliminate big-time sports programs. However, they represent serious and deep reforms. I assume that presidents and trustees want to do what is best for their school and students. Seeing the possible benefits of these changes is the first step in a reform process that could make athletics more compatible with their institutional mission and capabilities.

Chapter 1 · Commercialization, College Sports, and the Athletic Trap

1. Marklein (2013). In a related story, Kiley (2013) presented data showing differences in median academic spending levels per student and median athletic spending per athlete in the major and mid-major athletic conferences. He presented other data indicating how Division I schools distributed athletic revenue, what their sources of athletic revenue were, and how much they depended on institutional subsidies for athletics. Sports insiders, such as a former Ivy League director, have warned about the unsustainability of an economic model dependent on institutional subsidies, especially during periods of economic austerity (see Wolverton 2013).

2. *College* refers to the institutions of colleges and universities, except when explicitly noted otherwise. Similarly, *college sports, college sport, intercollegiate athletics, college athletics,* and simply *athletics* are generally used interchangeably, except when explicitly noted otherwise.

3. Troop (2013).

4. Bok (2003, preface).

5. See Cornwell (2011) for a British perspective of this uniqueness.

6. See Betts (1974) and R. A. Smith (1990) for more historical details about the first century of U.S. college sports.

7. Deford (2005).

8. Bok (2003, p. 35).

9. This brief overview of early college sports history is largely based on Betts (1974, pp. 101–105, 211–218, 346–352) and was briefly summarized by Nixon (1984, pp. 106–110; 2008, pp. 252–254).

10. See Pettegrew's (2007) analysis of how playing aggressive sports such as college football helped privileged young men learn about hypermasculine culture in the late nineteenth and early twentieth centuries.

11. See Rooney (1980, ch. 2).

12. Bok (2003, preface).

13. Rooney (1980, p. 14).

14. Bok (2003, p. 37).

15. Nixon (1984, p. 107; 2008, pp. 253–254).

16. Rooney (1980, p. 15).

17. Clotfelter (2011, p. 57).

18. Sack and Staurowsky (1998, p. 20).

19. Thelin (1994) and R. A. Smith (2010) document cycles of scandals and reform efforts in the history of college sports.

20. Bok (2003, p. 51).

21. See research presented by Clotfelter (2011, pp. 48–50).

22. A possible exception is the faculty athletics representative (FAR). The FAR is a faculty member at an NCAA member institution. The FAR is a link between academics and the athletic department and represents the institution at conference and NCAA-sponsored meetings. Specific duties of FARs vary across institutions. In general, a primary responsibility is to try to assure that academic integrity and the welfare of the student-athlete are protected and that the collegiate model is not overshadowed by the commercial model of athletics. More information can be found at the website for the FAR Association (FARA), www.farawebsite.org.

23. Data are from the 2011 NCAA Football Records website fs.ncaa.org for "Added and Discontinued Programs" and from National Football Foundation (2011).

24. NAIA refers the National Association of Intercollegiate Athletics. Its membership is much smaller than the NCAA, it sponsors fewer championships and is much less commercialized, and its members tend to be small colleges and universities.

25. The Football Championship Subdivision (FCS) level of the NCAA is often referred to as the "mid-major" level, and its football teams compete in a national postseason championship tournament. The highest and most commercialized level of college sports is the Football Bowl Subdivision (FBS). A competition in bowl games organized by the Bowl Championship Series (BCS) determines the national champion at this level.

26. See National Football Foundation (2011).

27. Chancellor is the name for president in the University of North Carolina system.

28. National Football Foundation (2011).

29. Edwards (1973).

30. Duderstadt (2000a, 2000b).

31. NCAA (2006).

32. Bauerlein (2010).

33. Women's college basketball is also a big-time sport on some campuses in its media connections, support from corporate sponsors, and escalating pay of top coaches. However, recent evidence reported by Berkowitz and Upton (2011a) revealed that even the most prominent women's basketball programs generate deficits, which are exacerbated by the high salaries of their coaches. These programs are not able to produce the revenue of the big-time men's programs.

34. Critics of Title IX have claimed that Title IX has been the *cause* of cuts in non-revenue men's sports. Others have counterargued that blaming Title IX for these cuts is misguided. They have contended that the primary reason for the cuts has been the drain on resources from the increasing costs of football and men's basketball in more commercialized athletic programs. See Nixon (2008, pp. 265–269) for more about this debate.

35. See Carey (2011).

36. See the Knight Commission website (www.knightcommission.org) for more information about this organization and its activities.

37. Yost (2010); Branch (2011).

38. E.g., Davis (2011).

39. Clotfelter (2011).

40. Clotfelter (2011) has shown how infrequently universities acknowledge the importance of this entertainment function of sports in their mission statement or even acknowledge sports at all as part of their mission.

41. Chronicle (2000); Nixon (2008, p. 288).

42. See Nixon (2008, pp. 24–26, 269–276) for a definition of this concept and how it applies to the business of college sports.

Chapter 2 · *The Intercollegiate Golden Triangle*

1. See Nixon (2008) for a definition of this concept (pp. 24–26) and specifically how it applies to the business of college sports (pp. 269–276).

2. Smart (2005, p. 144). The idea was inspired by Aris's (1990, p. xi) conception of commercial sponsors and television as the "twin props" of the "Sportbiz."

3. See Nixon (2008).

4. E.g., Maguire (1999) referred to the "global media-sport complex" in his analysis of global sport, and Messner, Dunbar, and Hunt (2000) wrote about the "sports/media/commercial complex" in their analysis of the influence of televised sports in the socialization of young males.

5. Clotfelter (2011, pp. 78–80).

6. Quoted in Wieberg (2006).

7. See Berkowitz (2012c). The NCAA reportedly derived 80 percent of its income in FY2012 from television and marketing rights contracts for the men's ($666 million) and women's ($18.8 million) basketball tournaments. Most of the rest of its revenue was from ticket and merchandise sales from its championships.

8. Of course, for-profit universities are an exception. Grand Canyon University is the rare case of a for-profit higher educational institution that competes in intercollegiate athletics (see Rohan, 2012b). This book focuses on more traditional nonprofit universities.

9. Berkowitz (2012a) reported a decline in attendance at college football bowl games for the 2011 season, which was projected to be the lowest per-game average in thirty years. Wolverton and Richards (2012) reported that more than seventy Division I men's basketball programs, or about 20 percent, saw their regular-season attendance drop by 20 percent or more over the past four seasons.

10. Nixon (2008, p. 258). Clotfelter (2011, p. 252, n. 16) left out the Big East for football. Clotfelter (ch. 3) discussed the meaning of "bigness" in "big-time" college sports and focused on revenue and exposure.

11. Non-AQ conferences in the BCS in 2012 were Conference USA (C-USA), and the Mid-American (MAC), Mountain West, Sun Belt, and Western Athletic (WAC) Conferences. AQ and non-AQ status generally reflected a conference's likelihood of having ranked teams.

12. See, e.g., the case of the University of California San Diego (UCSD). UCSD paid $28,000 to conduct a feasibility study to identify and assess options for reclassifying to NCAA Division I and adding football (UCSD, 2011). It appeared poised to move to Division I without football within two years after a student government vote in favor of the move in March 2012 (Schrotenboer, 2012). Student government explained its support in terms of the enhanced "qualify of life" it expected big-time sports to bring to the campus. UCSD was known more for its academic reputation than for a vibrant student life or a high level of student morale. However, a failed student referendum on increasing student fees put an end to these plans to move up the NCAA big-time level (Dailey, 2012). The university needed the additional funds to be able to finance the move to Division I. Student resistance to increased fees is understandable in view of the large tuition increases expected as UC institutions struggled with severe budget cuts prompted by huge state government deficits.

13. The move by institutions such as Harvard, Princeton, and Yale to form the Ivy League is interesting because this kind of league represented a retreat from the "big-time" status in sports that many of these academically prominent institutions formerly enjoyed.

14. These are among Shulman and Bowen's (2001) findings in their study of athletics and educational values at elite colleges and universities. They argued that making exceptions for or giving preferences to athletes is especially problematic for elite institutions, since admission is so competitive and academics is supposed to be valued so highly.

15. See U.S. Department of Education (2011). These data are cited in this section, unless otherwise noted. See Fusfeld (2011) for estimates of projected median per-school budgets in the top fifteen conferences that were based on his calculations using data submitted to the Department of Education.

16. Along with Texas, Ohio State, and Alabama, Michigan ($111.8 million) and Florida ($107.2 million) occupied the ranks of the top-five spenders in college sports for FY 2011, according to EADA data. According to financial or budget data on their university websites, the FY2012 budget for the University of Texas at Austin was $2.2 billion, for Ohio State University was $1.4 billion, and for the University of Alabama was $755.9 million. These numbers and the athletic budgets reflect the relative size of the universities, the relative wealth of the states, and the priority of athletics in the budgeting process.

17. Stating conference affiliations, even for established members, can be risky in light of recurring conference realignment.

18. Reported on its website ncaa.org in 2012.

19. M. Smith (2011).

20. Durkin (2012).

21. These figures are from an NCAA database reported in an article by Schnaars, Upton, Mosemak, and DeRamus (2012).

22. In 2012, two of the most successful members of the conference announced plans to leave. Basketball power Virginia Commonwealth was moving to the Atlantic 10, a more prestigious basketball conference than the CAA and with a history of more schools getting at-large bids to play in the NCAA tournament. Old Dominion was moving up to the FBS level to play in Conference USA. Their moves were part of the broader pattern of "churning" that is discussed later in this chapter.

23. See Schnaars, Upton, Mosemak, and DeRamus (2012). Note that Richmond and Villanova are private institutions and were not included in the database.

24. The data reported to the U.S. Department of Education underestimate the spending figures reported by the NCAA for 2011 by several million dollars for each institution, but reporting periods may have differed. The NCAA data are more recent. The subsidy data are from the NCAA database as reported by Schnaars, Upton, Mosemak, and DeRamus (2012).

25. See Wieberg (2012).

26. Quoted in Durkin (2012).

27. See "History" at ncaa.org.

28. The NCAA compensates its top officials well. In 2010 (the last year for which data are available), the NCAA's officers and five highest-paid employees earned $6.3 million. *USA Today* estimated that Mark Emmert, the president, earned approximately $1.6 million in his first year, beginning in October 2010 (Berkowitz, 2012c).

29. Regular season does not include postseason bowl games.

30. Gregory and Busey (1985). The Big Ten and Pac-10 left the group because they could not agree with its ideas for a television plan. The Pac-10 is now the Pac-12.

31. See Legal Information Institute (n.d.).

32. College Football (1996).

33. See Grasgreen's (2012c) report of the decision to create this new structure.

34. In 2012 four teams were transitioning into full FBS membership, and three other teams were waiting in the wings to ascend to this level.

35. See Wieberg (2011a).

36. Wieberg (2011a).

37. See the NCAA website (ncaa.org) for more information about its governance structure.

38. Grasgreen (2012a).

39. The college athletics online clipping service (collegeathleticsclips.com), which summarizes major news stories about college sports, published a series of realignment graphics updating the latest changes in conference affiliation. There were many updates over a relatively brief span of time. For example, Version no. 7 in June 2012 showed more than forty schools moving between nearly twenty Division I conferences, with some moves only for football. Version no. 17 was published less than six months later (Infante, 2012b), reflecting the increasing instability of the conferences.

40. These changes involved both forced and voluntary resignations, and two of the conferences had two leadership changes during this period.

41. See, e.g., Katz and McMurphy (2012). These schools were upset about the confirmed or rumored departure of West Virginia, Syracuse, Pittsburgh, Louisville, Rutgers, and Notre Dame. Of course, Notre Dame has always had a special status as a football independent.

42. Auerbach (2012). The seven universities were DePaul, Georgetown, Marquette Providence, St. John's, Seton Hall, and Villanova. In the ever-changing world of major conferences, these schools were to form an elite basketball league after the 2012–2013 season and retain the "Big East" name. Connecticut was among the four schools left floundering in the former Big East.

43. E.g., Rhoads (2004). Rhoads's research suggested that while competitive imbalance in a conference in regard to football may lead to churning to create more balance in football, it may not reduce competitive imbalance in basketball. The fact that conferences may be more concerned about being strong and nationally competitive in football than in basketball reflects the greater revenue potential of football than basketball. Of course, football is also a more expensive sport for individual institutions.

44. See, e.g., Mandel (2012) and Dodd (2012).

45. Fusfeld (2011) used data reported to the U.S. Department of Education for his statistical analysis.

46. Kramer and Trivette presented their work in a paper at the annual meeting of the Association for Institutional Research in 2012. The study was reported by Wolverton (2012a).

47. McGee (2011). This idea of super conferences figures prominently in the reform vision for big-time college sports that I present in chapter 7.

48. Grasgreen (2012c).

49. See Wieberg and Berkowitz (2011).

50. Quoted by Wieberg and Berkowitz (2011).

51. Wieberg and Berkowitz (2011) quoted Louis Caldera, who was president of the University of New Mexico from 2003 to 2006.

52. The Rose Bowl had a separate contract with ABC from 2007 to 2014, which paid $30 million each for ten games, including eight Rose Bowls and two BCS title games. Its reputation as the "Granddaddy of All Bowl Games" and its past relationship with ABC help explain why it was able to negotiate its own deal with ABC. See Martzke (2004).

53. These figures appeared in Grasgreen (2012c). Note that contracting with ESPN might create an access problem for some less affluent football viewers, since ESPN is a subscription cable network. See Tillman (2008).

54. Maloney (2011).

55. Some conferences did better than others. See, e.g., C. Smith (2012a, 2012b) about the ACC's media rights deal with ESPN and how it compared less favorably to TV deals made by other elite conferences. According to Smith, the ACC gave away more rights to attractive games than the other major conferences did and also made less money from its deal with ESPN. This less favorable deal caused speculation that top schools in the ACC, such as Florida State would try to find another conference with a better TV deal.

56. See Wieberg and Berkowitz (2011).

57. NCAA (2010).

58. Berkowitz (2012c).

59. NCAA (2010).

60. NCAA (2010).

61. Sawchik (2011). Articles by Tillman (2008) and Horrow and Swatek (2010) and from ESPN (2011b) and information from the Bowl Championship Series (BCS) website also provided information for this discussion of television money and college sports.

62. See evidence cited by Clotfelter (2011, pp. 78–79).

63. According to one of the biggest sports licensing firms, the Collegiate Licensing Company (CLC), the market for collegiate licensed merchandise was $4 billion in 2011. The CLC reports that its sports licensing business links together colleges, universities, athletic confer-

ences, bowl games, and other entities in college sports. Thus, the retail business of selling licensed sports gear to the public depends on its ties to members of the IGT. For more information about the CLC, see its website www.clc.com.

64. See Crupi (2011).

65. George Washington University (2012). Also see Berkowitz (2009) for an overview of the recent rise of IMG's power in college sports.

66. Berkowitz (2009).

67. See Capitol Broadcasting Company (2010), which reported a seven-year contract between Nike and Alabama for $3.75 million per year and a contract for eight years between Adidas and the University of Michigan for $8.3 million per year. Michigan had been a Nike customer.

Chapter 3 · The Business of College Sports

1. "The" golden triangle consists of a collection many loosely or tightly linked golden triangles organized around different commercialized sports in different locations with their own relationships to the media and corporate sponsors. They may have common or competing interests, just as members of a particular golden triangle may have different or competing interests. See Nixon (2008, pp. 24–25).

2. Knight Commission (2006). Research over the past twenty to twenty-five years has tested these kinds of beliefs. In one study, involving 233 institutions competing at the highest FBS and FCS levels of college football, D. R. Smith (2009) concluded that the positive effects of on-field success on the academic quality of entering classes over a twelve-year period were overshadowed by the more powerful effects of the enduring cultures and traditions associated with football at a school.

3. Among self-identified sports fans, this last number was 57 percent.

4. See Knight Commission (2006, nn. 2–5).

5. E.g., see Bennet (2012).

6. See Kerr (2001). This is the fifth edition of the classic *The Uses of the University*, which was first published in 1963.

7. There has not been much research about university governing boards, but Slaughter and Rhoades (2004) found a strong connection between sitting on corporate boards of directors and being on governing boards of major research universities.

8. On one of the campuses where I was a faculty member, a faculty colleague led a protest for several years to oppose building a new convocation center, which was to include a new basketball arena. His group had environmental, economic, and philosophical concerns. He was able to rally students, faculty members, and members of the community to lobby legislators on this issue. He ultimately lost his battle when a new president was hired and skillfully circumvented the opposition and got approval for construction of the center. A portion of the construction costs and annual operating costs were funded by state taxpayers.

9. Marklein (2012) reports on recent cases of college presidents at public universities who had been fired or forced to resign as a result of disagreements with boards.

10. In an interesting twist, the faculty senate effectively mobilized opposition to the board firing of a popular president at the University of Virginia in 2012. She was dismissed by business-minded board members in part because she was not entrepreneurial enough. Be-

cause of strong and widespread faculty opposition, the decision was reversed. I do not think that the president's stance or the faculty senate's effectiveness is typical for major research or comprehensive universities today. This case created a lot of public discussion about tensions between boards and presidents, which often pit business logic against traditional academic values.

11. Clotfelter (2011).

12. See Stone's (1955) classic piece on the transformation of sport from pure play into an entertainment spectacle.

13. See Clotfelter's (2011, pp. 85–90) data and analysis concerning advertising and the commercial value of televised sports.

14. See Clotfelter (2010; 2011, pp. 204–206).

15. Clotfelter (2011, pp. 38, 41–42) cited evidence showing that relatively few institutions with big-time sports programs included athletics in their formal mission statements or attributed any significant role to athletics in public pronouncements about major institutional purposes, initiatives, or achievements of the university. He argued that it was time for universities to be more explicit about the role of commercialized athletics on campus and to include it formally within their mission statements (p. 206).

16. This is how the festival describes itself. It is part of the internationally known Aspen Institute. See the festival website www.aspenideas.org/festival.

17. Bok (2003).

18. Newfield (2008, pp. 227–236).

19. Realms such as athletics may be called *self-support*, but relatively few athletic departments fully cover their expenses from external revenue sources. The norm is substantial subsidization by the university. As such, most athletic departments would be viewed as failures in strictly business or capitalistic terms.

20. Kirp (2003, p. 3). Slaughter and Leslie (1997, pp. 9–11) used the term academic capitalism to refer to the significant and growing influence of market forces in higher education. See also Slaughter and Rhoades (2004).

21. Clotfelter (2011, pp. 39–41).

22. Clotfelter (2011, p. 217).

23. Staples (2012).

24. According to the NCAA website (ncaa.org) section on athletic scholarships, the average annual value of a full athletic scholarship in 2009 for in-staters was $15,000 and for out-of-staters was $25,000. The average value of athletic scholarships at private institutions was $35,000.

25. See Staples (2012).

26. The session was moderated by ESPN correspondent Tom Farrey.

27. Branch (2011).

28. See, e.g., Nocera (2011a, 2011b).

29. See Bennet (2012).

30. Branch (2011) and Nocera (2011a) offered more elaborate and radical plans to pay Division I athletes. Zimbalist's (1999) book of "unpaid professionals" in the highly commercialized world of college sports remains one of the most thorough examinations of the roots of student-athlete exploitation issue.

31. Quoted by Staples (2012).

32. Quoted in Wieberg (2011a).

33. I am typically using the terms *athletic scholarship* and *grant-in-aid* interchangeably. The NCAA defines the grant-in-aid as financial aid based on athletic ability. Student-athletes in Division III are not permitted to receive athletically related financial aid. The NCAA stipulates the value of a full grant-in-aid but allows student-athletes to receive athletic grants-in-aid plus nonathletic financial aid including Pell Grants up to the cost of attendance. NCAA rules determine the types and amount of outside scholarship money received by student-athletes.

34. See Clotfelter (2011, p. 119).

35. Clotfelter (2011, p. 119).

36. See Grasgreen (2012e).

37. Wolverton (2012g). Notre Dame ultimately lost to the second-ranked team, Alabama, in the national championship game for the 2012 season. Alabama could not make such lofty academic claims.

38. See Nixon (2008, pp. 276–285) for an overview of extant knowledge about the academic performance of student-athletes.

39. Wolverton (2012h). Also see Nixon (2008, pp. 281–283) for a discussion of research about the racial gap in graduation rates.

40. According to the NCAA website (ncaa.org), the percentage of college football players who had become NFL players was 1.7 percent, and the percentage of men's basketball players who played professionally after college was 1.2 percent. Male hockey players (3.8 percent) and baseball players (8.9 percent) had a better chance of a pro sports career. The chances for women college basketball players was 0.9 percent. Professional sports careers are typically only a few years at most.

41. Adler and Adler's (1991) outstanding case study of the experiences of student-athletes in a big-time men's basketball program documented their role conflicts and their difficulties maintaining a serious academic commitment. Because their team was so successful, these young men developed an inflated and unrealistic sense of their talent and their likelihood of becoming professional basketball players. As a result, they were not well prepared for lives not involving basketball after their college sports careers ended.

42. I used this term in Nixon (2008, p. 285) to describe the pragmatic and often counterproductive way that big-time college athletes view their education.

43. The University of Notre Dame posted the NCAA definition of a *booster* on its athletics website (ncaacompliance.nd.edu/boosters.shtml). The term refers to individuals, agencies, or organizations known by a university to have been involved in promoting an institution's athletic program; to have made financial contributions to the athletic department or booster organization; to have been a season ticket holder; or to have given benefits to student-athletes, their families, or their friends.

44. Clotfelter (2011, pp. 142–144) looked at the guest lists of those who sat in the presidential box at football games in the 2008 season at the University of Washington, the University of Georgia, Texas A&M, Auburn, Florida State, Maryland, North Carolina, and NC State. The pattern was a common tendency to invite significant numbers of administrators and some faculty and many individuals from business and the professions, often presidents and CEOs of their companies.

45. Wolverton (2009).

46. Wolverton (2007) focused on the case of Appalachian State University, which became a football power in the FCS on the heels of an increased commitment to athletic fund raising. The new president who initiated a major athletic capital campaign stated that private donations were the only way to "close the gap between the programs at the top of college sports and the rest of us."

47. Chronicle (2009). Also see related article by Wolverton (2009).

48. Wolverton's (2009) drew from the *Chronicle* (2009) survey and other data in his examination of fundraising in big-time college sports.

49. Wolverton (2009).

50. Grasgreen's (2012b) report on research about athletic giving indicated that a major reason people donate to athletics is to get a tangible benefit such as game tickets. Bigger donors obviously want more than tickets.

51. See Wolverton (2009).

52. They also appreciate the financial rewards of being members of athletic boards or foundations. The Rams Club, the athletics foundation of the University of North Carolina at Chapel Hill reportedly paid its fifteen officers a total of $1.5 million several years ago (Fain 2007c).

53. ESPN (2011a).

54. Chronicle (2011).

55. See Fain's (2007c) and Rosenberg's (2011) reports of this case.

56. Reported in Grasgreen (2012b).

57. See Fain (2007c).

58. See Young's (2012) report of a statistical study by Michael Anderson about the benefits of college sports success, which was published by the *National Bureau of Economic Research*.

59. Sander (2011c).

60. Research by Tsitsos and Nixon (2011) showed a preponderance of public institutions among the football and men's basketball elite between 2003 and 2011, which is at odds with the preponderance of private institutions among the most highly ranked institutions in the *U.S. News & World Report* surveys.

Chapter 4 · The Arms Race, Inequalities, and the Pressures of the College Sports Business

1. Derber (2011) has written about the perversion of American values by the unrestrained pursuit of personal success at the expense of others. This kind of behavior can turn deviant as people try to win and be successful by any means necessary. This is a theme in the next chapter about deviance in college sports.

2. See Perko and Weiner (2009, chs. 2–3) for a report of NCAA data about typical expenses and revenues for the 119 FBS programs in 2007. Also see Clotfelter (2011, p. 98) for a model of the percentage breakdown of the key components of a typical athletic department, based on *USA Today* data from the 2007–2008 academic year.

3. The term *arms race* has frequently been used to refer to the pattern of escalating spending in college sport, and the existence of arms races regarding coaches' salaries and facilities has been well documented (e.g., see Orszag and Orszag 2005 and Orszag and Israel 2009).

4. Apparel, shoe, and equipment contracts have been controversial because they require

exclusive use of these items by university athletes and the display of company logos at athletic venues, in university publications, and on the shoes, clothing, or equipment used by athletes and coaches. These contracts have also been controversial because they have been lucrative for universities and many coaches but have provided no compensation to the athletes who use these items (Wieberg and Upton 2007).

5. Perko and Weiner (2009) provided a brief but informative overview of major financial issues in contemporary college athletics, including the arms race, under the auspices of the Knight Commission.

6. Bolton (2011) relied on 2009 data because that year was the most recent available when he wrote his article.

7. Bolton (2011).

8. Berkowitz and Upton (2011b); Isidore (2010).

9. We will look at some additional numbers from a *USA Today* database compiled from financial reports submitted to the NCAA. The numbers from this database were reported by Berkowitz and Upton (2011b). Their article is the basis for all of the numbers reported so far in this section. The NCAA report included information from public and private institutions, but Berkowitz and Upton focused mainly on the figures for the public institutions. Large public universities dominate the ranks of the big-time schools, especially in football.

10. Sander (2011a).

11. They were Penn State, Texas, Oklahoma, LSU, Texas A&M, Purdue, Nebraska, and Ohio State.

12. Baker (2010).

13. According to Wolverton (2012b), NCAA president Mark Emmert was being paid at a rate of approximately $1.6 million per year as NCAA president in 2010. As president of the University of Washington, his annual salary was $870,000.

14. Tsitsos and Nixon (2012).

15. Our salary database did not include information about several institutions, including the University of Southern California, Notre Dame, Stanford, and Brigham Young University, where coaches were likely to be highly paid. The 2011 *USA Today* database for football coaches put the Alabama coach behind the Texas coach, who was expected to earn nearly $5.2 million that year. See Brady, Upton, and Berkowitz (2011). Parenthetically, Saban moved past Brown in 2012 when his salary was bumped up to $5.5 million. Saban's team won the BCS championship game earlier in the year. See Berkowitz (2012b) and *USA Today*'s list of "Major-College Football Coaches Pay" in its November 20, 2012, issue (p. 8C Sports).

16. Moltz (2011).

17. Brady, Upton, and Berkowitz (2011).

18. Brady, Berkowitz, and Upton (2012).

19. Moltz (2011). According to the *USA Today* salary database for 2012 (March 29, p. 4C), the pay for the Louisville coach was $4.8 million, without the extravagant bonus he received the year before. The Duke coach's pay increased to $4.7 million from the previous year. However, both coaches were surpassed by the Kentucky coach's $5.4 million, which was a reward for winning the national championship.

20. See Langelett (2003) as well as the discussion of this research in Tsitsos and Nixon (2012).

21. See Perko and Weiner (2009, ch. 2) for a discussion of escalating coaches' salaries and the "social psychology" behind what drives athletic directors to spend "what it takes." Also see Sanserino (2011), who reports on the continuing escalation of coaches' salaries in the "star wars arms race."

22. Wolken (2012).

23. Gardner (2012) cites the research of Adler, Berry, and Doherty (2012), which found these patterns.

24. Moltz (2011).

25. Berkowitz and Upton (2011a). These figures are from *USA Today*'s first survey of women's basketball coach compensation. The coaches in their database were at the thirty-three institutions that had played in at least four of the previous five NCAA women's tournaments, up to 2011. The reported results are based on twenty-six of these thirty-three schools, since no compensation data were available for coaches at seven institutions, which were mostly private and were not required to release such information. Among those with no data were the coaches of the usually highly ranked Stanford and Duke. Five cases had data missing for nonuniversity income. Of the twenty-one cases with complete data, two-thirds (fourteen) earned $8,500 or less in nonuniversity income.

26. *USA Today* was not able to find information about nonuniversity income for about one-third of the coaches in its database.

27. Berkowitz and Upton (2011a).

28. Moltz (2011).

29. Eichelberger (2011).

30. See Tsitsos and Nixon (2012) for data challenging this assumption.

31. Berkowitz and Upton (2011a).

32. See Berkowitz and Upton (2011d) and Upton and Berkowitz (2011). The five "million dollar" athletic directors were at Florida, Louisville, Texas, Wisconsin, and Ohio State. At Vanderbilt, the athletic director's responsibilities were incorporated into the hybrid job of vice chancellor for university affairs and athletics, general counsel, and university secretary for the university and medical center. David Williams, who occupied this position in 2011, was also a tenured law professor and earned $2.6 million for carrying out these assorted duties.

33. Upton and Berkowitz (2011).

34. See Perko and Weiner (2009, ch. 4).

35. See Bennett (2012), who referred to the "recession-proof" nature of this arms race. The examples I cite here are from his article.

36. Perko and Weiner (2009, ch. 4).

37. Reported by CollegeAthleticsClips.com from NCAA and institutional statistics cited in the *SportsBusiness Journal*, January 9, 2012.

38. Details about the Michigan Stadium renovation were reported by Carty (2010).

39. The source is the Equity in Athletics Data Analysis (EADA) Cutting Tool, ope.ed .gov/athletics/. This site is linked to the U.S. Department of Education's Federal Student Aid site. The data cited here were from 2010–2011.

40. Figures cited by Zang (2012).

41. See Woo (2012).

42. Quoted in Carty (2010).

43. King (2005).

44. The relentless upward budgetary pressure of the arms race is seen in data showing a continuing pattern of budgetary increases across the major athletic conferences. M. Smith (2011) presented statistics showing that four (ACC, Big 12, Big East, and Big Ten) of the top six conferences had or were projected to have average double-digit budgetary increases, from 10.1 to 14.6 percent between FY2010 and FY2012. The expected increases for the other two conferences, the Pac-12 and SEC, were 9.1 and 8.4 percent, respectively.

45. Figures are from Moltz (2011).

46. See Tsitsos and Nixon (2012).

47. D. R. Smith (2009).

48. See Woo (2012).

49. Quoted in Moltz (2010), who uses the cases of Eastern Michigan University (of the Mid-American Conference) and the University of Michigan (of the Big Ten) to illustrate what it means to be a "have-not" (Eastern Michigan) as opposed to a "have" (Michigan).

50. Moltz (2010).

51. Berkowitz and Upton (2011c); Grasgreen (2011a).

52. Grasgreen (2011a).

53. Grasgreen (2012g).

54. Rutgers faced new challenges in 2013 with public revelations of a videotape showing verbal and physical abuse of players by the men's basketball coach. The videotape became known to athletic officials around the time Rutgers was seeking Big Ten membership. When the tape surfaced later, public reaction was quick and harsh, resulting in the firing of the coach. As a result of their relatively mild disciplining of the coach and general mishandling of this case, the athletic director and the university's senior lawyer resigned. Following the basketball scandal, the university initiated a comprehensive review of practices in its athletic department. Its first casualty was the men's lacrosse coach, who was suspended for allegedly verbally abusing his players. Rutgers obviously was finding its attempted rise up the sports hierarchy a slippery climb.

55. See Upton and Gillum (2010) and Upton, Berkowitz, and Gillum (2010). According to U.S. Department of Education EADA data, the discrepancy was greater in the following fiscal year, with Maryland spending $57.5 million and Towson spending $18.5 million.

56. Giannotto (2012).

57. See Grasgreen (2011b) and Giannotto (2012). The deficit was figured by subtracting university subsidies from the athletic budget.

58. Sander (2011b).

59. Schoenenberger (2011).

60. Schoenenberger (2011) suggested the interesting financial arrangements made between big-time athletic programs and corporate sponsors in the IGT. The multimedia corporation Comcast contributed $55 million toward the construction of the $110 million basketball arena. In return, it received naming rights—for the "Comcast Arena"—and the right to collect mandatory Comcast cable fees from each resident student. Unlike the university, its corporate partner was virtually assured that its investment would be fully repaid.

61. In an effort to generate more revenue, Maryland hired its popular and recently retired men's basketball coach to serve as a fundraiser, paying him $400,000 per year, apparently re-

flecting the belief that high-priced stars were needed to attract big donors in the institutional and athletic fundraising games (Barker [2011]).

62. Milhoces (2012).

63. McMillen (2012). Also see Prewitt (2012).

64. A commentary in the *Chronicle of Higher Education* is an example of his criticism of big-time college sports (McMillen, 2011).

65. Korman (2012).

66. McMillen (2012).

67. My insights about Towson University athletics are informed by my prior experience as the faculty athletics representative and my continuing tenure as an elected faculty member of the Intercollegiate Athletics Committee, which reports to the University Senate. I also relied on a steady stream of local news publications about the case.

68. Towson has a few applied doctoral programs in educational technology, information technology, audiology, and occupational therapy.

69. These statistics are from the *USA Today* College Athletics Finances database for 2006–2011.

70. Walker and Murray (2011).

71. The CAA has had several national FCS champions in football and has also placed two basketball teams, George Mason and Virginia Commonwealth, in the men's basketball Final Four.

72. Quotes from Walker and Murray (2011).

73. Quoted in Walker and Murray (2011).

74. Breazeale (2011).

75. Markus and Karpovich (2012).

76. This story continued to evolve beyond the details reported here. Political pressure from the governor and state comptroller, who were critical of the program cuts, produced some curious twists in this case. They raised concerns about the reportedly perfunctory and impersonal way the baseball and soccer players were informed by the president of their fate. They demanded that the president appear before them to explain her actions. After his own meeting with the president, the governor proposed a plan to give the university $300,000 to help save baseball—but not men's soccer—and another proposal surfaced to provide more than $2 million in funding for a women's softball field to help address Title IX concerns. Parenthetically, for a variety of reasons, supporters of the baseball team were more able than their soccer counterparts to mount a visible and effective lobbying campaign. The story continued to develop into the late spring 2013. The legislature set aside money for the University System of Maryland rather than specifically for Towson University. This may have been in response to the comptroller's claim that the $300,000 was a "bailout" of the university and baseball with public funds. The legislature also approved the funds for the softball facility. The political sparks kept flying, with the comptroller calling for the president's resignation after she failed to meet with him, the president refusing to resign, and the university engaging in a well-orchestrated public relations campaign in the media to counter the negative publicity that had arisen. This case illustrates how much the athletic trap can complicate the life and work of college presidents at institutions aspiring to push their athletic profile further into the big time. The most recent development as this book went to press was the departure

of the athletic director, who accepted a new position as a senior associate athletic director at the University of Arkansas. Thus, he got what he needed from his stint at Towson, a chance to move another step up the big-time college sports hierarchy. But he left behind a legacy of disruption as well as accomplishment.

77. See Knight Commission (2009) and Shipley (2009).

78. Knight Commission (2009). The study had an impressive response rate. There were 119 FBS members at the time, and the presidents of 95 of these institutions participated in a ten-minute phone interview. This was the quantitative part of the study. In the qualitative phase, 71 of the 95 presidents responding to the phone interviews also participated in a more open-ended interview, which averaged forty-five minutes. The extent and rate of participation reflected both the respect for the Knight Commission and the concerns that these presidents had about college sports or their programs.

79. Lederman, Kiley, and Jaschik (2012).

80. These findings regarding budget cutting priorities and strategies were from the first annual *Inside Higher Ed* survey of presidents in 2011, which was reported by Green, Jaschik, and Lederman (2011) .

81. See Bennett (2012).

82. See the discussion of Anderson's (2012) work in chapter 3.

83. See Tsitsos and Nixon (2012).

84. Sawchik (2011) raised the question of whether a financial bubble was forming as television contracts continued to escalate to levels far exceeding the real economic value of the investments. Real economic value is the actual return on investment that investors realize in the future. The implication is that since financial bubbles burst, the financial structure of big-time college sports today could be on a shaky foundation.

85. See Shiller's (2000) book about *irrational exuberance* among Wall Street investors. The term was coined by former Federal Reserve chairman Alan Greenspan.

Chapter 5 · Deviance, Corruption, and Scandals in College Sports

1. Lederman (2011).

2. CBSSports.com published a five-part series focusing on the pattern of repeated cheating in the history of big-time college sports. See, e.g., Dodd's (2011) lead article in this series.

3. The list includes Georgia Tech, Indiana University, Ohio State University, Purdue University, Rutgers University, University of Arizona, University of California at Berkeley, University of Colorado, University of Georgia, University of Illinois, University of Iowa, University of Kansas, University of Maryland, University of Michigan, University of Minnesota, University of Missouri, University of Oklahoma, University of Oregon, University of Southern California, University of Texas, University of Washington, and University of Wisconsin. The University of North Carolina and the University of Miami were among those institutions that joined the list in the next two years.

4. Miringoff, Carvalho, and Azzoli (2012).

5. Pilon (2011). In a parallel move, penalized schools such as Ohio State have beefed up their compliance staff to try to stay out of trouble. Their annual compliance budget in 2012 was $1.1 million (Wolverton, 2012i).

6. Thamel (2011). In 2012 the NCAA revamped its enforcement structure, which created more levels of violations, streamlined investigations to make them more efficient, increased penalties for the worst offenders, and put more responsibility on coaches to get their staff members to be more attentive to NCAA rules (Brown, 2012). Some worried that the richer schools would have more resources to argue for less serious sanctions (Wolverton, 2012e).

7. The primary source for the description of this case is Charles Robinson's (2011) lengthy and carefully researched exposé for *Yahoo! Sports.*

8. Wetzel (2011).

9. Federal Bureau of Investigation (2012).

10. Garvin (2011).

11. Quoted by Robinson (2011).

12. E. Smith (2011).

13. Miami's record in football was 6–6 in 2011. It was not permitted to play in a bowl game. In the previous two seasons, the team's record was 9–4 (2009) and 7–6 (2010), with bowl game losses. Except for 2009, these are not the records that devoted fans and boosters expect from a University of Miami football team, which created more pressure to do what was necessary to win.

14. Forde (2011).

15. Foote and Shalala were quoted in Wolff (2011).

16. Quoted in Robinson (2011).

17. Basken (2011).

18. Albany, Buffalo, and Stony Brook all competed at the Division I level.

19. Thamel (2009a) reported the recognition and regret associated with Binghamton's rapid rise in athletics. I draw from his report to describe reactions to the move to Division I.

20. Brady and Wieberg (2009) and Thamel (2009a, 2009b, 2010a, 2010b, 2012) provide excellent background about this case, and I have relied on these articles, along with a commissioned report by Judith Kaye (2010), for my description and analysis. Kaye's report was prepared for the Board of Trustees and chancellor of the State University of New York, and it clearly and thoroughly documents the facts of this case.

21. See Kaye (2010).

22. See SUNY (2010). Binghamton was expected to reimburse SUNY for 50 percent of the cost.

23. Brady and Wieberg (2009) also pointed out that one other school moved up to Division I and then dropped back down for financial reasons and that another moved up and then decided to drop athletics.

24. Quoted in Brady and Wieberg (2009).

25. Sander (2011d).

26. Binghamton had lost twenty-seven consecutive games, starting with the final game of the previous season, before winning a game in the 2011–2012 season. At the time of its victory, it was the only Division I men's team without a win that season.

27. Thamel (2012).

28. Freeh (2012).

29. See Proffitt and Corrigan's (2012) analysis of how the "success with honor" idea was

related to the institutional structures and brand logic that blocked disclosure in the Penn State scandal.

30. Potuto (2012).

31. There were many news stories about this case in *USA Today* and in newspapers around the country. The *Chronicle of Higher Education* and *Inside Higher Ed* also published thoughtful stories and commentaries. *Sports Illustrated* provided bookend cover stories, "The Failure and Shame of Penn State" in November 2011 (McCallum, 2011; Verducci, 2011; and Wertheim and Epstein, 2011) and "We Were Penn State" in late July 2012, after the release of the Freeh Report (Freeh, 2012) and the imposition of sanctions by the NCAA (Wolff, 2012). The college sports clipping service, College Athletics Clips, regularly reported and published articles about this case from a wide range of sources.

32. Quoted in Lash, Hall, and Darragh (2012).

33. It appears that the athletic staff was generally unaware of the Clery Act, which required college employees to report to the police information about possible crimes such as Sandusky's acts.

34. Wolverton (2012c).

35. See Wertheim and Epstein (2011, p. 46) about Penn State. The results of the entire *Sports Illustrated/CBS News* investigation were reported by Dohrmann and Benedict (2011).

36. Quoted in Fitzpatrick (2012).

37. *Sports Illustrated* senior writer Alexander Wolff (2011) called for the end of the Miami football program in 1995 and again in 2011 in letters to the university's president prominently featured in his magazine.

38. Eder (2012).

39. An interesting footnote to his story is that at a time in January 2011 when Paterno became aware of the criminal investigation of Sandusky, he negotiated a $3 million deal to finish coaching at the end of the upcoming season instead of in 2012 as his contract stipulated (Becker, 2012).

40. Rohan (2012a).

41. Price (2012).

42. See Wieberg (2011b).

43. See Grasgreen (2011c).

44. Smiley (2012).

45. Cited in Wolff (2012).

46. Wolff (2012).

47. M. Smith (2011).

48. Wolverton (2012f).

49. Cited by Van Natta (2012).

50. Moran (2012).

51. See Hutchens (2009). Brand died in 2009.

52. See DeCourcy (2010).

53. See Littwin (1985).

54. USA Today (2012).

55. Aubrey (2012).

56. CBSSports (2012). Nearly one hundred coaches were interviewed by CBSSport.com's college basketball staff.

57. Quoted in Barra (2012).

58. However, Calipari and other coaches have a vested interest in getting players who leave early to do so in good academic standing. They do not want to run afoul of the NCAA academic progress rate (APR), which is meant to anticipate graduation rates by measuring academic eligibility and retention. If their team has a substandard APR, they will face NCAA sanctions, including of loss of scholarships, postseason opportunities, and ultimately their NCAA membership status. The seriousness depends on how many years their team fails to meet the APR standard.

59. Branch (2011).

60. Bazerman and Tenbrunsel (2011).

61. Bartlett (2011).

62. These observations from the Freeh Report were reported by Belson (2012).

Chapter 6 · Control and Reform in Big-Time College Sports

1. See Duderstadt and Womack's (2003, pp. 18–19, ch. 8) discussion of governance and governing boards.

2. Wolverton and Fuller (2012).

3. See Kiley (2012b).

4. Duderstadt and Womack (2003, p. 137). Duderstadt was the president of the University of Michigan and Womack was the chief financial officer at Michigan and the University of North Carolina.

5. See, e.g., Hersh and Merrow (2005).

6. Spellings (2006).

7. Hacker and Dreifus (2010) presented a scholarly but especially harsh recent critique of both higher education and big-time athletics. They said that all institutions sponsoring intercollegiate athletics were infected with a "virus." They argued that commercialization in athletics had compromised academic integrity and the moral authority of educators, and consumed resources that could have been used for more academic pursuits (p. 156).

8. See Green, Jaschik, and Lederman (2011); Lederman, Kiley, and Jaschik (2012).

9. See Sander (2009).

10. Knight Commission (2009).

11. Knight Commission (2009).

12. Dodd (2012).

13. See Peterson (2008). Harry L. Peterson was the president emeritus of a small college in Colorado who had been a senior administrator at the big-time University of Wisconsin. He wrote an opinion piece for the *Chronicle of Higher Education* about "Why Presidents Fail—and How They Can Succeed." He wrote that presidents often arrived on the job with limited understanding of athletic administration or in some cases of intercollegiate athletics.

14. See Powers (2008). While presidents may benefit from experience with athletics, it appears that institutions hiring athletic directors are becoming more impressed with a resume built in the business world than with experience only in athletics administration (Thomas, 2010).

15. Quoted in Lederman, Kiley, and Jaschik (2012). Kirwan got caught in his own athletic trap when he was involved in the Maryland regents' decision to back the University of Maryland's money-driven move to the Big Ten. He was on record as a frequent critic of commercialism in college sports, and he recognized that financial factors drove this move. However, he also wanted to support the Maryland president and improve the financial status of its athletic program. Thus, he failed to take a strong stand against the move and did not join regent Tom McMillen in his public outcry about the secret process the board used in making this decision (Grasgreen, 2012f).

16. Dobel (2012) argued that the Penn State case showed that coaches become more powerful than the campus president because coaches are paid more, are better known to the public, and are treated more as celebrities and symbols of the university than the president is.

17. See Wickersham's (2011) profile of Gordon Gee.

18. Tkach (2012) cited data from the *Chronicle of Higher Education* annual survey of public university presidents in his report. Spanier's pay was about one-third of the amount Joe Paterno was to be paid at the end of the 2011 season if he agreed to step down at that time. This contractual arrangement was negotiated in the midst of the brewing Sandusky scandal but before the scandal became public and Paterno was fired (Becker, 2012). Spanier received a very extravagant golden parachute when he was fired in 2011. He reportedly was paid $3.3 million in salary, severance, and deferred compensation (Stripling, 2012).

19. Dohrmann and Epstein (2011).

20. Quoted in Wickersham (2011).

21. Gee was quite extravagant in his discretionary spending to court prospective donors. According to OSU records, between October 2007 and the end of June 2012, he spent $1.09 million for travel, $813,000 for tailgating, and $2.17 million for special events as well as $1.6 million for his office expenses and $2.1 million for the operation of his 9,600-square-foot presidential mansion. By comparison, the president of the University of Texas spent $310,000 for travel and entertainment between 2007 and 2011, and the University of Michigan president spent $410,000 on travel and entertainment during this period. The Texas president ($663,000) and the Michigan president ($860,782) earned far less than Gee's $1.9 million. The Ohio State endowment slipped from twenty-seventh to thirty-first nationally during Gee's tenure and ranked behind the endowments of Northwestern, Minnesota, and Michigan in the Big Ten. See Bischoff (2012).

22. Knight Commission (1991).

23. Wickersham (2011).

24. Gee (2005, p. 12).

25. Gee (2005, p. 13).

26. Vanderbilt continues to strive for success at the highest levels of football and men's basketball, though.

27. See Selingo (2007) and Fain (2010).

28. See Selingo (2007).

29. More than 80 percent of board members in the *Chronicle* survey reported meeting two to four times a year (Selingo, 2007, p. A20).

30. See, e.g., Stripling (2011).

31. See Fain (2007b) in Selingo's (2007) survey article.

32. See Fain (2007a).

33. Grasgreen (2012d).

34. According to its website (agb.org), the AGB is the only national association representing the interests and serving the needs of academic governing boards, foundation boards, and campus CEOs and other high-level campus administrators on issues concerning higher-education governance and leadership. Its stated mission is "to strengthen, protect, and advocate on behalf of citizen trusteeship that supports and advances higher education."

35. I focus on the 2009 document, which can be found on the AGB website, and in Lederman's (2009) article about the board role in athletics spelled out by the AGB.

36. They were general oversight responsibilities, presidential leadership, the mission of the athletic department, fiscal responsibility, academics and the welfare of student-athletes, compliance with NCAA rules, personnel, and communications.

37. Knight Commission (2010).

38. Their accountability document stated that boards should support bold moves by presidents that were consistent with the overall institutional mission; require that athletic departments develop mission statements consistent with the institutional mission; be sure that their institution was investing in athletics at a level they could afford and that salaries of athletic personnel, such as coaches and athletic director, were in line with compensation elsewhere in the institution; and ensure that student-athletes received adequate academic support but were treated overall like other students in admissions and in the classroom.

39. Casteen and Legon (2012). The survey of presidents was by email in the spring 2012. The 143 presidents who responded represented around 42 percent of the Division I institutions. Three additional, smaller surveys generated responses from fifteen system heads, nine system board chairs, and twenty-five other board chairs. The survey featured the responses from the presidents' survey. Presidents and board chairs agreed on most issues.

40. Casteen and Legon (2012, pp. 6–7).

41. Casteen and Legon (2012, p. 7).

42. See Lederman (2009).

43. Casteen and Legon (2012, p. 3).

44. Kiley (2012a).

45. In a study for AGB, Schwartz (2010) found that 15 percent of private institutions and 13 percent of public institutions had faculty trustees with voting power. An additional 14 percent of private institutions and 10 percent of public institutions had nonvoting faculty trustees. A survey of faculty trustees by the Cornell University Higher Education Research Institute (Ehrenberg, Patterson, and Key, 2012) showed a limited amount of self-perceived influence, especially outside the area of academic affairs. Athletics was not explicitly mentioned as an area of influence.

46. Knight Commission (2007).

47. See, e.g., Sperber (1991, 2001). Yost (2010) and Branch (2011) emphasize the exploitation of student-athletes in this entertainment industry in their critiques of big-time college sports.

48. Wolverton (2010).

49. Schackner (2007).

50. Lederman (2012).

51. Branch (2012).

52. Feinstein (2011).

Chapter 7 · Reforming College Sports

1. Among the many serious and thoughtful publications of the Knight Commission on Intercollegiate Athletics (Knight Commission) over the past decade are Knight Commission (2001, 2006, 2007, 2009, 2010) as well as Friday and Hesburgh (2001) and Perko and Weiner (2009).

2. Maisel (2012).

3. Wilson (2012). Many on campus were also unhappy that the NCAA had used the Freeh Report as the basis of its actions. They thought the penalties were excessive and the characterization of the campus culture as a culture of reverence was oversimplified. Protesters called for the resignation of the governor, university president, and members of the board of trustees in a rally at the beginning of the 2012 school year (Tully 2012).

4. Green, Jaschik, and Lederman (2011).

5. Sack (2012).

6. See the Drake Group website (www.thedrakegroup.org). This organization disseminates information, contributes opinion pieces, and lobbies in various other ways to try to assure a quality education for college athletes. It also supports outspoken faculty and faculty whistle-blowers who have endangered their job security by raising academic issues and problems in athletics. Along with the Coalition on Intercollegiate Athletics (COIA), it has been the most prominent faculty voice for change in the college sports reform movement. See Benford (2007) for an overview of the role of the Drake Group and COIA in this movement.

7. Groves (2012) wrote about the blurring of this line in a game between football powers Alabama and Michigan that was played at the opening of the 2012 season in Cowboys Stadium, home of the NFL Dallas Cowboys. He argued that, although these teams would have made as much money playing in their own mammoth stadiums, there was a certain cachet that was associated with playing in a venue that was the most spectacularly glitzy and high-tech stadium in professional sports and was the home of one of the legendary NFL franchises. This game reflects the nature of big-time college sports in its detachment from the home bases of both competitors in the interest of impressing the fans and boosters who could afford to attend as well as future recruits.

8. Cited in Lederman (2012).

9. See, e.g., McCann's (2012) story about the lawsuit against the NCAA's licensing of names, images, and likenesses of big-time college athletes without their permission or compensation.

10. Clotfelter (2011) discussed various types of hypothetical reform scenarios in the concluding pages of his book under the title "Prescriptions for Reform." He saw the most realistic as more of an accommodation than reform. It would begin with a formal acknowledgment in the institutional mission statement of the importance to the campus of commercialized sports. He thought that this acknowledgment would lead to a more open and fruitful discussion of how to integrate big-time athletics into the academic enterprise and how to deal with its excesses and problems while retaining its benefits as entertainment.

11. Wieder (2013).

12. See the IOC website (www.olympic.org/athletes-commission) for information about this commission.

13. Estler and Nelson (2005, p. 3).

14. Feinstein (2011) cited Krzyzewski's ideas for reform in an article evocatively called "Fixing College Sports Requires Less Talk, More Action."

15. Lederman (2012).

16. I assume that following the implementation of this model, the New NCAA would simply be called the "NCAA." It would embody the principles the NCAA has always said it valued. I use "New NCAA" here to avoid confusion between the current organization and the new one I am proposing.

17. The idea of reconfiguring college sports along these lines is not entirely new. See, e.g., Lederman (2012).

18. Wolverton (2012d) incorporated similar ideas into his model for reinventing college sports.

19. See Stevens (2007). Even sports teams of academically elite institutions such as Harvard may experience the fallout of big-time college sports. In 2012 an academic cheating scandal occurred at Harvard, and the co-captains of the men's basketball team were reportedly implicated in it. The basketball team had achieved its first ranking in the top twenty-five in 2012 season and earned its first trip to the NCAA tournament in sixty-six years (see Pennington, 2012).

20. Clotfelter (2010, 2011).

21. The 400 targeted subscribers included 55 presidents, 135 athletic directors, 15 conference commissioners, 40 other conference executives, 60 faculty athletics representatives, 30 bowl executives, 25 Division I CFOs, and 40 others (Infante, 2012a).

22. The current March Madness field is sixty-eight teams, with a number of highly competitive teams waiting in the wings.

23. A legal expert proposed that a way to make NCAA enforcement more fair and effective would be to outsource investigations of major infractions to a law firm, investigative agency, or similar type of organization (Miller, 2012).

24. Division I schools significantly trimmed their rule book at the 2013 NCAA convention and deregulated recruiting to allow more flexibility and freedom in communication. However, the changes were thought mostly to benefit larger programs and to intensify the arms race. It shifted from a guiding philosophy of "competitive equity" making sure that one program did not have an advantage over another to "fairness of competition" in which teams do not have an advantage over their opponent in actual competition on the field. These changes were unlikely to change the basic commercial structure of college sports (see Grasgreen, 2013).

25. See Duderstadt and Womack (2003, pp. 116–117).

26. See Nixon (2008, pp. 263–265).

27. E.g., Lopiano (2005) argued that those unhappy with cuts to men's nonrevenue sports ostensibly to create more gender equity should redirect their criticism from women's sports to the most expensive men's sports, such as football. She argued that football (and men's

basketball) ate up a disproportionate amount of athletic budgets, hurting women but also men in nonrevenue sports.

Epilogue

1. I am borrowing from Zimbalist (1999) here. His "unpaid professionals" term refers to college athletes who are economically exploited by big-time college sports. This is a central focus of Branch's (2011) harsh critique of the "shame of college sports."

2. Pargman (2012) proposed that one way to end the "charade" of big-time athletes being students is to create a "sports performance major" with serious academic content but with an intrinsic appeal to students interested in a career playing, or perhaps coaching, sports. He was a retired professor of educational psychology at Florida State.

Adler, E. Scott, Michael J. Berry, and David Doherty. 2012. "Pushing 'Reset': The Conditional Effects of Coaching Replacements on College Football Performance." *Social Science Quarterly* 93, October 26. Retrieved November 29, 2012 (onlinelibrary.wiley.com).

Adler, Patricia A., and Peter Adler. 1991. *Backboards and Blackboards: College Athletes and Role Engulfment.* New York: Columbia University Press.

Anderson, Michael L. 2012. "The Benefits of Athletic Success: An Application of the Propensity Score Design with Instrumental Variables." *National Bureau of Economic Research.* Working Paper No. 18196, June.

Aris, Stephen. 1990. *Sportsbiz: Inside the Sports Business.* London: Hutchinson.

Aubrey, Will. 2012. "College Basketball: Kentucky's John Calipari Voted Biggest Cheater by His Peers." *Examiner.com*, August 12. Retrieved August 14, 2012 (www.examiner.com).

Auerbach, Nicole. 2012. "'Catholic 7' Announce Official Departure from Big East." *USA Today*, December 16. Retrieved December 16, 2012 (www.usatoday.com).

Baker, Linda. 2010. "Oregon's Poorly Funded Universities Revolt." *OregonBusiness*, February. Retrieved July 10, 2012 (www.oregonbusiness.com).

Barker, Jeff. 2011. "Gary Williams Gets Salary of $400,000." *Baltimore Sun*, August 24, p. 6 ("Sports").

Barra, Allen. 2012. "Both the NBA and the NCAA Want to Keep Athletes in College for Too Long." *Atlantic*, April 6. Retrieved August 14, 2012 (www.theatlantic.com).

Bartlett, Tom. 2011. "'Motivated Blindness': One Take on What Went Wrong at Penn State." *Chronicle of Higher Education*, November 25, p. A9.

Basken, Paul. 2011. "Miami's Shalala Has Track Record of Dealing Deftly with Controversy." *Chronicle of Higher Education*, August 25. Retrieved August 26, 2011 (www.chronicle.com).

Bauerlein, Mark. 2010. "'The Ivory Tower'—Who Does He Play For?" *Wall Street Journal*, January 22. Retrieved February 18, 2011 (online.wsj.com).

Bazerman Max E., and Ann E. Tenbrunsel. 2011. *Blind Spots: Why We Fail to Do What's Right and What to Do about It.* Princeton, NJ: Princeton University Press.

Becker, Jo. 2012. "Paterno Won Sweeter Deal Even as Scandal Played Out." *New York Times*, July 14. Retrieved August 8, 2012 (www.nytimes.com).

Belson, Ken. 2012. "Abuse Inquiry Faults Paterno and Others at Penn State." *New York Times*, July 12. Retrieved July 12, 2012 (www.nytimes.com).

Benford, Robert D. 2007. "The College Sports Reform Movement: Reframing the 'Edutainment' Industry." *Sociological Quarterly* 48: 1–28.

Bennet, James. 2012. "'Just Imperfect as Human Beings': How the NCAA Sees Itself and Its Future." *Atlantic*, June 28. Retrieved July 2, 2012 (theatlantic.com).

Bennett, Brian. 2012. "Arms Race Proves Recession-Proof." *ESPN.com*, June 14. Retrieved July 2, 2012 (espn.go.com).

Berkowitz, Steve. 2009. "IMG Jolts Campus Scene to Give Schools a Cash Boost." *USA Today*, April 2. Retrieved May 17, 2012 (www.usatoday.com).

———. 2012a. "College Football Bowl Game Attendance Takes a Dip." *USA Today*, January 4. Retrieved May 30, 2012 (www.usatoday.com).

———. 2012b. "Alabama Opens Bank to Make Nick Saban the Nation's Top-Paid Coach." *USA Today*, March 26. Retrieved March 27, 2012 (www.usatoday.com).

———. 2012c. "NCAA Assets Pass $500M, Including $260M Fund." *USA Today*, October 15. Retrieved October 22, 2012 (www.usatoday.com).

Berkowitz, Steve, and Jodi Upton. 2011a. "Salaries Dramatically Rise for Top Women's Basketball Coaches." *USA Today*, April 5. Retrieved April 11, 2011 (www.usatoday.com).

———. 2011b. "Athletic Departments See Surge Financially in Down Economy." *USA Today*, June 16. Retrieved August 11, 2011 (www.usatoday.com).

———. 2011c. "Rutgers Athletic Department Needs Fees, Funds to Stay Afloat." *USA Today*, June 28. Retrieved August 25, 2011 (www.usatoday.com).

———. 2011d. "Demands on College Ads Resemble CEO Challenges." *USA Today*, October 6. Retrieved October 14, 2011 (www.usatoday.com).

Betts, John R. 1974. *America's Sporting Heritage, 1850–1950*. Reading, MA: Addison-Wesley.

Bischoff, Laura A. 2012. "OSU President Expenses in the Millions." *Dayton Daily News*, September 22. Retrieved December 17, 2012 (www.daytondailynews.com).

Bok, Derek. 2003. *Universities in the Marketplace: The Commercialization of Higher Education*. Princeton, NJ: Princeton University Press.

Bolton, Jason. 2011. "College Football Elite Spend to Win." *Memphis Business Journal*, September 1. Retrieved October 4, 2011 (www.bizjournals.com/memphis/news).

Brady, Erik, Steve Berkowitz, and Jodi Upton. 2012. "'Average' Salary: $1.64 Million." *USA Today*, November 20, pp. 1A, 5A.

Brady, Erik, Jodi Upton, and Steve Berkowitz. 2011. "Salaries for College Football Coaches Back on Rise." *USA Today*, November 16. Retrieved November 21, 2011 (www.usatoday.com).

Brady, Erik, and Steve Wieberg. 2009. "Binghamton Mess a Recurring Tale for Schools' D-I Dreams." *USA Today*, October 13. Retrieved February 18, 2011 (www.usatoday.com).

Branch, Taylor. 2011. "The Shame of College Sports." *Atlantic*, October. Retrieved September 14, 2011 (www.theatlantic.com).

———. 2012. "The NCAA Entrenches Itself as Part of the Problem." *Chronicle of Higher Education*, August 1. Retrieved September 6, 2012 (www.chronicle.com).

Breazeale, Helene. 2011. "Letter: New Athletic Arena Is Absurd." *Towerlight*, April 17. Retrieved April 18, 2011 (www.thetowerlight.com).

Brown, Gary. 2012. "Board Adopts Tougher, More Efficient Enforcement Program." *NCAA*, October 30. Retrieved November 7, 2012 (www.ncaa.org).

Capitol Broadcasting Company. 2010. "Heels Second to Alabama on Nike Pay Scale." *wral sportsfan.com*, May 16. Retrieved August 11, 2011 (www.wralsportsfan.com).

Carey, Kevin. 2011. "The Dangerous Lure of the Research-University Model." *Chronicle of Higher Education*, February 25, pp. A32, A33.

Carty, Jim. 2010. "Renovated Michigan Stadium Is Set to Open." *New York Times*, September 3. Retrieved January 19, 2012 (www.nytimes.com).

Casteen, John T., and Richard D. Legon. 2012. *Trust, Accountability, and Integrity: Board Responsibilities for Intercollegiate Athletics*. Association of Governing Boards. Washington, DC, August 15. Retrieved October 10, 2012 (agb.org/reports/2012).

CBSSports. 2012. "Critical Coaches: Who Is Perceived to Be the Biggest Cheater in the Sport?" *CBSSports.com Eye on College Basketball*, August 10, 2012. Retrieved August 14, 2012 (www.cbssports.com).

Chronicle. 2000. "'One Plus Three': The Knight Commission's Legacy for College Athletics." *Chronicle of Higher Education*, June 16, p. A45.

———. 2009. "Fund Raising for Athletics in 6 Major Conferences." *Chronicle of Higher Education*, January 23. Retrieved January 23, 2009 (www.chronicle.com).

———. 2011. "If You Pay, Do You Get to Play?" *Chronicle of Higher Education*, "The Briefing," February 4, 2011, p. A3.

Clarke, Liz. 2011. "Maryland Athletic Department May Have to Cut Sports to Address Budget Shortfall." *Washington Post*, August 19. Retrieved August 22, 2011 (www.washingtonpost.com).

Clotfelter, Charles T. 2010. "Commentary: Is Sports in Your Mission Statement?" *Chronicle of Higher Education*, October 24. Retrieved November 30, 2010 (www.chronicle.com).

———. 2011. *Big-Time Sports in American Universities*. New York: Cambridge University Press.

College Football. 1996. "College Football; Its Power Eroding, C.F.A. Will Disband." *New York Times*, June 1. Retrieved June 4, 2012 (www.nytimes.com).

Cornwell, Rupert. 2011. "Unlike Our Boat Race, US College Sport Is Big Business." *Independent*, March 27. Retrieved March 28, 2011 (www.independent.co.uk).

Crupi, Anthony. 2011. "March Madness Still One of the Biggest Sports Franchises." *Adweek*, March 1. Retrieved February 2, 2012 (www.adweek.com).

Dailey, Phil. 2012. "UC San Diego's Move to Division I Gets 'No' Vote." *La Jolla Light*, March 27. Retrieved June 2, 2012 (www.lajollalight.com).

Davis, Seth. 2011. "Should College Athletes Be Paid? They Already Are." *SI.com*, September 21. Retrieved September 30, 2011 (sportsillustrated.cnn.com).

DeCourcy, Mike. 2010. "A Look Back at Bob Huggins' Final Years at Cincinnati." *Sporting News*, February 1. Retrieved August 14, 2012 (aol.sportingnews.com).

Deford, Frank. 2005. "America's Modern Peculiar Institution." Pp. 145–154 in *Declining by Degrees: Higher Education at Risk*, edited by R. H. Hersh and J. Merrow. New York: Palgrave and Macmillan.

Derber, Charles. 2011. *The Wilding of America: Money, Mayhem, and the New American Dream*. 5th ed. New York: Worth Publishers.

Dobel, J. Patrick. 2012. "Penn State: When Coaches Are More Powerful than College Presidents." *Point of the Game: Conversations on Sports, Ethics and Culture*, July 13. Retrieved July 16, 2012 (pointofthegame, blogspot.com).

Dodd, Dennis. 2011. "Championships without Cheating? History Is against It." *CBSSports. com*, July 6. Part 1 of 5-part series. Retrieved July 18, 2011 (cbssports.com).

———. 2012. "Considering Their Track Record, Don't Expect Presidents to Get Playoff Right." *CBSSports.com*, June 19. Retrieved June 20, 2012 (cbssports.com).

Dohrmann, George, and Jeff Benedict. 2011. "Sports Illustrated and CBS News Special Report: Rap Sheets, Recruits and Repercussions." *Sports Illustrated*, March 7, pp. 31–39.

Dohrmann, George, with David Epstein. 2011. "The Fall of Jim Tressel." *Sports Illustrated*, June 6, pp. 40–48.

Duderstadt, James J. 2000a. "Some Observations on the Current State and the Future of Intercollegiate Athletics." Presented to the Knight Commission, October 18, Washington, DC. Retrieved April 13, 2004 (milproj.ummu.umich.edu/publications/knight_commis sion/index.html).

———. 2000b. *Intercollegiate Athletics and the American University: A University President's Perspective*. Ann Arbor: University of Michigan Press.

Duderstadt, James J., and Farris W. Womack. 2003. *The Future of the Public University in America: Beyond the Crossroads*. Baltimore: Johns Hopkins University Press.

Durkin, Erin. 2012. "Small Athletics Budgets Makes NCAA Division I Play a Challenge." *USA Today*, May 15. Retrieved May 31, 2012 (www.usatoday.com).

Eder, Steve. 2012. "Former Penn State President Is Charged in Sandusky Case." *New York Times*, November 1. Retrieved November 2, 2012 (www.nytimes.com).

Edwards, Harry. 1973. *Sociology of Sport*. Homewood, IL: Dorsey Press.

Ehrenberg, Ronald G., Richard Patterson, and Andrew Key. 2012. *Faculty Members on Boards of Trustees: The 2012 Cornell Higher Education Research Institute Survey of Faculty Trustees*. Cornell Higher Education Research Institute. Retrieved December 18, 2012 (www.ilr .cornell.edu).

Eichelberger, Curtis. 2011. "Women Basketball Programs Lose Money as Salaries Break College Budgets." *Bloomberg*, April 1. Retrieved April 4, 2011 (www.bloomberg.com/news).

ESPN. 2011a. "Robert Burton Ends Dispute with UConn." *ESPN.com*, February 12. Retrieved July 5, 2012 (espn.go.com).

———. 2011b. "Pac-10 Announces ESPN/Fox TV Deal." *ESPN.com*, May 4. Retrieved August 11, 2011 (espn.go.com).

Estler, Suzanne E., and Laurie J. Nelson, eds. 2005. *Who Calls the Shots? Sports and University Leadership, Culture, and Decision Making*. Special Issue. *ASHE Higher Education Report* 30(5), pp. 1–125.

Fain, Paul. 2007a. "Accountability and Athletics Top Agenda at Meeting of Trustees." *Chronicle of Higher Education*, March 16. Retrieved February 18, 2011 (www.chronicle.com).

———. 2007b. "For Trustees, Faith in College Presidents Lies at the Heart of Good Relationships." *Chronicle of Higher Education*, May 11, pp. A14–A15.

———. 2007c."Oregon Debates Role of Big Sports Donors." *Chronicle of Higher Education*, October 26, pp. A38–A41.

———. 2010. "Diversity Remains Fleeting on Colleges' Governing Boards, Surveys Find." *Chronicle of Higher Education*, November 29. Retrieved August 21, 2012 (www.chronicle.edu).

Farrey, Tom. 2011. "Big Changes Coming to NCAA." *ESPN.com*, August 6. Retrieved August 8, 2011 (espn.go.com).

Federal Bureau of Investigation. 2012. *Largest Recruiter of Investors to Nevin Shapiro's $930 Million Ponzi Scheme Sentenced to Prison for Lying to the IRS about Millions in Related Income.* FBI Newark Division, January 10. Retrieved August 7, 2012 (fbi.gov).

Feinstein, John. 2011. "Fixing College Sports Requires Less Talk, More Action." *Washington Post*, August 18. Retrieved August 29, 2011 (www.washingtonpost.com).

Fitzpatrick, Frank. 2012. "Louis Freeh Report on PSU Attacks Joe Paterno's Judgment and Integrity." *Philadelphia Inquirer*, July 13. Retrieved August 7, 2012 (www.philly.com).

Forde, Pat. 2011. "Miami Takes Its Turn on Wheel of Scandal." *ESPN.com*, August 18. Retrieved August 8, 2012 (espn.go.com).

Freeh, Louis. 2012. *Report of the Special Investigative Counsel Regarding the Actions of the Pennsylvania State University Related to the Child Sexual Abuse Committed by Gerald A. Sandusky*, July 12. Freeh Sporkin & Sullivan, LLP. Retrieved July 14, 2012 (www.The FreehReportonPSU.com).

Friday, William C., and Rev. Theodore Hesburgh. 2001. *A Call to Action: Reconnecting College Sports and Higher Education.* Knight Commission on Intercollegiate Athletics, June 18. Retrieved February 18, 2011 (www.knightcommision.org).

Fusfeld, Adam. 2011. "How Much Do the NCAA's Top 15 Conferences Spend on Athletics?" *Business Insider*, January 11. Retrieved February 18, 2011 (www.businessinsider.com).

Gardner, Lee. 2012. "The Tricky Economics of Firing a Football Coach." *Chronicle of Higher Education*, November 30. Retrieved November 30, 2012 (www.chronicle.com).

Garvin, Glenn. 2011. "Reporter's Exposé on Miami Hurricanes Was Surreal Journey." *Miami Herald*, August 23. Retrieved August 23, 2011 (MiamiHerald.com).

Gee, Gordon. 2005. "A New (Old) Philosophy of Intercollegiate Athletics." *Phi Kappa Phi Forum* 85 (Fall): 11–13.

George Washington University. 2012. "George Washington Athletics, IMG College Strike Corporate Sponsorship Rights Agreement." *cstv.com*, May 10. Retrieved May 17, 2012 (www.cstv.com).

Giannotto, Mark. 2012. "Maryland Cut Seven Sports on 'Sad Day' in College Park." *Washington Post*, July 2. Retrieved July 10, 2012 (www.washingtonpost.com).

Grasgreen, Allie. 2011a. "Another Round at Rutgers." *Inside Higher Ed*, August 24. Retrieved August 25, 2011 (www.insidehighered.com).

———. 2011b. "Maryland Will Cut Eight Teams to Mitigate Athletic Budget Deficit." *Inside Higher Ed*, November 22. Retrieved November 22, 2011 (www.insidehighered.com).

———. 2011c. "Poll Shows Concern over Penn State and Other Athletic Programs." *Inside Higher Ed*, November 23. Retrieved November 23, 2011 (www.insidehighered.com).

———. 2012a. "Division I Divisiveness." *Inside Higher Ed*, February 16. Retrieved February 23, 2012 (www.insidehighered.com).

———. 2012b. "Athletic Giving Crowds Out Academic Donations, Research Finds." *Inside Higher Ed*, April 27. Retrieved April 27, 2012 (www.insidehighered.com).

———. 2012c. "After Months of Build-Up, BCS Presidents Approve College Football Playoff." *Inside Higher Ed*, June 27. Retrieved June 27, 2012 (www.insidehighered.com).

———. 2012d. "After Freeh Report, Some Say a Grand Gesture Is Needed." *Inside Higher Ed*, July 17. Retrieved July 17, 2012 (www.insidehighered.com).

———. 2012e. "NCAA Athlete Graduation Rates Up in Football and Men's Basketball,

but Down over All." *Inside Higher Ed*, October 26. Retrieved October 28, 2012 (www
.insidehighered.com).

———. 2012f. "Maryland Departs ACC for Big Ten Conference." *Inside Higher Ed*, November 20. Retrieved November 20, 2012 (www.insidehighered.com).

———. 2012g. "Struggling Rutgers Follows Maryland to Big Ten." *Inside Higher Ed*, November 21. Retrieved November 21, 2012 (www.insidehighered.com).

———. 2013. "Division I Trims Rulebook, Deregulates Recruiting." *Inside Higher Ed*, January 21. Retrieved January 21, 2013 (www.insidehighered.com).

Green, Kenneth C., with Scott Jaschik and Doug Lederman. 2011. "Presidential Perspectives: The 2011 Inside Higher Ed Survey of College and University Presidents." *Inside Higher Ed*, March 4. Retrieved March 4, 2011 (www.insidehighered.com/news/survey/president2011).

Gregory, Byron I., and J. Craig Busey. 1985. "Alternative Broadcasting Arrangements after NCAA." *Indiana Law Journal* 61 (1): article 5. Retrieved June 4, 2012 (www.repository
.law.indiana.edu/ilj/vol61/iss1/5).

Groves, Roger. 2012. "College Professionals at Cowboys Stadium? Alabama vs. Michigan." *Forbes*, September 3. Retrieved September 4, 2012 (www.forbes.com).

Hacker, Andrew, and Claudia Dreifus. 2010. *Higher Education? How Colleges Are Wasting Our Money and Failing Our Kids—and What We Can Do about It*. New York: Times Books.

Hersh, Richard H., and John Merrow, eds. 2005. *Declining by Degrees: Higher Education at Risk*. New York: Palgrave Macmillan.

Horrow, Rick, and Karla Swatek. 2010. "College Football's Golden Bowl Series." *Bloomberg Businessweek*, October 21. Retrieved August 11, 2011 (www.businessweek.com).

Hutchens, Terry. 2009. "Brand, Knight Forever Linked by Coach's Dismissal at Indiana." *USA Today*, September 16. Retrieved August 14, 2012 (www.usatoday.com).

Immerwahr, John, and Jean Johnson. 2010. *Squeeze Play, 2010: Continued Public Anxiety on Cost, Harsher Judgments on How Colleges Are Run*, February. New York: Public Agenda Report for the National Center for Public Policy and Higher Education.

Infante, Nick. 2012a. "A New Paradigm for Conference Realignment?" *College Athletics Clips*, November 25. Retrieved November 26, 2012 (www.collegeathleticsclips.com).

———. 2012b. "Conference Realignment, Version #17." *College Athletics Clips (Graphics)*, December 15. Retrieved December 17, 2012 (www.collegeathleticsclips.com).

Isidore, Chris. 2010. "College Football's $1.1 Billion Profit." CNNMoney.com, December 29. Retrieved March 24, 2011 (money.cnn.com).

Katz, Andy, and Brett McMurphy. 2012. "Big East Fate Vexes Catholic Schools." *ESPN.com: NCAA*, December 10. Retrieved December 11, 2012 (espn.go.com).

Kaye, Judith S. 2010. *Report to the Board of Trustees of the State University of New York*, February 11. Skadden, Arps, Slate, Meagher & Flom, LLP. Retrieved August 8, 2012 (www
.suny.edu).

Kelderman, Eric. 2008. "Colleges Foot a Large Share of Athletics Expenses, New NCAA Data Show." *Chronicle of Higher Education*, March 15. Retrieved March 15, 2008 (www
.chronicle.com).

Kerr, Clark. 2001. *The Uses of the University: The Godkin Lectures on the Essentials of Free Government and the Duties of the Citizen, 1963*. Cambridge, MA: Harvard University Press.

Kiley, Kevin. 2012a. "Trustees Are Different than They Used to Be, and U.Va.-like Clashes

Will Be More Common." *Inside Higher Ed*, July 2. Retrieved July 2, 2012 (www.inside highered.com).

———. 2012b. "Pennsylvania Officials Examining President's Role on Board in Wake of Sandusky Scandal." *Inside Higher Ed*, September 5. Retrieved September 5, 2012 (www .insidehighered.com).

———. 2013. "Universities Spend More on Athletics per Athlete than on Academics per Student, Report Finds." *Inside Higher Ed*, January 16. Retrieved January 16, 2013 (www .insidehighered.com).

King, Bill. 2005. "Race for Results." *SportsBusiness Journal*, December 5–11. Retrieved August 17, 2011 (www.sportsbusinessdaily.com).

Kirp, David L. 2003. *Shakespeare, Einstein, and the Bottom Line: The Marketing of Higher Education*. Cambridge, MA: Harvard University Press.

Knight Commission. 1991. *Keeping Faith with the Student-Athlete: A New Model for Intercollegiate Athletes*, March. Knight Commission on Intercollegiate Athletics. Retrieved May 26, 2007 (www.knightcommission.org).

———. 2001. *A Call to Action: Reconnecting College Sports and Higher Education*, June. Knight Commission on Intercollegiate Athletics. Retrieved May 26, 2007 (www.knight commision.org).

———. 2006. *Public Poll: Americans Are Concerned about College Sports. Executive Summary*, January. Knight Commission on Intercollegiate Athletics. Retrieved May 26, 2007 (www .knightcommission.org).

———. 2007. *Faculty Perceptions of Intercollegiate Athletics Survey. Executive Summary*, October 15. Knight Commission on Intercollegiate Athletics. Retrieved October 30, 2007 (www.knightcommission.org).

———. 2009. Quantitative and Qualitative Research with Football Bowl Subdivision University Presidents on the Costs and Financing of Intercollegiate Athletics, October. Knight Commission on Intercollegiate Athletics. Baltimore: Art and Science LLC. Retrieved July 12, 2012 (www.knightcommissionmedia.org).

———. 2010. *Restoring the Balance: Dollars, Values, and the Future of College Sports*, June 17. Knight Commission on Intercollegiate Athletics. Retrieved June 20, 2010 (www.knight commission.org).

Korman, Chris. 2012. "Big Ten Targeted Maryland Partly because It Feared Losing Penn State." *Baltimore Sun*, December 7. Retrieved December 8, 2012 (www.baltimoresun.com).

Langelett, George. 2003. "The Relationship between Recruiting and Team Performance in Division IA College Football." *Journal of Sports Economics* 4: 240–245.

Lash, Devon, Peter Hall, and Tim Darragh. 2012. "Freeh: Penn State Leaders Agreed to Hide Abuse." *Morning Call*, July 12. Retrieved July 13, 2012 (www.mcall.com).

Lederman, Doug. 2009. "The Board Role in College Sports." *Inside Higher Ed*, April 8. Retrieved February 18, 2011 (www.insidehighered.com).

———. 2011. "Bad Apples or More?" *Inside Higher Ed*, February 7. Retrieved February 7, 2011 (www.insidehighered.com).

———. 2012. "Calls for Major Reform of College Sports Unlikely to Produce Meaningful Change." *Inside Higher Ed*, January 10. Retrieved January 10, 2012 (www.insidehighered.com).

Lederman, Doug, Kevin Kiley, and Scott Jaschik. 2012. "Concerns about Sports, Back for

Obama: A Survey of Presidents." *Inside Higher Ed*, March 8. Retrieved July 13, 2012 (www .insiderhighered.com).

Legal Information Institute. n.d. *National Collegiate Athletic Association, Petitioner v. Board of Regents of the University of Oklahoma and University of Georgia Athletic Association.* Cornell University Law School. Retrieved June 4, 2012 (www.law.cornell.edu/supremecourt/ text/468/85).

Littwin, Mike. 1985. "The Tulane Scandal." *Los Angeles Times*, April 29. Retrieved March 25, 2011 (articles.latimes.com).

Lopiano, Donna. 2005. "The Real Culprit in the Cutting of Men's Olympic Sports." Pp. 294–296 in *Sport and Contemporary Society: An Anthology*, 7th ed., edited by D. S. Eitzen. Boulder, CO: Paradigm Publishers.

Maguire, Joseph. 1999. *Global Sport*. Cambridge: Polity Press.

Maisel, Ivan. 2012. "Knight Commission's Losing Battle." *ESPN.com*, October 10. Retrieved October 22, 2012 (espn.go.com).

Maloney, Brendan. 2011. "Texas' Longhorn Network Sparks Debate in College Athletics." *USA Today*, August 12, 2011. Retrieved August 12, 2011 (www.usatoday.com).

Mandel, Stewart. 2012. "Marinatto Resignation Latest Proof Presidents Have Too Much to Say." *SI.com*, May 7. Retrieved June 5, 2012 (sportsillustated.cnn.com).

Marklein, Mary Beth. 2012. "Disputed Ouster of UVa. President Could Be 'Teachable Moment.'" *USA Today*, June 23. Retrieved June 26, 2012 (www.usatoday.com).

———. 2013. "Division I Schools Spend More on Athletes than Education." *USA Today*, January 16. Retrieved January 16, 2013 (www.usatoday.com).

Markus, Don, and Todd Karpovich. 2012. "Towson Athletic Department Recommends Cutting Baseball and Men's Soccer." *Baltimore Sun*, October 2. Retrieved October 3, 2012 (www.baltimoresun.com).

Martin, Dave. 2011. "Ohio State: Pryor Would've Been Ineligible for All of 2011." *USA Today*, July 27. Retrieved July 27, 2011 (www.usatoday.com).

Martzke, Rudy. 2004. "ABC Bundles Up Rose Bowl through 2014." *USA Today*, August 5. Retrieved August 11, 2011 (www.usatoday.com).

McCallum, Jack. 2011. "A Legacy in Tatters." *Sports Illustrated*, November 21, pp. 50–51.

McCann, Michael. 2012. "O'Bannon Expands NCAA Lawsuit." *SI.com*, September 1. Retrieved September 9, 2012 (sportsillustrated.cnn.com).

McGee, Ryan. 2011. "The Rise of NCAA Superconferences." *ESPN.com: NCAA*, November 2. Retrieved November 3, 2011 (espn.go.com).

McMillen, C. Thomas. 2011. "Eliminate the Profit Motive." *Chronicle of Higher Education*, December 11. Retrieved December 13, 2012 (www.chronicle.com).

———. 2012. "Big Ten, Big Mistake." *Washington Post*, November 21. Retrieved December 12, 2012 (www.washingtonpost.com).

Messner, Michael A., Michele Dunbar, and Darnell Hunt. 2000. "The Televised Sport Manhood Formula." *Journal of Sport & Social Issues* 24: 380–394.

Mihoces, Gary. 2012. "Maryland Leaves ACC for More Money." *USA Today*, November 19. Retrieved November 20, 2012 (www.usatoday.com).

Miller, Stephen A. 2012. "The NCAA Needs to Let Someone Else Enforce Its Rules." *Atlantic*, October 23. Retrieved November 30, 2012 (theatlantic.com).

Miringoff, Lee M., Barbara L. Carvalho, and Mary E. Azzoli. 2012. *Majority Thinks Colleges Break NCAA Rules*. Marist College Institute for Public Opinion, March 29. Retrieved March 30, 2012 (www.maristpoll.edu).

Moltz, David. 2010. "The Athletics Tax." *Inside Higher Ed*, June 1. Retrieved November 18, 2010 (www.insidehighered.com).

———. 2011. "Rich Get Richer in Athletics." *Inside Higher Ed*, June 16. Retrieved June 16, 2011 (www.insidehighered.com).

Moran, Robert. 2012. "Penn State Is Told Its Accreditation 'Is in Jeopardy.' " *Philadelphia Inquirer*, August 14. Retrieved August 15, 2012 (www.philly.com).

National Football Foundation. 2011. "Colleges Continue to Add Football Teams." *National Football Foundation & College Football Hall of Fame*. Retrieved February 11, 2012 (www.footballfoundation.org).

NCAA. 2006. *The Second-Century Imperatives: Presidential Leadership—Institutional Accountability*. A Report from the Presidential Task Force on Division I Intercollegiate Athletics. Retrieved October 31, 2006 (www2.ncaa.org).

———. 2010. "NCAA Signs New 14-Year Deal for D1 Men's Basketball." *NCAA News*, April 22. Retrieved August 11, 2011 (www.ncaa.org).

Newfield, Christopher. 2008. *Unmaking the Public University: The Forty-Year Assault on the Middle Class*. Cambridge, MA: Harvard University Press.

Nixon, Howard L., II. 1984. *Sport and the American Dream*. New York: Leisure Press.

———. 2008. *Sport in a Changing World*. Boulder, CO: Paradigm.

Nocera, Joe. 2011a. "Let's Start Paying College Athletes." *New York Times*, December 30. Retrieved December 31, 2011 (www.nytimes.com).

———. 2011b. "The College Sports Cartel." *New York Times*, December 30. Retrieved December 31, 2011 (www.nytimes.com).

Orszag, Jonathan, and Marl Israel. 2009. *The Empirical Effects of Collegiate Athletics: An Update Based on 2004–2007 Data*. February. Compass Lexecon (Commissioned by the National Collegiate Athletic Association). Retrieved August 26, 2011 (www.ncaa.org).

Orszag, Jonathan M., and Peter R. Orszag. 2005. *The Empirical Effects of Collegiate Athletics: An Update*. April. Compass (Commissioned by the National Collegiate Athletic Association). Retrieved August 26, 2011 (www.ncaa.org).

Pargman, David. 2012. "End the Charade: Let Athletes Major in Sports." *Chronicle of Higher Education*, November 26. Retrieved November 27, 2012 (www.chronicle.com).

Pennington, Bill. 2012. "Cheating Scandal Dulls Pride in Athletics at Harvard." *New York Times*, September 18. Retrieved September 19, 2012 (www.nytimes.com).

Perko, Amy, and Jay Weiner. 2009. *College Sports 101: A Primer on Money, Athletics, and Higher Education in the 21st Century*, October. Knight Commission on Intercollegiate Athletics. Retrieved April 19, 2010 (www.knightcommission.org).

Peterson, Harry L. 2008. "Why Presidents Fail—and How They Can Succeed." *Chronicle of Higher Education*, June 13, p. A40.

Pettegrew, John. 2007. *Brutes in Suits: Male Sensibility in America, 1890–1920*. Baltimore: Johns Hopkins University Press.

Pilon, Mary. 2011. "Scandals Test the N.C.A.A.'s Top Rules Enforcer." *New York Times*, December 16. Retrieved December 18, 2011 (www.nytimes.com).

Potuto, Josephine. 2012. "The NCAA's Brave New World." *Chronicle of Higher Education*, July 23. Retrieved August 6, 2012 (www.chronicle.org).

Powers, Elia. 2008. "Sports and the Presidential Pedigree." *Inside Higher Ed*, February 20. Retrieved February 15, 2011 (www.insidehighered.com).

Prewitt, Alex. 2012. "Tom McMillen Rails on Decision-Making Process, Confidentiality Agreement in Washington Post Op-Ed." *Washington Post*, November 21. Retrieved December 12, 2012 (www.washingtonpost.com).

Price, S. L. 2012. "We Are Still Penn State." *Sports Illustrated*, November 5, pp. 61–65.

Proffitt, Jennifer M., and Thomas F. Corrigan. 2012. "Penn State's 'Success with Honor': How Institutional Structures and Brand Logic Disincentivized Disclosure." *Cultural Studies— Critical Methodologies*, May 14. Pre-publication Online Version. Retrieved May 24, 2012 (csc.sagepub.com).

Rhoads, Thomas. 2004. "Competitive Balance and Conference Realignment in the NCAA: The Case of the Western Athletic and Mountain West Conferences." Presented at the annual meeting of the Southern Economic Association Annual Meeting, November, New Orleans.

Robbins, Lenn. 2011. "Big East Officially to Invite Six Schools." *New York Post*, November 2. Retrieved November 4, 2011 (nypost.com).

Robinson, Charles. 2011. "Renegade Miami Football Booster Spells Out Illicit Benefits to Players." *Yahoo! Sports*, August 16. Retrieved August 23, 2011 (sports.yahoo.com).

Rohan, Tim. 2012a. "Sandusky Gets 30 to 60 Years for Sexual Abuse." *New York Times*, October 9. Retrieved October 10, 2012 (www.nytimes.com).

———. 2012b. "For-Profit University's Shift to Division I Stokes Debate." *New York Times*, November 29. Retrieved November 29, 2012 (www.nytimes.com).

Rooney, John F., Jr. 1980. *The Recruiting Game: Toward a New System of Intercollegiate Athletics*. Lincoln: University of Nebraska Press.

Rosenberg, Michael. 2011. "Nike's Phil Knight Has Branded Oregon into National Power." *SI.com*, January 7. Retrieved July 5, 2012 (sportsillustrated.cnn.com).

Sack, Allen L. 2012. "After Penn State Scandal, Congress Should Make NCAA Put Students, Education First." *Christian Science Monitor*, August 24, 2012. Retrieved August 27, 2012 (www.csmonitor.com).

Sack, Allen L., and Ellen J. Staurowsky. 1998. *College Athletes for Hire: The Evolution and Legacy of the NCAA's Amateur Myth*. Westport, CT: Praeger.

Sander, Libby. 2009. "Presidents Favor Reining in Athletic Costs, but Feel Powerless to Effect Change." *Chronicle of Higher Education*, October 26. Retrieved February 18, 2011 (www.chronicle.com).

———. 2011a. "22 Elite College Sports Programs Turned a Profit in 2010, but Gaps Remain, NCAA Report Says." *Chronicle of Higher Education*, June 15. Retrieved June 16, 2011 (www.chronicle.com).

———. 2011b. "Maryland's Fiscal Woes Should Be a Wake-Up Call to Governing Boards, Regent Says." *Chronicle of Higher Education*, July 26. Retrieved July 27, 2011 (www.chronicle.com).

———. 2011c. "University Presidents to Weigh Major Changes in College Sports at NCAA Summit." *Chronicle of Higher Education*, August 4. Retrieved August 5, 2011 (www.chronicle.com).

————. 2011d. "NCAA Penalizes Boise State U. for Violations in 5 Sports." *Chronicle of Higher Education*, September 13. Retrieved September 13, 2011 (www.chronicle.com).

Sanserino, Michael. 2011. "College Coaches' Salaries Continue to Soar." *Pittsburgh Post-Gazette*, January 15. Retrieved March 23, 2011 (www.post-gazette.com).

Sawchik, Travis. 2011. "Lucrative Television Contracts Turn College Football into Big Business." *Post and Courier*, July 19. Retrieved August 11, 2011 (www.postandcourier.com).

Schackner, Bill. 2007. "College Presidents' Tenure Grows: Report Says Leaders of Nation's Colleges Holding Jobs Longer than Any Time since the Mid '80s." *Pittsburgh Post-Gazette*, February 12. Retrieved March 30, 2011 (www.post-gazette.com).

Schnaars, Christopher, Jodi Upton, Jerry Mosemak, and Kristin DeRamus. 2012. "NCAA College Athletics Department Finances Database." *USA Today*, May 14. Retrieved May 31, 2012 (www.usatoday.com).

Schoenenberger, Todd M. 2011. "College Park Suffers from Bad Bet on Basketball." *Baltimore Sun*, November 28, p. 17.

Schrotenboer, Brent. 2012. "UCSD Planning to Move to Division I Sports." *Union Tribune*, March 7. Retrieved June 2, 2012 (www.utsandiego.com).

Schwartz, Merrill P. 2010. "Board Composition: Student and Faculty Trustees." *Trusteeship* 18 (July–August): 36–38.

Selingo, Jeff. 2007. "Chronicle Survey: What Trustees Think." *Chronicle of Higher Education*, May 11, pp. A11–A21.

Shiller, Robert J. 2000. *Irrational Exuberance*. 2d ed. Princeton, NJ: Princeton University Press.

Shipley, Amy. 2009. "University Presidents Sound Alarm at Expenses." *Washington Post*, October 27. Retrieved October 27, 2009 (www.washingtonpost.com).

Shulman, James L., and William G. Bowen. 2001. *The Game of Life: College Sports and Educational Values*. Princeton, NJ: Princeton University Press.

Slaughter, Sheila, and Larry L. Leslie. 1997. *Academic Capitalism: Politics, Policies, and the Entrepreneurial University*. Baltimore: Johns Hopkins University Press.

Slaughter, Sheila, and Gary Rhoades. 2004. *Academic Capitalism and the New Economy: Markets, State, and Higher Education*. Baltimore: Johns Hopkins University Press.

Smart, Barry. 2005. *The Sport Star: Modern Sport and the Cultural Economy of Sporting Celebrity*. London: Sage.

Smiley, Tavis. 2012. "Interview of NCAA President Mark Emmert." *Tavis Smiley Show*. PBS, July 16. Retrieved July 17, 2012 (www.pbs.org).

Smith, Chris. 2012a. "Say Your Goodbyes: The ACC's Days Are Numbered." *Forbes.com*, May 29. Retrieved June 11, 2012 (www.forbes.com).

————. 2012b. "The ACC's Third Tier Rights and Why They're Killing the Conference." *Forbes.com*, June 4. Retrieved June 11, 2012 (www.forbes.com).

Smith, D. Randall. 2009. "College Football and Student Quality: An Advertising Effect or Culture and Tradition." *American Journal of Economics and Sociology* 68: 553–579.

Smith, Erick. 2011. "Eight Miami Players Suspended by NCAA for Improper Benefits." *USA Today*, August 30. Retrieved August 31, 2011 (www.usatoday.com).

Smith, Michael. 2011. "Athletic Budgets Continue to Climb." *SportsBusiness Journal*, August 22–28. Retrieved August 29, 2011 (www.sportsbusinessdaily.com).

Smith, Ronald A. 1990. *Sports and Freedom: The Rise of Big-Time College Athletics*. New York: Oxford University Press.

———. 2010. *Pay for Play: A History of Big-Time College Athletic Reform*. Champaign: University of Illinois Press.

Spellings, Margaret. 2006. *A Test of Leadership: Charting the Future of U.S. Higher Education*. A report of the commission appointed by Secretary of Education Margaret Spellings. Washington, DC: U.S. Department of Education. Retrieved August 17, 2012 (www2.ed.gov).

Sperber, Murray. 1991. *College Sports, Inc.: The Athletic Department vs. the University*. New York: Henry Holt.

———. 2001. *Beer and Circus: How Big-Time College Sports Is Crippling Undergraduate Education*. New York: Henry Holt.

Staples, Andy. 2012. "Full Cost-of-Attendance Scholarship Debate Breaks Up the FBS." *SI.com*, March 8. Retrieved March 14, 2012 (sportsillustrated.cnn.com).

Stevens, Mitchell L. 2007. *Creating a Class: College Admissions and the Education of Elites*. Cambridge, MA: Harvard University Press.

Stone, Gregory. 1955. "American Sports: Play and Display." *Chicago Review* 9: 83–100.

Stripling, Jack. 2011. "Few Trustees Challenge Their President or Push Major Changes, Study Finds." *Chronicle of Higher Education*, December 14. Retrieved December 14, 2011 (www.chronicle.com).

———. 2012. "Penn State Paid Spanier $3.3-Million in 2011." *Chronicle of Higher Education*, November 28, 2012. Retrieved November 29, 2012 (www.chronicle.com).

SUNY. 2010. "Statement from SUNY Board of Trustees Chairman Carl T. Hayden and Chancellor Nancy L. Zimpher." *SUNY*, February 11. Retrieved August 14, 2012 (www.suny.edu).

Thamel, Pete. 2009a. "At Binghamton, Division I Move Brings Recognition and Regret." *New York Times*, February 22. Retrieved February 23, 2009 (www.nytimes.com).

———. 2009b. "SUNY Board to Oversee an Audit of Binghamton." *New York Times*, October 3. Retrieved October 4, 2009 (www.nytimes.com).

———. 2010a. "Report Faults Binghamton's Leaders in Scandal." *New York Times*, February 12. Retrieved February 18, 2011 (www.nytimes.com).

———. 2010b. "Binghamton Coach Gets $1.2 Million to Resign." *New York Times*, October 29. Retrieved March 9, 2011 (www.nytimes.com).

———. 2011. "College Football's Ugly Season, Facing Scandals of Every Stripe." *New York Times*, August 21. Retrieved August 22, 2011 (www.nytimes.com).

———. 2012. "After a Costly Scandal, Binghamton Begins Rebuilding." *New York Times*, February 29. Retrieved March 1, 2012 (www.nytimes.com).

Thelin, John R. 1994. *Games Colleges Play: Scandal and Reform in Intercollegiate Athletics*. Baltimore: Johns Hopkins University Press.

Thomas, Katie. 2010. "Experience in Sports Optional for New Leaders." *New York Times*, February 2. Retrieved May 17, 2012 (www.nytimes.com).

Tillman, Spencer. 2008. "Latest BCS-TV Deal Likely to Pilfer Fans' Pockets in Future." *CBSSports.com*, November 21. Retrieved August 11, 2011 (www.cbssports.com).

Tkach, John. 2012. "College Presidents Lag Behind Coaches in Pay." *USA Today*, May 22, p. 3C.

Troop, Don. 2013. "Near-Term Outlook Is Bleak for All of Higher Education, Moody's Says." *Chronicle of Higher Education*, January 16. Retrieved January 16, 2013 (www.chronicle .com).

Tsitsos, William, and Howard L. Nixon II. 2012. "The Star Wars Arms Race in College Athletics: Coaches' Pay and Athletic Program Status." *Journal of Sport & Social Issues* 36: 68–88.

Tully, Jessica. 2012. "Rally at Penn State Calls for President's Resignation." *USA Today*, September 15. Retrieved September 16, 2012 (www.usatoday.com).

UCSD. 2011. *University of California San Diego Feasibility Study: Options for Reclassifying to NCAA Division I & Adding Football*. Athletics Staffing and Consultants, March 11.

Upton, Jodi, and Steve Berkowitz. 2011. "Athletic Directors Seeing Major Increase in Salaries." *USA Today*, October 6. Retrieved October 14, 2011 (www.usatoday.com).

Upton, Jodi, Steve Berkowitz, and Jack Gillum. 2010. "Big-Time College Athletics: Are They Worth the Big-Time Costs?" *USA Today*, January 15. Retrieved March 23, 2011 (www .usatoday.com).

Upton, Jodi, and Jack Gillum. 2010. "USA TODAY Database: What NCAA Schools Are Spending on Athletics." *USA Today*, April 2. Retrieved August 24, 2011 (www.usatoday .com).

U.S. Department of Education. 2011. *The Equity in Athletics Data Analysis Cutting Tool*. Washington, DC: Office of Postsecondary Education. Retrieved January 31, 2012 (ope.ed .gov/athletics/InstDetails.aspx).

USA Today. 2012. "John Calipari Gets $400K Pay Increase from Kentucky." *USA Today*, May 4. Retrieved August 14, 2012 (www.usatoday.com).

Van Natta, Don. 2012. "On Death's Door." *ESPN: The Magazine*, August 20. Retrieved as advance copy on August 6, 2012 (www.collegeathleticsclips.com).

Verducci, Tom. 2011. "A Place Apart." *Sports Illustrated*, November 21, pp. 48–49.

Walker, Childs, and Ken Murray. 2011. "Seeking a Turnaround in Towson Athletics." *Baltimore Sun*, April 10, pp. 1, 17.

Wertheim, L. Jon, and David Epstein. 2011. "Special Report: Scandal. Shame. A Search for Answers. This Is Penn State." *Sports Illustrated*, November 21, pp. 40–53.

Wetzel, Dan. 2011. "Miami Scandal Is Symptom of NCAA Flaws." *Yahoo! Sports*, August 17. Retrieved August 23, 2011 (sports.yahoo.com).

Wickersham, Seth. 2011. "Is Gordon Gee Serious?" *ESPN.com*, August 8. Retrieved August 26, 2011 (espn.go.com).

Wieberg, Steve. 2006. "Brand, in Change of Heart, Seeks More Name Recognition for NCAA." *USA Today*, January 19. Retrieved May 17, 2012 (www.usatoday.com).

———. 2011a. "NCAA Could See 'Fundamental Changes' in Way It Operates." *USA Today*, July 6. Retrieved July 11, 2011 (www.usatoday.com).

———. 2011b. "USA TODAY/Gallup Poll: Penn State Football Too Powerful." *USA Today*, November 16. Retrieved November 17, 2011 (www.usatoday.com).

———. 2012. "Texas President: Finances Could Cause Split in NCAA Football." *USA Today*, May 15. Retrieved June 1, 2012 (www.usatoday.com).

Wieberg, Steve, and Steve Berkowitz. 2009. "Has College Sports Marketing Gone Too Far?" *USA Today*, April 2. Retrieved May 17, 2012 (www.usatoday.com).

———. 2011. "Is ESPN the Main Force behind Realignment in College Sports." *USA Today*, November 1. Retrieved November 4, 2011 (www.usatoday.com).

Wieberg, Steve, and Jodi Upton. 2007. "Success on the Court Translates to Big Money for Coaches." *USA Today*, March 8. Retrieved April 27, 2007 (www.usatoday.com).

Wieder, Ben. 2013. "College Enrollment Expected to Slip." Pew Charitable Trusts, January 16. Retrieved January 22, 2013 (www.pewstates.org).

Wilson, Robin. 2012. "Penn State Faculty Leaders Attack NCAA's Use of Freeh Report." *Chronicle of Higher Education*, August 28. Retrieved August 29, 2012 (www.chronicle.com).

Wolff, Alexander. 2011. "16 Years Later, It's Time to Get Real." *Sports Illustrated*, August 20, pp. 33–35.

———. 2012. "We Were Penn State." *Sports Illustrated*, July 30, pp. 38–41.

Wolken, Dan. 2012. "SEC Even Does Coaches' Buyouts Big." *USA Today*, November 26. Retrieved November 27, 2012 (www.usatoday.com).

Wolverton, Brad. 2007. "For Small Programs, Fund Raising Can Be a Ticket to the Big Time." *Chronicle of Higher Education*, October 26, p. A41.

———. 2009. "For Athletics, a Billion Dollar Goal Line." *Chronicle of Higher Education*, January 23. Retrieved July 3, 2012 (www.chronicle.com).

———. 2010. "Faculty Reps Botch Sport-Oversight Role." *Chronicle of Higher Education*, November 1. Retrieved February 18, 2011 (www.chronicle.com).

———. 2012a. "Does Switching Athletics Conferences Lead to Academic Gains." *Chronicle of Higher Education*, June 5. Retrieved June 7, 2012 (www.chronicle.com).

———. 2012b. "NCAA's President Paid at Nearly $1.6 Million per Year." *Chronicle of Higher Education*, July 10. Retrieved July 10, 2012 (www.chronicle.com).

———. 2012c. "Investigators Find 'Total Disregard for Safety' of Child Victims by Penn State Officials." *Chronicle of Higher Education*, July 12. Retrieved July 12, 2012 (www.chronicle.com).

———. 2012d. "How Would You Reinvent College Sports." *Chronicle of Higher Education*, October 15. Retrieved October 15, 2012 (www.chronicle.com).

———. 2012e. "Tough New NCAA Penalties Could Hit College Teams Unevenly." *Chronicle of Higher Education*, October 30. Retrieved October 30, 2012 (www.chronicle.com).

———. 2012f. "Penn State Enrollment and Gifts Seem Unaffected by $20-Million Scandal." *Chronicle of Higher Education*, November 2. Retrieved November 2, 2012 (www.chronicle.com).

———. 2012g. "Notre Dame Scores a First: No. 1 in Football and in Graduating Its Players." *Chronicle of Higher Education*, November 20. Retrieved November 21, 2012 (www.chronicle.com).

———. 2012h. "Report Describes Disturbing Racial Inequalities in 6 Powerful Sports Conferences." *Chronicle of Higher Education*, December 3. Retrieved December 3, 2012 (www.chronicle.com).

———. 2012i. "Ohio State's Sports Program Aims to Play It Straight." *Chronicle of Higher Education*, December 10. Retrieved December 14, 2012 (www.chronicle.com).

———. 2013. "In Time of Budget Austerity, Athletics Programs Need a Reset." *Chronicle of Higher Education*, January 17. Retrieved January 17, 2013 (www.chronicle.com).

Wolverton, Brad, and Andrea Fuller. 2012. "Who's in Charge of Sports? Maybe Not the

President." *Chronicle of Higher Education*, September 3. Retrieved September 5, 2012 (www.chronicle.edu).

Wolverton, Brad, and Alex Richards. 2012. "Crowds Shrink at Men's Basketball Games." *Chronicle of Higher Education*, March 25. Retrieved May 30, 2012 (www.chronicle.com).

Woo, Stu. 2012. "The State of Affairs That Is Boise State." *Wall Street Journal*, October 21. Retrieved October 29, 2012 (online.wsj.com).

Yost, Mark. 2010. *Varsity Green: A Behind the Scenes Look at Culture and Corruption in College Athletics*. Palo Alto, CA: Stanford University Press.

Young, Elise. 2012. "Report Finds Alumni Giving, among Other Areas, Correlated with Football Success." *Inside Higher Ed*, July 3. Retrieved July 3, 2012 (www.insidehighered.com).

Zang, Frank. 2012. "Boise State Breaks Ground on New Football Complex." *Update*, April 12. Retrieved July 10, 2012 (news.boisestate.edu).

Zimbalist, Andrew. 1999. *Unpaid Professionals: Commercialism and Conflict in Big-Time College Sports*. Princeton, NJ: Princeton University Press.

Page numbers in **boldface** indicate definitions of terms

ABOUT THE AUTHOR

Howard L. Nixon II is a pioneer in the field of sports sociology. He has written and spoken widely about the sociology of sport, small groups and support networks, and the sociology of disability. His most recent research and
writing have focused on the sociology of pain and injuries, disability sport,
and social change in higher education. Nixon has also taught courses in
introductory sociology, sociological analysis (an advanced writing course),
the sociology of sport, and higher education, along with courses in various
other areas of sociology.

He received his B.A. (Social Relations) from Lehigh University and
Ph.D. (Sociology) from the University of Pittsburgh. He has been a faculty
member and administrator at the University of Vermont and Appalachian
State University as well as at Towson University.